D0946767

Between two worlds

Critical Social Thought

Series editor: Michael W. Apple
Professor of Curriculum and Instruction and of Educational Policy Studies, University of Wisconsin-Madison

Already published

Critical Social Psychology Philip Wexler
Reading, Writing and Resistance Robert B. Everhart
Arguing for Socialism Andrew Levine

LC
2801
.W36
1985

BETWEEN TWO WORLDS

Black students in an urban community college

Lois Weis

Routledge & Kegan Paul
Boston, London, Melbourne and Henley

To my father
and in memory of my mother

First published in 1985
by Routledge & Kegan Paul plc

9 Park Street, Boston, Mass. 02108, USA

14 Leicester Square, London WC2H 7PH, England

464 St Kilda Road, Melbourne,
Victoria 3004, Australia and

Broadway House, Newtown Road,
Henley on Thames, Oxon RG9 1EN, England

Set in Linotron 202 Times, 10 on 12pt
by Inforum Ltd, Portsmouth
and printed in Great Britain
by T.J. Press (Padstow) Ltd
Padstow, Cornwall

Copyright © Lois Weis 1985

No part of this book may be reproduced in
any form without permission from the publisher,
except for the quotation of brief passages
in criticism

Library of Congress Cataloging in Publication Data

Weis, Lois.
Between two worlds.
(Critical social thought)
Bibliography: p.
Includes index.
1. Afro-Americans—Education (Higher)—United States—Case studies. 2. Community colleges—United States—Case studies. 3. Education, Urban—United States—Case studies. 4. Cultural conflict—United States—Case studies. I. Title. II. Series.
LC2801.W36 1985 378'.1982 84–24960

British Library CIP data also available

ISBN 0–7100–9980–0

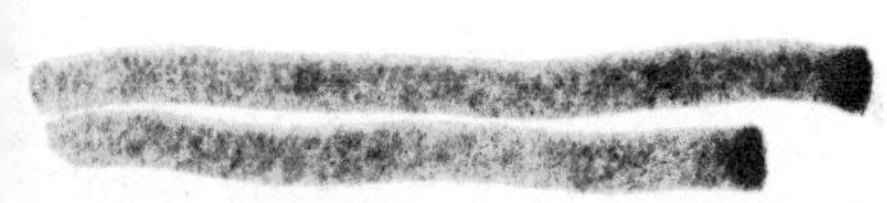

Contents

Tables

Series editor's introduction

During the past decade, there has been a major shift in many of the ways our dominant institutions have been critically analyzed. We have moved from a focus on the manner in which social control works to an emphasis on resistance and contestation. In the former the point was to document how, for example, dominant ideologies seemed to work their way through the workplace, family, school, government and elsewhere. In the latter, the aim was to show that existing modes of control and ideological forms are not monolithic. They are continually resisted and struggled over.[1] The movement away from theories of social control – where "agents" exist but have no real agency and where elite groups always get their own way in the economic, political and cultural spheres in some straightforward fashion – can readily be seen in the recent history of literature on the labor process. Harry Braverman's classic volume, *Labor and Monopoly Capital*, provides a case in point.[2]

In Braverman's analysis, the power of capital is such that there is inexorable management pressure on workers that ultimately depowers and deskills them. Conception is successfully separated from execution. The labor process is transformed so that management, through the use of Tayloristic strategies, ultimately succeeds both in "removing the brains from under the worker's hat" and in appropriating these skills and knowledge for its own use.

While the debates over Braverman are still intense, one thing has been made clear. The processes and pressures he pointed to illuminate only one side of the picture. Workers in our stores, factories, and offices have had a long history of mediating, resisting and even transforming management techniques so that a good deal of the brains do in fact remain under their own hats.[3]

A similar case in point can be found in the arguments about what historically has been called the hidden curriculum of elementary and secondary schools in capitalist countries. Early work stressed the role of schooling in socializing students to the norms and values that were "appropriate" to their prospective rungs in the labor market and the class structure. Schools sorted and selected students, and in the process students learned – again in some supposedly straightforward manner – to be obedient operatives who pursued the goals and internalized the perspectives necessary for the reproduction of the social division of labor. Such a position has been demonstrated to be exceptionally mechanistic both empirically and conceptually. Students, like the workers mentioned above, are not passive recipients of the knowledge and values "given" by capital. They too actively mediate and transform these values and knowledge based on their own class, gender, and race biographies and trajectories. A series of provocative studies, from the work of Willis and McRobbie in England to that of Everhart and Valli in the United States, has enabled us to go a long way toward gaining a more dynamic and realistic picture of the lived culture of students. It is a picture that has been very effective in moving us away from simplistic models of social control and socialization, while at the same time clearly recognizing the realities of the relations of domination and exploitation that do exist.[4] I have no doubt that *Between Two Worlds* will take its place alongside these other excellent studies.

Similar tendencies have become visible in work on the state, on patriarchal relations and in other areas of analysis. With these very real empirical and conceptual gains, however, it has become apparent that the mere fact that workers, students and others, say, resist does not guarantee either that they will be successful or, and this is very important, that their resistances will necessarily lead in a progressive direction. That is, side by side with elements of "good sense" in their activity and consciousness will be elements of "bad sense" as well. Sometimes their attempts at resisting dominant cultural, economic and political relations will turn back upon them, hurting as well as helping, in much the same way as the lads in Paul Willis's now famous book subverted the ideological and social relations of the school while at the same time reproducing at an even deeper level the distinctions between mental and manual labor and between men's and women's labor that lie at the heart of our social formation.

This more dialectical picture, one which recognizes the tension (perhaps contradiction is a better word) between good and bad sense in consciousness and ideology, has been exceptionally productive. It reintroduces notions of agency, of real people responding to real material conditions with their own real interests in real institutions, back into discussions of the way power works in our society. One is tempted to say "thank goodness," since the debates over culture and economy and over ideology and agency have been particularly arid at times. The flesh and blood of living, breathing people is made more visible and, hence, can be an effective counterbalance to the overly deterministic theories that are still too readily accepted.

In all of this emerging work, a particular position has been taken on how we might best think about culture, ideology and social relations. Rather than conceiving of culture as a given, it is seen as *produced* in particular sites. Structure and subjectivity are ongoingly produced in institutions as ordinary people go about working, consuming, educating themselves and so on. Culture, then, is relatively autonomous, not a mere reflection of economic determinations.[5] It has its own efficacy, as will be made strikingly clear in *Between Two Worlds*.

Thus, we have made considerable conceptual and empirical progress in generating alternatives to the earlier onesided models that neglected culture and agency. We do know a good deal about working class culture and resistance in schools and workplaces. We are well on our way to more fully understanding struggles over gender relations as well. Yet, while sensitive to class and gender dynamics, even these newer perspectives are often strikingly incomplete. They are too often silent on one of the most constitutive of all dynamics. Here I am speaking of *race*. The impressive feminist criticisms of traditional marxist approaches have made many investigators less apt to be class reductionist, surely a healthy sign.[6] Patriarchal forms do have their own specificities and are not reducible to class and economic relations. Surely the same must be admitted for race. Indeed, just noting that the very history of capitalism is so intimately connected with that of the exploitation of people of color in what is now called the third world should make us pause and reflect about it. We cannot really fully understand either the historical or existing economic, cultural or political structures of American society (and many others as well, of course) without thoroughly integrating race into the analysis. In essence, it is the absent presence behind our work.

The past and current experiences of black people in the United States can serve as an essential lens through which to view class, gender and race dynamics as they interact, reproduce and contradict each other.[7] Furthermore by taking these experiences seriously as *structural* forces – that is, by seeing race as being a truly constitutive building block of why this society is the way it is – we can learn considerably more about the social formation as a whole. In essence, I want to claim that the politics of the ways blacks have been and are treated economically and culturally can, "like a barium meal," illuminate the entire organism of a society.[8]

But how has our society thought about race in large part? The very language that permeates the dominant discourse of race speaks to the fact that this exploitative history is still very much present. In many ways, in countries such as the United States and England, a set of common-sense images of black people has evolved that is shot through with racist imagery. Linkages are made among "cultures of deprivation," the "inadequate family," youth criminality and so on, each element forming a part of a larger whole that is constantly being compared in its very discourse to the "natural" family and "good" culture. The authors of a recent study of racism put it this way:

> Where the common-sense images of white family and white youth are naturalized through reference to gender-specific "natural" roles, attributes and characteristics of women and men, the images of black families and black youth are the outcome of *double* naturalization. Blacks are pathological once via their association with the "cultures of deprivation" of the decaying "inner cities" and again as the bearers of specifically *black* cultures.[9]

We can only counter such imagery through a recognition of what Afro-Americans have had to work against and for, how they struggled, and the failures and successes of the vast river of such struggles. The notion of a river, as Vincent Harding so eloquently reminds us, is apt. Such a metaphor conveys "its long, continuous movement, flowing like a river, sometimes powerful, tumultuous, and roiling with life; at other times meandering and turgid, covered with ice and snow of seemingly endless winters, all too often streaked and running with blood."[10] But even when seemingly frozen, it is still ongoing, providing the cultural grounding of day-to-day experience for the people who make up that great river. It has provided a cultural and political depth that speaks powerfully to the creativity embodied in the black experience, creativity that may seem less visible to those who do not see it close up. As Omi and Winant suggest, account must be taken "of the ways in which minority cultures have remained flexible and adaptive, both in their capacity to carry out traditions of resistance to subjection along racial lines, and in responsiveness to shifting demands made upon group members by the majority culture."[11]

The black experience in the north, where Lois Weis's book takes place, has in part grown out of the soil of a society that found substitutes for the overt slavery of the south. A widespread system of economic, political and cultural discrimination, segregation and what can only be called cruel repression developed. These conditions may have at times been uneven and varied, but they were there. Black men and women may have found a system in which overt slavery was absent, but – again in the words of Harding – it was not a promised land. "Canaan was by no means sweet."[12] Any sweetness that arose had to be won, often at great cost, as the river moved on toward today.

Just as black slaves developed cultures of resistance based on music, family ties, religion and African traditions and in the process sustained a free black identity, so too in all periods have such people struggled to "accept or reject, to strengthen or undermine, the definitions and social situations within which [they] discover [themselves]."[13] To define oneself as a black person within existing institutions, then, continues to be an *active project*, not a set of foregone conclusions to be known in advance. It is this "active project" in all its contradictions and tensions that Lois Weis enables us to see.

Between Two Worlds takes us inside one of these institutions, a community college located in one of the large urban areas in the northeastern part of the United States. Weis focuses on the students and the culture they construct. She shows us what programs they take and why, their creative uses of bureaucratic rules, and finally the tightrope they must walk between life in an urban black community with its own valued styles, culture and linguistic forms and the dream of upward mobility through education. The community college she examines is not seen as an isolated entity, however. It is instead seen relationally. Its meaning is in its varied uses by both the state (to increase the state's legitimacy and extend limited opportunities for mobility) and the students (who often use it for their own purposes).

Weis goes beyond many of the previous arguments about the relationship between education and mobility in general and the role of the community college in particular. Her exceptionally sensitive ethnography partly confirms others' claims that such institutions are not the great engines of democracy and mobility we might think. Yet because this is an ethnography, we are led to see why this is the case. We can uncover the ways the students, most of whom are Afro-Americans, partly help to create these unequal outcomes in ways that both give these same students strength and catch most of them in the cycle of unequal power, education and jobs at one and the same time.

The basic arguments, both political and cultural, of *Between Two Worlds* can best be summarized in Weis's own words:

> Community colleges *are* structurally designed to offer opportunities for mobility. As a response to contest in the racial state, they had to be. On the other hand, community colleges may well serve fundamentally to reproduce structured social inequality. My investigation of Urban College suggests that this is the case. The way in which this occurs, however, is tied in contradictory ways to the culture students themselves produce within the institution – a culture that is rooted in but not "determined" by the existing social structure.

The themes of agency and cultural production, in the context of a structural analysis of how the economy and race interact, are clear here. They are what sets this argument apart from previous investigations. As she says in her introductory chapter:

> I focus on the self-formative process of cultural production lived by blacks. . . . Paradoxically, it is the culture which students *produce* within the college that helps to ensure the continued structural bases of their own "superexploitation." Despite intentions to the contrary, students forge a collective culture

> that ensures that the vast majority of them will return to the ghetto streets. This process is not conflict-free, however. It is fraught with contradictions and partial understandings as to the "true" role education plays in the reproduction of structure.

Yet to talk about students in general is also to miss something of importance. There are significant structural differences among them, especially in terms of gender. *Between Two Worlds* enables us to clarify this as well.

By focusing on the experiences not only of black men but also of black women in the community college, Weis has accomplished two important things. First, she has recognized the fact that divisions exist within the black community that are not only based on class, without assuming that white patriarchal relations are simply reproduced there. Second, and just as crucial, she takes us in her analysis beyond some of the limitations of a good deal of existing feminist work. While feminist theory has been of exceptional importance in its own right, it has tended to ignore the experiences of black women. Since racism "ensures that black men do not have the same relations to patriarchal/capitalist hierarchies as white men," and hence black men have not actually "held the same patriarchal positions of power that white males have established," a focus on the lives of black women cannot but help to reveal important similarities and differences between both black men and women *and* white and black women.[14] Weis's treatment of these phenomena could provide real opportunities for further empirical and theoretical advances.

Between Two Worlds, then, is a rare kind of book since it advances our understanding in a wide array of areas. First, as an analysis of how race operates in one of our major institutions, it is a real contribution to the debate over how class, race and gender actually work in advanced capitalist societies. Second, as a "culturalist reading" of the lived contradictions within black culture, it goes a good deal further than previous examinations of the role and efficacy of resistance in local institutions. This will prove to be extremely helpful in the current arguments among those who study the relationship between culture and social structure over the very meaning of resistance itself and over a potential politics that might result from it. Third, and this and the next points are of major importance to those readers who are specifically interested (as I think we all should be) in our educational institutions, as an ethnography Weis's volume lets us see what happens to faculty and students within formal school programs. The effects of the curriculum, of the teaching, of the institution itself, are made visible. Such an investigation should be significant to those of us who are concerned with the effects of educational programs. Finally, by taking seriously possibilities for reform, *Between Two Worlds* raises issues that policy makers, educators, government officials and community members cannot ignore. By making contributions in all these areas, the volume is a very welcome addition.

Michael W. Apple
The University of Wisconsin-Madison

Notes

1 For a review of these tendencies, see Michael W. Apple, *Education and Power* (Boston: Routledge & Kegan Paul, 1982).
2 Harry Braverman, *Labor and Monopoly Capital* (New York: Monthly Review Press, 1974).
3 The works of Richard Edwards, Michael Burawoy, Stanley Aronowitz and similar figures represent this argument. See Apple, *Education and Power*, for further discussion and Tony Manwaring and Stephen Wood, "The Ghost in the Machine: Tacit Skills in the Labor Process," *Socialist Review* 14, 2 (March–April 1984): 57–83.
4 Paul Willis, *Learning to Labour* (Westmead, England: Saxon House, 1977); Angela McRobbie, "Working Class Girls and the Culture of Femininity," in Women's Studies Group, ed., *Women Take Issue* (London: Hutchinson, 1978), pp. 96–108; Robert Everhart, *Reading, Writing and Resistance* (Boston: Routledge & Kegan Paul, 1983); and Linda Valli, "Becoming Clerical Workers: Business Education and the Culture of Femininity," in Michael W. Apple and Lois Weis, eds, *Ideology and Practice in Schooling* (Philadelphia: Temple University Press, 1983), pp. 213–34.
5 See Michael W. Apple, ed., *Cultural and Economic Reproduction in Education* (Boston: Routledge & Kegan Paul, 1982) and Apple and Weis, *Ideology and Practice in Schooling*.
6 Michele Barrett, *Women's Oppression Today* (London: New Left Books, 1980).
7 For further arguments about the necessity of seeing class, race, and gender dynamics as a totality, see Apple and Weis, *Ideology and Practice in Schooling* and Goran Therborn, *The Power of Ideology and the Ideology of Power* (London: New Left Books, 1980).
8 Centre for Contemporary Cultural Studies, *The Empire Strikes Back: Race and Racism in 70s Britain* (London: Hutchinson, 1982), p. 146.

9 Ibid., p. 56.
10 Vincent Harding, *There is a River: The Black Struggle for Freedom in America* (New York: Vintage Books, 1981), p. xix.
11 Michael Omi and Howard Winant, "By the Rivers of Babylon: Race in the United States," *Socialist Review* 13, 5 (September–October 1983): 49.
12 Harding, *There is a River*, p. 118.
13 Omi and Winant, "By the Rivers of Babylon," 50.
14 Centre for Contemporary Cultural Studies, *The Empire Strikes Back*, pp. 213–17.

Acknowledgments

The field research for this book was conducted in 1979–80. It is now 1985. During the past six years numerous individuals have contributed in one way or another to the outcome. Students, faculty and staff at Urban College allowed me into their lives for a full academic year. While they must remain nameless, I express my deep appreciation. Bob Dischner, Maryann Dorgan, Eva Rathgeber, Faith Campbell and Gunilla Holm-Lundberg acted as my research assistants, spending countless hours collecting data without which this book could never have been written. Phil Altbach, Steve Brown, Henry Giroux, Gail Kelly, Lionel Lewis, John Ogbu and Sheila Slaughter read drafts of the manuscript and contributed to my thinking in a number of ways. Michael Apple supported the project from the very beginning and helped me think through a series of difficult points. Carol Baker of Routledge & Kegan Paul offered encouragement and suggestions when I needed them most. Pat Gless typed and re-typed the manuscript until we both were tired. My husband, Tereffe Asrat, never lets me forget that what I am doing needs to be done. His questions sharpen my thinking; his love and encouragement strengthen my resolve and make difficult tasks worth doing. Sara Asrat and Woinam and Welela Tereffe remind me daily that the future is worth fighting for. Thanks to those mentioned above for encouraging my capacity to wonder. There is no greater gift.

Key to transcripts

*	From field notes, not transcription
#	Interview conducted by person other than LW
[ ]	Background Information
. . .	Pause
(. . .)	Material edited out

Coffee shop adjacent to Urban College

Joan (1st white waitress): I can't believe they are in *college*. This is supposed to be *college*. I could see if they were just kids off the street, but these are *college* students!
Sue (2nd white waitress): They are stupid. They are just going to college because they're getting *paid*. It's ridiculous! We are closing public schools and keeping this one open.
Robert (a black male customer): Well, if they're getting paid to do it, then maybe they're not so stupid.

1
Introduction

The 1950s and 1960s witnessed unprecedented militancy among black Americans. Blacks and supportive whites marched on Washington, held "sit-ins," and boycotted buses in the segregated south to demonstrate opposition to an unjust social order. Violence erupted in the 1960s in Detroit, Milwaukee and major cities throughout the country. H. Rap Brown cried, "America won't come around, so we're going to burn America down." The struggle of the 1950s and 1960s led to new efforts in housing, welfare, education and employment. It looked as if blacks would, at last, get their share of the American dream.[1]

This did not happen, however. There has been little change in income inequality between blacks and whites since the early 1950s. As the 1980s drew near, the situation looked bleak. Inflation and recession had eroded some of the moderate expansion in the small group of black professionals and managers. There were, in fact, few tangible economic gains as a result of the massive struggle of the 1950s and 1960s.

However, to argue that nothing changed for blacks in America is too simple. There were gains in education, and the ideology of "equality of opportunity" was extended to include blacks in direct response to the struggle of previous decades. The last vestiges of legal discrimination and segregation were dismantled, and blacks gained the opportunity to compete for positions previously denied to them. There was also large-scale expansion in tertiary level education and the success of the community college movement is linked directly to demands for education among previously excluded groups.

Substantial gains in education did not result in equality in the economic arena. While there are many reasons for this (some of which I will discuss more fully in this chapter), it is becoming increasingly apparent that the culture students produce in educational institutions makes a significant contribution to the maintenance of an unequal social structure. The present study explores this issue. Specifically, through the use of ethnographic techniques, I focus on the self-formative process of cultural production lived by blacks in an urban community college in a large northeastern city in the United States. Paradoxically, it is the culture which students *produce* within the college that helps to ensure the continued structural bases of their own "superexploitation." Despite intentions to the contrary, students forge a collective culture that ensures that the vast majority of them will return to the ghetto streets. This process is not conflict-free, however. It is fraught with contradictions and partial understandings as to the "true" role education plays in the reproduction of structure. Culture is also not free-floating. It takes its shape and form from the existing distribution of power and wealth in America – a distribution that is strikingly unequal by class, race and gender. Chapter 1 provides a description of the general position of blacks in American society; situates the study within a larger set of debates on culture, the economy and the state; and introduces the reader to students at what I call Urban College.[2]

Blacks in US society

The most extensive analysis to date on the position of blacks in the economy is provided by Michael Reich. Reich argues that while race relations have generally improved since 1918, racism, the systematic subordination of one race, is still a major problem in the United States. Rather than becoming narrower, important racial income differences have persisted throughout the century.[3] In spite of optimistic expectations resulting from the struggles of the 1950s and 1960s, the median income of black families in 1978 remained at only 57 per cent of that of white families. In fact, "the median income of blacks was at approximately the same relative level found in the early 1950s and remarkably close to estimates of black–white income ratios in 1900."[4] This is in spite of the struggles of the 1950s and 1960s, whose gains were expected to produce significant changes in the economic position of black Americans. While there is evidence to suggest that the black professional and managerial strata has expanded considerably since the 1960s (mostly as a result of employment in the state sector), the vast majority of blacks were left far behind.

The black class structure has changed, however, most notably in terms of the "decline of blacks as an agrarian class of small-holding and tenant farmers and their incorporation into the urban working class and professional and managerial strata." These developments rather than eliminating racial inequality, served to reproduce it in another setting. As Reich points out, much of the change observed in national data with respect to black employment reflects either "cyclical ups and downs in the economy or the movement of blacks *between* economic sectors," out of the agrarian south and into the urban and industrial north and south. Few declines in racial income inequality have taken place *within* urban areas and industries.[5]

The poverty levels of black Americans are striking. As of 1980, one in three blacks lived in poverty, as compared to one in ten whites. Nearly two-thirds of all black families living in poverty are one-parent homes headed by women, and the proportion of female-headed households jumped from 23.7 per cent in 1965 to 40 per cent in 1980. In contrast, the proportion of white families headed by women has remained at approximately 10 per cent during this same time period. In 1978, 50 per cent of all one-parent black households lived in poverty as compared to less than one-third of similarly situated white families.[6]

There have also been few changes in patterns of residential segregation, the persistence of which, argue Reich and others, result primarily from racial discrimination.[7] Census data indicate that residential segregation has increased by race in most cities since 1940. Despite a modest decline in segregation in northern cities between 1950 and 1960, residential segregation increased in most large cities in both the north and south during the 1960s and 1970s.[8]

The persistence of racial differentials is particularly noteworthy in light of changes in other areas. In education, there has been substantial improvement in both the quantity and quality of schooling. "The gap in median years of schooling completed between black and white males aged 25 to 29 fell from 6.5 years in 1890 to 3.3 years in 1940, and 0.5 years in 1970." Department of Labor Statistics suggest that approximately 75 per cent of the gap in 1960 was closed between 1960 and 1970. The gap for females, which had been even greater (7.2 years in 1890), stood at 0.3 years in 1970. Since black students in southern schools attended school only two-thirds as many days as whites until the 1950s, these figures understate the narrowing that has occurred.[9] While educational opportunities are not yet equal (particularly in terms of quality of school attended), changes that did occur did not exert a substantial upward force on relative income or residence patterns.

Major changes have also taken place in other arenas. Since 1945 most racial barriers to equal political and civil rights have been torn down; the sharecropping system in the south that served to maintain blacks at a level little better than slavery for so many decades has been largely dismantled. Most blacks now reside in metropolitan areas and work for a wage or salary. Yet substantial inequalities by race persist in the United States in the economic, cultural and political spheres.[10]

In fact, a high proportion of blacks are now trapped in what has been called the urban underclass. As Douglas Glasgow describes it,

> The term *underclass* does not connote moral or ethical unworthiness, nor does it have any other pejorative meaning; it simply describes a relatively new population in industrial society. It is not necessarily culturally deprived, lacking in aspirations, or unmotivated to achieve. Many of the long-term poor, those who have been employed for most of their productive lives but who have never moved from the level of bare subsistence living, are essentially part of the underclass. They try to keep body and soul together and maintain a job, but they remain immobile, part of the static poor. Others who could make this adaptation fail to do so, often preferring to remain unemployed rather than accept a job that demands their involvement for the greater part of each day but provides only the barest minimum of financial reward. They seek other options for economic survival ranging from private entrepreneurial schemes to working the welfare system. Hustling, quasi-legitimate schemes, and outright deviant activity are also alternatives to work. And still there are those who do wish to work but cannot find any meaningful employment. They spend a large part of their time hunting for jobs. They try many low-level jobs, some seasonal, others part-time, but always for a

> limited period. They may also seek alternatives for survival, sometimes unemployment insurance or welfare when they can meet the eligibility criteria.[11]

Notice what Glasgow is arguing here. On the one hand, entrapment in the urban underclass is related to employment in what Richard Edwards and others call the secondary labor market. Jobs in this sector are marked by the casual nature of the employment and the fact that work almost never requires previous training or education beyond basic literacy. In contrast to jobs in the primary market, they provide virtually no job security, and movement in and out of such jobs is common. They are typically dead-end jobs with few prospects of advancement. Most important is the fact that such work is not regular, and pervasive wagelessness is linked to employment in the secondary market.[12]

Glasgow also alludes to the fact that persons trapped in the underclass survive through a combination of transfer payments (such as welfare), seasonal or sporadic work, and "hustling." Ethnographic studies consistently suggest that whether working or receiving some form of public assistance, incomes for urban ghetto dwellers are far from sufficient. Bettylou Valentine's study of Blackston, for example, indicates that a typical pattern in a two-parent wage-earning household (which is *not* the norm for the underclass) is a husband who works at a trade, a wife who does domestic service or factory work, and two teenage children who may have part-time service jobs such as waitressing or clerking. The loss of employment for just one member of the unit often means the loss of property.[13] Such losses occur frequently given the casual nature of employment in the secondary market.

In order to supplement their income, individuals, whether working or not, often participate in a variety of illegal and quasi-legal activities such as gambling ("numbers") and the buying and selling of stolen merchandise like food, clothing and jewelry. Others sell drugs such as methodone, heroin, marijuana and cocaine. Glasgow's comments on hustling are well substantiated by field work. Valentine describes Bernice, a resident of Blackston, as follows:

> Bernice worked, occasionally in an office, always in her home, but she worked hardest at keeping Hank working too. She received her welfare payments, dealt with the welfare

> department and the case workers, and even arranged to receive welfare subsidized rents for their old home. And last but not least, Bernice knows she had hustled – buying "hot" goods, selling commercial products, playing the numbers, giving card parties and dances. Bernice and other Blackstonians found all this acceptable and indeed necessary in order to make it.[14]

It is not only black Americans who are entrapped in the underclass. Jagna Sharff's ethnography indicates that the situation of hispanics in urban areas is much the same. Like Valentine, she finds that life is saturated with "irregular" work.

> The clumps of young men, six to ten daily, who seemed to be socializing on the corner of Battery Avenue, from early morning into late at night were not there solely for convivial reasons. Nor was a little hole-in-the-wall cigarette store near the corner selling only tobacco cigarettes. Nor was the store-front next to ours just the home of a popular bachelor with lots of friends continually dropping by, nor was the mechanic next door simply repairing cars.
>
> The social club across the street was selling more than drinks and the bodega [small grocery store] next to it was selling more than groceries. And finally, as we discovered much later, the mothers conversing in small groups and calling out the windows were not simply occupied with housework and child care. . . .
>
> As we were to discover with the arrival of colder weather almost every man, woman, and older child on the block was actively engaged in providing services or securing additional goods and income for its household through licit or illicit occupations.[15]

Besides providing rich ethnographic material, Sharff documents that households could not survive if they did not participate in the "irregular" sector. An average family of four at the time of her study was receiving $258 a month from the Department of Welfare and $88 in food stamps, a total of $346 a month. Although this money was to cover gas, food, electricity, telephone, school supplies, clothing, transportation, and so forth, the estimated cost of food in New York City alone (where the study was conducted) for a family of four was $352 a month.[16] Since the structure of the illegal economy closely parallels that of the legal one, with high monopolistic earnings at the top, and low-paid, unstable, risky jobs at the bottom, residents in poor neighborhoods must continually hustle in order to make ends meet.[17]

While this situation does not apply to all raced persons in the United States, it characterizes life for those trapped in central city poor neighborhoods. As Harvard Sitkoff points out, two unequal societies developed within black cities: a small black middle class struggling to maintain its present status and a black underclass mired in poverty and despair. The latter is precisely the area from which Urban College draws a majority of its students. The fact that there is some tension between these two groups makes it difficult for individuals to attempt social mobility unless they are certain of success. I will address this point more fully in chapters 4 and 5.

Before proceeding to a discussion of Urban College and its students, it is important to locate the study within a larger set of debates on culture, the economy and the state. It is only then that we will be able to understand the way in which the self-formative process of cultural production is linked in contradictory ways to an unequal social structure.

Schools and the reproduction of structure

The role of education in the reproduction of structure has received considerable attention in recent years. While the debates in this area are still intense and there are points of severe (and healthy) disagreement among scholars, progress has been exceptional. It is now apparent, for example, that no one-way, simple, base-superstructure model will do to explain what goes on in schools. Schools are seen as *sites* where cultures and ideologies are produced in ongoing interactions rather than places where ideologies are imposed upon students. This does not mean that economists like Bowles and Gintis are entirely wrong when they argue that schools reproduce a division of labor and a set of ideological characteristics favorable to the maintenance of capitalism.[18] What it does mean is that this process is characterized by tension and contradiction, and that ideological hegemony is never secure.[19]

It is not my intention here to review the work in the area of culture, the economy and the state; others have done that well.[20] However, it is important to highlight two points which bear directly on the Urban College study: (1) schools are subject to contradictory demands, and (2) students, as classed, raced and gendered persons work on and through these contradictions at the level of their own culture. Both ensure that the outcomes of domination are less than total.

Schools are called upon to "mediate" inherent contradictions in the base. As Martin Carnoy argues, "under capitalism the return to capital must come from labor, and labor neither owns capital nor controls its investment and deployment."[21] This leads to struggle in the base, which, in turn, leads to attempts by capitalists to control this struggle. Mediation takes place in large part through the state supported educational system.[22]

Michael Apple and Roger Dale point out that schools, as mediators, are expected to perform rather contradictory "functions."[23] On the one hand, schools must assist in the capitalist accumulation process by providing some of the conditions for the reproduction of an unequal economy. Schools are expected to sort and certify a hierarchically organized student body and at the same time provide students with appropriate levels of knowledge and skill. Schools also assist in the creation of a context amenable to the capitalist accumulation process in that they keep children off the street, ensuring that for at least part of each day, they cannot engage in activities which will disrupt this process. While in school, students are also subject to attempts at socialization into ways compatible with the maintenance of this context.[24]

Schools also perform a "legitimation" function in that they are expected to sustain a meritocratic ideology, this reinforcing ideological forms necessary to the maintenance of an unequal economy. As Apple points out, these functions may be contradictory:

> (T)he needs of capital accumulation may contradict the needs for legitimation, a situation that is currently rather intense. In the school we can see this in the relative overproduction of credentialed individuals at a time when the economy no longer "requires" as many high salaried personnel. This very overproduction calls into question the legitimacy of the ways schools function. On a more concrete level, we can see the contradictions of the institution in the fact that the school has different ideological obligations that may be in tension. Critical capacities are needed to keep our society dynamic; hence

> schools should teach students to be critical. Yet critical capacities can challenge capital as well. This is not an abstract idea. These ideological conflicts permeate our educational institutions and are worked out every day in them.[25]

This situation is even more intense given that schools are state institutions and that the state has its own needs for legitimacy. Since the state is also subject to contradictory demands (support of the capitalist accumulation process which guarantees a context for its continued expansion as well as the legitimation of the capitalist mode of production and increasingly the state's role in it), schools are cross-pressured in a variety of ways. They cannot respond to the needs of capital accumulation in any simple sense. Indeed, the accumulation needs are themselves increasingly contradictory given that the state plays a more central role in the maintenance of capitalist accumulation than ever before.[26] As the state becomes more and more central to this process, it is likely that the legitimation and accumulation functions will clash even further.

Given the above points, it is significant that racial minorities have made the most gains in the state sector, particularly in education. In order to preserve its legitimacy in the face of mounting criticism, the state had to generate consent from competing groups. As Michael Omi and Howard Winant argue, the racial order has become more a terrain of struggle in the state than any time previously. Historically racial domination in the United States was enforced by terrorism, Jim Crow laws in the South (which were openly discriminatory), and "oppressive custom."[27] Since 1950, the state has been the focus of collective demands for democratic reforms as well as the enforcement of existing privileges. The racial state is itself a site of conflict and its own legitimacy depends to some extent on the mediation of such conflict. Omi and Winant further note that

> (t)he postwar black movement, later joined by other racially based minority movements, has sought by a strategy of war of position to transform the dominant racial ideology in the United States, to rearticulate its elements in a more egalitarian and democratic discourse. It has also sought to confront the manner in which state institutions enforce the pre-existing system of racial categories and practices.[28]

Minorities demanded access to educational institutions and a restructuring of those institutions and policies that had prevented such access. Increased quantity of education in the 1960s, in particular, must be seen as a direct result of racial contest in the state.

The fact that there have been few economic returns to gains in the educational sector can be linked, on the one hand, to the relative autonomy of the cultural, political and economic spheres. Increased access to education is a *political* response to racial contest in the state sector – it need not be linked in any direct fashion to the economy. Since, as I argued above, the needs for legitimation and accumulation may be contradictory, increased access may actually contradict needs for capital accumulation. This is not to deny the effects of racism *per se* in the economic sphere, but rather to argue that at least *some* of the disjunction between education and jobs, for example, is due to the relatively independent legitimation needs of the state and the fact that these needs may contradict the needs of accumulation. There is no guarantee that expansion in educational access will serve any other purpose except *temporary* legitimation.

One other factor needs to be considered here: the cultural level itself exhibits a degree of autonomy. No matter what the imperatives of capital or the state, for example, students do not passively accept meanings distributed through schools. They "act back" on such meanings depending on their own classed, raced and gendered subjectivities.

Paul Willis's study of working class boys provides an excellent example of the way in which students may reject and partially or totally transform meanings embedded within schools. *Learning to Labour* is an ethnographic account of a group of working class boys at an all-male comprehensive school in an industrial area of England.[29] Rather than internalize messages distributed through schools, the "lads" self-consciously reject such meanings and spend their time "working the system" in order to gain some measure of control over obligatorily spent time. They use school time to "have a laff." In contrast, the "ear 'oles" comply with educational authority and the notion of qualifications and credentials. The lads actively differentiate themselves from the "ear 'oles" and school culture in general, categorizing them as effeminate and unrelated to the masculine world of work. In Willis's terms, "the adult world, specifically the adult male working class world, is turned to as a source of material for resistance and exclusion."[30]

Willis's ethnography demonstrates that we cannot assume that meanings distributed through schools are necessarily internalized by students. His analysis goes further in important ways. By rejecting the world of the school and what the "ear 'oles" do, the lads reject mental labor as effeminate and celebrate manual labor as masculine, therefore better. As Harry Braverman and others have argued, hierarchical capitalist social relations demand the progressive divorce of mental from manual labor; the lads' rejection of the world of the school reproduces at an even deeper level the social relations of production necessary for the maintenance of a capitalist economy.[31] Although the lads live their rejection of the school as a form of cultural autonomy and freedom, the seeds of reproduction lie in this very rejection.

Angela McRobbie's research on working class girls in England examines the role of gender as it intersects with class in the production of culture and ideologies.[32] While McRobbie's "girls" fundamentally endorse traditional "femininity," they do so as a creative response to their own lived conditions rather than passively accept meanings imposed by others (family and school, specifically). In spite of the fact that they know that marriage and housework are far from glamorous simply by virtue of the lives of female relatives and friends, they construct fantasy futures and elaborate an "ideology of romance." They create a specifically *female* anti-school culture which consists of interjecting sexuality into the classroom, talking loudly about boyfriends, and wearing makeup. As McRobbie argues,

> Marriage, family life, fashion and beauty all contribute massively to this feminine anti-school culture and, in doing so, nicely illustrate the contradictions inherent in so-called oppositional activities. Are the girls in the end not doing exactly what is required of them – and if this *is* the case, then could it not be convincingly argued that it is their own culture which itself is the most effective agent of social control for the girls, pushing them into compliance with that role which a whole range of institutions in capitalist society also, but less effectively, directs them towards? At the same time, they are experiencing a class relation, in albeit traditionally feminine terms.[33]

McRobbie illustrates the relatively independent dynamic of gender as it intersects with class. While both Willis's lads and McRobbie's girls are working class, they elaborate, simply by virtue of gender, different cultures. Where McRobbie and Willis are alike, however, is in the fact that both see culture as relatively autonomous. Paradoxically, it is culture itself as elaborated by distinctly different groups which helps to sustain, in contradictory ways, an unequal base.

The present study builds on work by Willis, McRobbie and others who have studied lived cultural forms in schools.[34] While numerous scholars have noted the importance of race as a factor in the production of culture and ideologies, no one has investigated these processes directly.[35] The present study will begin to fill a significant void in the literature on education and cultural and economic reproduction.

The qualitative methods and participant-observation techniques employed in the Urban College study (see Appendix A for a full description of method) were dictated by my interest in the interplay between culture and economics. As Willis notes, "these techniques are suited to record this level and have a sensitivity to meanings and values as well as the ability to represent and interpret symbolic articulations, practices and forms of cultural production."[36] During the academic year 1979–80 I attended classes, conducted in-depth interviews with both students and faculty, and in general immersed myself in Urban College for three days a week for one full academic year. A record was kept of the day-to-day experiences and comments of students and faculty in classrooms, corridors, stairwells, offices, cafeteria and the local coffee shop and bar. This allowed me to explore both the direct experiences of education and the way in which these experiences are worked over and through the praxis of cultural discourse.[37]

The community college in the United States provides an excellent site in which to explore cultural production and the reproduction of class and race antagonisms. More than any other institution, the community college has been heralded as the great equalizer and it is generally viewed as the leading edge of an open and egalitarian system of education. The growth of the community college system coincided with the struggles of the 1960s: community colleges must be seen at least partially as a response to racial contest in the state.[38] Proponents argue that community colleges respond to demands for access and equality of opportunity through (1) a comprehensive curriculum; (2) an open-door admission policy; (3) a convenient location whereby 95 per cent of the students may commute; (4) a publicly stated attempt to give students a "second chance"; and (5) a community orientation whereby students will see the value of higher education and choose to attend college.[39]

While this is the official version of the role of community colleges, scholars such as Jerome Karabel and Burton Clark argue that community colleges serve primarily to reproduce structured social inequality.[40] Clark, for example, points to the high attrition rate in the transfer program (the liberal arts track) at a community college in California, and Karabel notes that community colleges draw primarily from the working class and train students for working class jobs. Universities, on the other hand, draw from the middle class and train for middle class jobs.

As I will argue here, the above positions are both partially correct. Community colleges *are* structurally designed to offer opportunities for mobility. As a response to contest in the racial state, they had to be. On the other hand, community colleges may well serve fundamentally to reproduce structured social inequality. My investigation of Urban College suggests that this is the case. The way in which this occurs, however, is tied in contradictory ways to the culture students themselves produce within the institution – a culture that is rooted in but not "determined" by the existing social structure. I now turn to Urban College itself.

Urban College and its students[41]

Urban College is located on the edge of the urban ghetto in a large northeastern city in the United States.[42] It opened its doors in 1971, and became the first multi-campus public community college in the state. It began with 342 students, eighteen full-time faculty, four department chairs, and five additional administrators. It offered Associate of Applied Science degree programs in Business Administration and Secretarial Science, Associate of Arts programs in Humanities and Social Sciences, and an Associate of Science degree program in Mathematics. By the spring of 1981, Urban College had a student headcount of 1552 and a full-time equivalent count of 1383 students.[43] Curriculum offerings were expanded to include Associate degree programs in Criminal Justice, Paralegal Assistant,

Fashion Merchandising, Science Laboratory Technology, Child Care and Radiologic Technology. Unlike the California system as described by Clark, credits obtained in even ostensibly "terminal" programs transfer to state colleges and universities.[44]

The mission of Urban College reflects that of the broader community college movement. The 1981–2 college catalog states the following:

> The threefold mission of Urban College is to develop and provide high-quality, low-cost, public post-secondary educational programs and related services which are geographically accessible to county residents; to maintain an admissions policy whereby students academically qualified as well as academically deficient, may fulfill College requirements toward certificate or degree program options and to comply with affirmative action, equal opportunity, and special education requirements in terms of student admissions and faculty and staff recruitment.[45]

More specifically, Urban College has the following objectives:

– To provide students with general education courses to complement courses in their areas of concentration.

– To provide instructional programs which parallel the first two years of study in a four-year institution.

– To provide occupational educational programs which prepare students for realistic employment upon graduation.

– To offer skills re-training and pertinent state-of-the-art courses for individuals who seek promotion within the businesses and industries at which they are currently employed.

– To assure that graduates demonstrate competency in reading, mathematics, and comprehension.

– To provide quality instruction at each campus [in the multi-campus unit] by instituting evaluation mechanisms that assess instructional programs and staff.

– To provide continuing education and community service

programs to accommodate expressed individual or organizational needs.

– To provide limited use of College facilities to the public for educational, cultural, recreational, and avocational activities.[46]

Of these, providing instructional programs which parallel the first two years of those in four-year institutions, and providing vocational programs which prepare students for employment upon graduation are the most important. In general, however, these objectives reflect the goals of the broader movement.

The college itself is designed to promote equal educational opportunity. For this reason it advocates full opportunity in its admissions policy, and all high school graduates are accepted at Urban College. As stated in the handbook, "Adults, veterans, the unemployed, housewives, transfer students, military personnel, businessmen, blue-collar workers and those self-employed are encouraged to apply to and attend the variety of programs and courses offered at Urban."[47] In line with an open admissions policy, applications are accepted until the first day of class every semester.

As noted earlier, Urban College is located on the edge of the urban ghetto. Over 70 per cent of the students are black and the vast majority reside in surrounding ghetto neighborhoods.[48] Approximately 39 per cent of black students and 50 per cent of white students are 22 or younger, and 42 per cent and 30 per cent of black and white students respectively are between the ages of 23 and 29. Twenty per cent of both black and white students are over 29; of these, less than 5 per cent of blacks (all females) and 14 per cent of whites are between the ages of 40 and 61.[49] The process of cultural production explored in this book is generally applicable to black students, both male and female. Women who are returning to school after they have raised their families (this characterizes approximately 4.5 per cent of black female students) are largely exempt from the group logic examined here. While students below the age of 22 may be somewhat less "serious" about school than their older, non-traditional counterparts, there is little difference between the two groups in terms of the culture that they produce and live within the institution.[50]

Although Urban College students do not, by and large, attend college directly from high school, over 90 per cent are attending on a full-time basis.[51] Since the college is a Full Opportunity Program (FOP) branch of State University, all applicants who have high school or general equivalency diplomas are admitted. More than 90 per cent of the students receive some form of financial aid. In the Fall of 1980, 90 per cent of Urban College students received Tuition Assistance Program (TAP) benefits; 87 per cent received Basic Educational Opportunity Grant (BEOG); and 27 per cent received Educational Opportunity Program (EOP) benefits. Ten per cent of students received Veterans' benefits in spring of 1981.[52]

An overwhelming number of students at Urban College intend to continue their education after completing the Associate degree. Ninety-four per cent and 90 per cent of black men and women respectively state that they intend to continue their education.[53] The comparable figures for white males and females are 90 per cent and 66 per cent. These data reflect higher aspirations than the national average for community college students. I will pursue student affirmation of education at some length in chapter 2.

Urban College does not draw from the black middle class. Based on results of a survey questionnaire administered in March 1980, it can be estimated that fathers of students, if employed, are concentrated disproportionately in production and service – well over 75 per cent of employed fathers are rooted in these sectors. A relatively small percentage of this group have stable, unionized jobs. Twelve per cent of students report that their father is not in the labor force. Data on mother's occupation largely parallel these findings: 38 per cent of mothers have low-paying jobs in the clerical, production or service sectors, and 40 per cent are not in the labor force.[54]

The high percentage of students who did not respond to the question or who indicated that they "don't know" their father's occupation, in particular, is noteworthy. A full 15 per cent of black students said that they did not know what their father did for a living, and over 17 per cent did not respond to the question. The comparable figures for mothers are 10 per cent and 9.6 per cent. While it is possible that students genuinely lack such information, it is likely that a number of fathers and mothers are engaged in quasi-legal activities that would not be revealed on a questionnaire. As Glasgow, Valentine, Sharff and others remind us, the interplay between the "legitimate" and the "irregular" economy exerts a powerful influence on the day-to-day lives of ghetto residents. Out of necessity, even those who hold legitimate jobs often participate in the irregular sector.

The parents of Urban College students are, for the most part, rooted in the secondary labor market and students tend to exhibit the same economic marginality as their parents. While most have families of their own, they have not had, nor do they have, steady employment. Those who work generally have part-time employment in either service or production, engaging in casual hourly wage labor that offers neither security nor benefits. In point of fact, such employment is increasingly difficult to obtain in the city in which Urban College is located and the majority of students, both men and women, survive through a combination of transfer payments (such as welfare), occasional jobs in production or service, and "hustling." Like their parents, then, Urban College students exhibit characteristics that destine them to become part of a permanently trapped population of poor people – the industrial underclass.

Students are aware of this and they actively perceive Urban College as a mediator between two worlds – the ghetto and the cultural mainstream. Attendance at Urban College must be understood at least in part as a rejection of "street" life and an attempt to embrace what students see as "legitimate" society. As Anthony, a Business Administration student states, the streets mean "heroin, cocaine, marijuana, armed robbery, petty theft and direct rip-offs – con games." They also mean "pimps, prostitutes and numbers dealers." "Going legit" (entering the cultural mainstream) means, in the words of another student, a "good" job, a "three piece suit, and lunch on ______ Avenue."

That students employ this dichotomy is clear from the taped interviews. Although the question was never broached directly, time and time again students indicate that they view the community college as a way off the streets and, by implication, out of the urban underclass. Students see the college functioning exactly as its proponents argue – as offering them a "second chance." In the context of the urban ghetto, this means a chance to *reverse* a mode of living they feel they "chose" at a younger age. George, a former student, describes the role of Urban College as follows:

> "[Ghetto kids] are always looking out of a window; looking for money and power and not really knowing where to get it. . . .

At a very young age these kids are faced with a choice; they can go the easy way as a pimp, numbers dealer, prostitute, or they can try to make it another way – through the schools. [Urban College] represents a way back for those who took the left fork first and became disillusioned."

The following transcriptions clarify this point. Students repeatedly indicate that they view the community college as a way off the streets – as a way of disassociating *themselves* from certain aspects of the urban black community.

James, for example, was born and raised in Columbus, Ohio and is enrolled in the paralegal curriculum. A black male aged about 45, he is back in school because his mother, dead twenty years, wanted him to be a lawyer, doctor or teacher. For him,

"Everything moves in its own time and I ran the streets enough. Ripping and running back and forth across the country and now it's time for me to take myself back to school and try to fulfill a promise that I made to her [my mother].

(. . .) I am going back to school, to get enough expertise relative to handling oneself, to raise one's employability level because you can. Because you are not going to get a job *legally* expediting skills that you have learned street-side way, and this is what I and a number of others [here] were about – street players . . . standing on the corner matching wits with the authorities, that sort of stuff. And you simply don't find jobs doing that so you got to go back to school, either technical school or you got to be involved in academia in order to raise your employability level."

For James, Urban College is a way of entering a new world – a way of gaining skills, thereby changing his own culture so that he will fit into another sector of society. In order to gain skills that will enable participation in the "legitimate" economy and the cultural mainstream, the individual must cut himself or herself off totally from former contacts:

"When one *opts* [my emphasis] to change one's lifestyle, he lets go of the streets. I do not go to ______ and ______ any more although I haven't cancelled out on my friendships such as they are, in any way over there, but I simply feel that I don't have anything in common with the fellas involved in those crap games in those buildings out there. I don't have anything in common with those fellas who want to hang around the pool hall shooting pool for money all day long. I don't do that any more. I can always find something that I have to do relative to furthering my education."

This feeling is further illustrated by Anthony, a black male of about 27, who is working on an Associate degree in Business Administration. His was a conscious decision to disassociate himself from street life for fear of its consequences:

Anthony: I did well living on the streets. I made more money living on the streets than after I went back to school, got me a job and was living the way I guess society expects me to live.
LW: Why did you decide to go back to school?
Anthony: I chose school and society over Attica, because the things I was doing on the streets, they eventually would bring you to Attica, Elmira, or any correctional institution you care to name. I said I better get myself out of this and go straight.
LW: Can you elaborate on that?
Anthony: Nothing I did was legal when I was on the streets. (. . .) Eventually there was gonna come a time when I was going to have my first bust, my second bust, and I was gonna maybe suspend a sentence, maybe probation, but eventually it was gonna lead to incarceration somewhere. So rather than seeing myself being put into a cage, I started weighing the benefits. I said I don't think it should be that hard for me to go back to school. I was no dummy in the streets, why should I think I'm going to be a dummy in school?

(. . .) In the black community it [attending Urban College] is an attempt to identify with another group of people and still do what we call "hang" – you know, "be in." [The community] puts a lot of pressure on you. By going back to school, believe me, I have lost friends in the community.

By virtue of lived realities related to gender (and the way in which gender intersects with race and class), the experience of black female students is somewhat different. Like their male counterparts, however, women attend school to escape life in the ghetto. Odessa, a 25-year-old single mother of three, explains her plight.

> *Odessa:* I have to send two [children] off to school and one to a babysitter and really the money [BEOG] I get from school doesn't even cover the babysitting charges. I'm not gainin' nothin'. I pay my babysitter a hundred dollars a month. . . . It's rough. I feel as if I'm in the war. And I still do the laundry and get clothes straightened out each day. It's hard. (. . .) I dropped out last semester because there was no where to keep the baby, and I know that if I brought the baby I might as well have stayed at home.

Despite these hardships, Odessa also sees the school as a way out:

> (. . .) [The college] turned me against the wrong crowd. Before I was, you know, with people who really didn't care about their education, but now since I've been going to school I've been with more people who did care about their education and their futures. (. . .) It keeps me alive.
> *LW:* If you had not gone back to school, what would you be doing?
> *Odessa:* Well, I'd probably be goin' out all weekend (. . .), just wastin' my time, not really gettin' anything, you know, playin' around. I'm more settled now than I ever was – settled in my mind, not in material things.
> *LW:* So, coming back to school allowed you to meet other people like yourself?
> *Odessa:* [It allowed me] to keep going, instead of going back to not doin' nothin', sittin' around, waitin' on some man, or something like that.

It is apparent that blacks at Urban College view the institution as a way of escaping aspects of their immediate environment. The college is the vehicle through which students perceive that they can enter the cultural mainstream and at the same time "hang" – that is, "be in." This is important, and attending Urban College should not be interpreted as a wholesale denial or rejection of the black cultural experience. In spite of their desire to escape the urban underclass, students are very much part and parcel of the urban black community, and this is a determining factor in the production of located cultural form.

Gender and student culture

Men and women in the urban ghetto, like men and women elsewhere, experience different lived realities. As Joyce Ladner argues in her excellent study of black women in the United States, most black females view the duties of the woman as those associated with keeping the home intact. This includes caring for children, cleaning house and providing financial support. Black women *expect* to be strong, and parents socialize their daughters with this end in mind.[55] Loretta, a Business Administration student at Urban College, reinforces this point when she states: "The women work harder [than the men]; they've been liberated a long time. . . . Black women have *had* to be serious – the men have not."

Women assume primary responsibility for children. While this is certainly true in many communities, a high percentage of women with children in the urban ghetto are no longer married or never were married. Child bearing and rearing are regarded as natural and highly desirable activities, whether one is married or not. While the acknowledged father has certain rights and responsibilities with respect to his children, children generally reside with the mother and her kin network. Mothers expect little from the father; they just "hope that he will help out."[56] This is not to suggest that men are "absent" or that children are raised by women alone. Indeed this is not the case. Numerous studies remind us that fathers, as well as lovers and friends, play an important role in children's lives. As Carol Stack argues, however,

> The emptiness and hopelessness of the job experience for black men and women, the control over meager [AFDC] resources by women, and the security of the kin network, militate against successful marriage or long-term relationships. . . . Women and men nonetheless begin buoyant new relationships with one another and fall in love, as all races and classes do. But they must wager their relationships against the insurmountable forces of poverty and racism.[57]

This is not to say that ghetto residents do not wish it were otherwise; it simply reflects the stark realities of America's urban poor.

This is borne out by survey data collected at Urban College. Thirty per cent of black male students claim responsibility for children as compared with 70 per cent of black female students. Seventy per cent of females also refer to themselves as "head of household." While there are certainly married students with children at Urban College, the majority of students with children are no longer married or never were married.

The desire to provide a better life for children constitutes a major reason why females attend Urban College. While they, like their male counterparts, wish to escape the ghetto streets themselves, they also express great concern over the future of their children. Women repeatedly suggest that they are attending school to make a better life for themselves and their sons and daughters. The comments below, drawn from conversations and student essays, clarify this point. They illustrate not only the extent to which single women are raising children, but also the fact that the desire for a better life for these children is what motivates women, in particular, to go back to school.

*Friday September 7, 1979 2:00 p.m.**

After Public Speaking class Eloise and Jessie were talking. They were talking about the required speech and Eloise said she was nervous about giving speeches (she had just given hers). Jessie asked her what the speech was about and she said it was about their lives – why they are at Urban College and what they want in the future.

Eloise said she wanted a better life for her and her daughter (in the speech she had said that her "9-year-old daughter is the most important thing in the world to me"). She wants to take care of herself – "don't trust no man." Jessie agreed, "Yeah, they keep running out; you got to make a better life for yourself."

* * *

Jennifer: I was born in ______ (. . .) and have lived here all my life. I'm divorced and have a daughter 3½ years old. I'm attending Urban College full-time days and I'm majoring in Business Administration.

(. . .) Becoming a CPA [certified public accountant – she intends to go to State University] is very important to me. I came from a broken home and I know how hard things can be while growing up. And I want to be able to give my daughter every possible chance in life that she deserves. (. . .) I'm not only doing it for my own satisfaction, but also so I can raise and support my daughter to the best of my ability. (from a student essay)[58]

* * *

Jayette: I am enrolled in the Fashion Merchandising curriculum. (. . .) I'm 22 years old . . . I have three children now. ______ age 7, ______ age 3, and ______ age 1. I'm trying to create a stable situation for myself and family. Without dependence on welfare for life. Just myself and society can and will get me by in years to come. (from a student essay)

* * *

Caroline: I am going back to school because I have a little boy and my little boy is now in the second grade and he has made me so very proud of him, he gets very good grades in school. And I tells him how important it is to do your very best in whatever you do in life. I had to quit school because I was having a baby and now my son is old enough so I can go back and get my education because I believe in practice what you preach. (from a student essay)

* * *

Sarena: My reasons for being here are many. I'm a single parent of four children, trying to improve my education. This will help me to move up in the world. I want the feeling of independence. (from a student essay)

* * *

Lena: At 24 with one girl child, I am constantly tired, because of incompletion of education, taking penny-anny jobs. Surviving presently on assistance from welfare and grant money, I have now realized what it takes to get where I want to be. (from a student essay)

* * *

Tara: At the age of 26 and having a son at the age of 7, I feel kind of strange going back to school. I quit school at the age of

> 15. Eleven years later I am back in school. One of the reasons I quit school is because I did not know what I wanted to do. Now I know and it is to get a degree in Business Administration. In order to make a better life for my son and myself. No one in my family have a degree in anything except having babies. (from a student essay)

There is no question but that the majority of female students attend Urban College to ensure a better life for themselves and their children. This in itself differentiates them from male students since the majority of men do *not* have primary responsibility for children, whether financial or emotional. In this sense then, the lived realities of women and men are different.

As Stack and others argue, the urban poor form extensive networks of kin and friends who support and reinforce each other – constructing schemes for self-help, strategies for survival in a community of scarce resources. It is these very networks (which I will discuss more fully in chapter 5) that enable women to attend school. Despite the lack of a day care facility on campus, women with small children are able to attend classes by virtue of their kin. As ghetto residents say, "you have to have help from everybody and anybody," and, "The poorer you are, the more likely you are to pay back."[59] Michele, an Urban College student and mother of a 4-month-old child, states "As long as I go back to school and am doing something, my momma said she'd take care of my child."

Cooperative arrangements among kin are common. Odessa, who earlier stated that she feels as if she is "in the war," says "usually I'm by myself [in school]. See, most of the women have someone to help them and I don't. My mind is totally into what the teacher is saying." Odessa was born in South Carolina and raised in the northeast by an aunt and uncle. She differs from other students in that her aunt and uncle do not help her and she has no other kin to rely upon. The father of her children was recently killed. Although he did not live with her and "wasn't that much help," he did help "sometimes." She has no kin network and therefore relies only upon herself:

> "Most of them [younger women][60] think that some man is going to do it for them. I know that if you don't do it for yourself, there's no man that's going to take all that weight off you. . . .

Most women already have children and that causes a little bit of confusion, 'cuz if the man scolds the child, she'll say 'You're doing that 'cuz he's not yours.' "

While the majority of women at Urban College work at low-paying jobs in the secondary market or are "on aid" (which prevents them from taking "legitimate" employment), they, like the men, must constantly "hustle" in order to make ends meet. The form of work available in the "legitimate" sector differs to some extent by gender, but the fact remains that *neither* males nor females are able to earn a living wage in this sector alone. Both are trapped in the secondary market; both are dependent upon transfer payments; and both must hustle in order to survive. The conversations below reinforce the point that hustling is not confined to men:

Lena: I have great business knowledge. I learned from the streets. Those in higher positions play for greater stakes. The rules for both are the same. I figure that if I add technical knowledge to street knowledge, my results should be those of a winner. Financially I want to be able to pay for my bills without having to steal from Peter to give to Paul.

* * *

Belinda: These people [students] are *expert* in what they do and they learn it from the school of hard knocks, as we call it. They are expert in what they do and they have expert minds. They have to be retrained, but they can be retrained and they can be put out into a market for businessmen, or whatever.

(. . .) If a prostitute or pimp takes that step to come here [Urban College] I think that is a person that needs to be encouraged most. That's a whole different thing. People that are encouraged by their families, pushed by their families, because they want daddy to buy them a car, they want a boyfriend, they want to be secure – their drive, their reasoning is not as intense as when they come from a different lifestyle. That's the kind of person who needs a little help, some special kind of help.

(. . .) We have here [at Urban] what you call the quasi-prostitute. They do it to a degree. I'd say that 50 per cent of the females and 86 per cent of males are trying to get changed among the blacks.

* * *

Anthony: It is not uncommon to see women dealing on the

> streets in the black community.
> *LW:* Are there more men or women dealing in the streets?
> *Anthony:* It doesn't make any difference. It's getting harder to find a job.(. . .) With the unemployment ratio as great as it is, what do you turn to to get this money and get these things that you want to do? So, if I can get enough money together to get my first quarter pound, or my first pound, I can go from there.
> (. . .) Unemployment in the black community is not this fictitious figure they have 11 or 12 per cent [official figures for the city]. It is more like 40, 45 or 50 per cent.

While the lived realities of men and women differ in some rather important ways, in the final analysis black men and women share the lived reality of urban poverty. They share entrapment in the urban ghetto and racist America. *These shared experiences lead students to forge a collective culture within Urban College that is not bound strictly by gender.* The culture produced in the college ensures that the vast majority of students will return to the ghetto streets. It is these shared aspects of existence that give rise to this culture – a culture that helps to ensure the continued structural bases of their own "superexploitation" as blacks. In so doing, students help to reproduce the structural bases for the distinct form that gender relations take within this class fraction. While the reproduction of gender-based tensions and antagonisms is in itself an important topic for research, I do not address this question here. Wherever appropriate, I point out areas where the logic may work differently by gender.

In the remainder of the book I articulate elements of black student culture as produced within Urban College, and explore factors both within and outside the institution that contribute to the production of located cultural form. Chapters 2 through 5 constitute a more traditional ethnography of Urban College. Chapters 6 and 7 are largely theoretical. Like Willis's latter chapters, they analyze the rationality and dynamic of the cultural processes recorded in chapters 2 through 5, and the ways in which these cultural processes are linked to the maintenance of an unequal social structure. This is not total, however: the culture students produce has elements of both "good" and "bad" sense which suggest that ideological hegemony is never secure. There is, therefore, a capacity for serious political action. Chapter 8 explores this possibility.

2
Elements of culture

"Most of these people [students at Urban College] have no basic skills; they can't read or write, can't do math, they don't know Malcolm X, John Coltrane, Bobby Seale, Huey Newton. They just don't know. (. . .) I am continually shocked. My own people can't read, write, and know nothing about their own history. We have no heroes. Our heroes become Abraham Lincoln and the Emancipation Proclamation – all the rest are dead and buried (. . .).

Black people are going back to being slaves. That's why I wear this bracelet [locked]; I don't intend to take it off until we get out of slavery." (An Urban College graduate)

This chapter details elements of black student culture at Urban College. As I will argue, these elements are themselves contradictory: students embrace and reject schooling at one and the same time. Students affirm the process that is education but drop in and out of school, arrive late to class, exert little effort and engage in extensive drug use. The effects of the culture are twofold: (1) an exceedingly low graduation rate per entering class; and (2) the reproduction of deeply rooted race/class antagonisms in the broader society. In the latter case, it is black culture acting in concert with white culture that is linked to the reproduction of fundamental antagonisms.

I will briefly compare elements of black student culture with those noted among the white working class. The comparison rests primarily on Paul Willis's data on working class boys in England and Howard London's data on white working class students in a community college in the United States.[1] Unlike the students in Urban

College, those in London's study have fathers who are members largely of what Edwards calls the Traditional Proletariat. These jobs are located within the subordinate primary market; they are better paying than secondary market jobs and involve long-term stable work with prospects for advancement. In the United States they are distinguished from secondary market jobs most fundamentally by the presence of unions.[2]

Willis's "lads" are also of the white manual labor working class. While the fathers of students are engaged in generalized rather than in skilled labor, pervasive wagelessness is not a feature of the class landscape.[3] The English equivalent of the wagelessness and economic marginality noted for Urban College students lies with immigrant groups, particularly West Indians. The lads' economic position is therefore closer to that of London's students than that of Urban College students.

It is noteworthy that white working class students at Urban College (who constitute approximately 30 per cent of the student body) do not manifest a culture similar to that noted by London and Willis. While it is difficult to assess the depth of this difference given that I did not study white culture directly, it can be argued that white lived culture in Urban College takes a different shape and form from that noted in previous investigations given that it emerges dialectically in relation to that of the black urban underclass as produced in the college as well as the larger white working class. I will address the reproduction of race/class antagonisms toward the end of the chapter.

Attitudes toward authority and knowledge

One dimension of black student culture at the community college is the affirmation of both the idea of teachers and the content of school knowledge. In contrast, investigators of working class white cultural forms note a distinctly negative attitude toward authority and school knowledge, manifested in incivility toward faculty.

The most obvious dimension of the lads' culture, for example, is "entrenched general and personalized opposition to authority." The lads engage in behavior designed to show resentment while stopping just short of outright confrontation. There is, notes Willis,

> an aimless air of insubordination ready with spurious justification and impossible to nail down. If someone is sitting on the radiator, it is because his trousers are wet from the rain, if someone is drifting across the classroom he is going to get some paper for written work, or if someone is leaving class, he is going to empty the rubbish "like he usually does". . . . A continuous hum of talk flows around injunctions not to, like the inevitable tide over barely dried sand and everywhere there are rolled-back eyeballs and exaggerated mouthings of conspirational secrets.[4]

While it is tempting to relate these behaviors to adolescence rather than social class *per se*, it is important to note that adult white working class males in the community college exhibit similar attitudes toward authority and engage in comparable behavior.[5] About a month or so after school opened, students in London's study began injecting *sotto-voce* taunts into classroom lectures and discussions. This opposition took a distinctly class form in that, for the most part, it was done by students in manual training programs and aimed at liberal arts teachers or vocational training teachers who were considered too abstract. Law enforcement students did not harass teachers who were ex-detectives, for example, but they did harass the lawyer who taught legal aspects of police work. Students reacted negatively only in those classes that were "too intellectual," that is, too centered on mental labor.[6]

The case of Urban College students, both male and female, is substantially different. Rather than rejecting the idea of teachers or the content of school knowledge, Urban College students criticize teachers only in so far as they do not encourage what students consider a fair transaction. In return for respect or obedience on the part of students, students expect faculty to share their knowledge. As the following transcriptions suggest, negativity is expressed only in terms of faculty not caring enough or not working hard enough to ensure that students learn. In contrast to the white working class, Urban College students steadfastly affirm what the faculty have to offer – they simply want them to offer it and hold teachers at least partially responsible for student failure.[7]

> *Anthony:* See what it is that, for one thing the instructor – he doesn't present the class to make anyone feel comfortable. He could be a much more influential force in the class if he would

emphasize certain things and de-emphasize things that he emphasizes right now. As far as participation, don't be so sarcastic because people that are hesitant to get up in class right now are afraid more so of him than they are of the class.

(. . .) They are afraid of his critical judgment on them as a human being and an individual and a student, instead of him using his influence to make these people feel comfortable.

LW: Could you elaborate?

Anthony: He would, I imagine, have a much better class, a greater attendance record and fewer drop out if he would put himself in the position to realize that the students don't have confidence within themselves yet, and a little more personal understanding. (. . .) It's a monotone, monotonous type of class, no fluent conversation, no fluent inter-relationship between the instructor and the student. (a Business Administration student)

* * *

James: I would like to see more dedication on the part of the faculty.

LW: In what sense?

James: There is a vast difference between a pro and a novice in anything. If you are a professional, you take pride in whatever your specialty is; you take pride in doing a good job. The old-fashioned shoe cobbler, he took immense pride in turning out or trying to turn out the perfect pair of shoes. I feel a professional person can look at the situation no different. That you must take pride in whatever you are doing and try to do the best possible job. I feel that any teacher over there should be concerned about his students more than the others, and enough to look down the line and pick the paper a student has achieved and he can see his handiwork in the achievement of the individual students.

When I went to school (. . .) the teacher held the same place of honor and respect that the black preacher did who came to the house on Sunday to eat up all the chicken. Well a teacher held the same esteem that he did. In my household I *had to study and I had to learn, but in exchange for this my teachers were dedicated*. [My emphasis]

LW: When you say that teachers here are not dedicated, what do you mean?

James: (. . .) There may be some who don't have what I consider a dedication, they are just there to get the money. They are not unlike the students themselves [referring to the commonly held notion that many students attend school simply to obtain grant money]. They are there to get paid and they are going to do as less they can. . . This works to the detriment of the student because what it does is lower standards and makes the person think that they are getting an education when they are not. Then they leave this facility and go some place else; they get a job, go to another school, then they cannot pass the entrance test, or they get in class then they can't maintain because the proper groundwork hasn't been laid over there . . . I feel that the ones [teachers] who are not dedicated should be held to performance within the scope of their employment. If they cannot perform, then it's about standing aside and allowing someone to assume the position who can. (. . .) I want my teachers to be dedicated in teaching me, not just there to get the dollar. (a Paralegal student)

* * *

[an informal group discussion]
Johnnie: As far as the professors I'd attempt to keep their attendance in line (. . .) because the professors at Urban College tend to just take for granted the students in this school.

(. . .) They take the attitude that the student at this school doesn't really want to learn. He's here for some reason or another other than to learn. "So I'm going to miss this day and I'm going to miss that day."
Claude: It's bias.
Johnnie: (. . .) This is my first semester. I started off with five classes and now I'm presently at four. Out of four classes I have two good instructors that are there when they are supposed to be and the way they go about instructing is compatible. You know, you can really get into it. But I have two other instructors that are hardly ever there; what they teach they don't test on, and they use attendance as their chain on you or something. He says if you don't attend, you don't get a good grade, but if you attend and he's not there, your motivation about getting to this class tends to drop somewhat. You go to class; you break your neck to get there at 9:00 [a.m.] and you go to class and the instructor's not there and he told you you were going to have a

test and you studied *all* night – stuff like that.

(. . .) If they [faculty] couldn't handle the job in the beginning they shouldn't have took the job. 'Cuz you can't go out here and get a job in industry and then expect somebody else to do your job 'cuz that's too much for you. You shouldn't be there in the beginning (. . .). You see, a lot of these professors use teaching as a second job or even a third job. There's a lot of good instructors there but they don't apply themselves. I know the students don't either and that has the instructor's motivation drop somewhat. (. . .) I can understand that, but *that is their job* [emphasis mine]. And as far as the students are concerned, they are paying to go to school and if they show up or not, that's their fault.

* * *

Jerome: At Urban College the instructors tend to make that assumption that everybody is on the same footing when they're not. Certain people can't even understand whiteys, so there's a communications breakdown. Then you have a personality clash between some teachers and students. (. . .) You know, I take the attitude you're white, you don't care, you get paid anyway. I know you don't care if I learn. That don't caring attitude – it's transmitted over a period of time. (. . .) Students are off into that, so there's no communication between students and teachers.
LW: (. . .) Could you be a bit more specific?
Jerome: In a sense, like, you have various wealth of people, most of them are people you can categorize as being unemployed, underemployed, social service recipients, you know, uh, poorly educated in the sense that the reading level and the math skills are below par of most high school kids now. So you know that with that knowledge that most instructors up there have, they are still around there with that Harvard school attitude and that's not Harvard. So to me that's cold and impersonal. "I'm going to do my job and fail three quarters of them and the two/three good ones can just slip through," you know. (a Fashion Merchandising student)

The above discussions suggest that Urban College students do not reject the idea of teachers, nor do they question the legitimacy of their knowledge. They are willing to admit that faculty possess worthwhile knowledge and that they, as students, would like to obtain it. Within the context of Willis's teaching paradigm (which is only partially related to a class paradigm), students resent the lack of what they consider a fair exchange.[8] Some students, like Jerome, attribute the lack of a fair exchange to racism. As he states, "You know, I take the attitude, you're white, you don't care, you get paid anyway. I know you don't care if I learn."[9] Even those who are most critical, however, adhere strongly to the notion that the content of knowledge is legitimate. Not only do they see knowledge as legitimate, but they also envision it as power. College knowledge has an immediacy and potency that is readily verbalized; it is not an abstract set of codes or principles but rather leads to personal enhancement and collective improvement directly. This is clear in the interviews with Anthony, Jerome and James below.

Anthony: [on a Salesmanship class]
[I've learned] how to make a presentation. It made me aware of public speaking. (. . .) It made me aware of "know yourself before you try to sell anyone else."

(. . .) There is a few people in this particular class that are still a little withdrawn. I guess you know from being in the class, a few of them are still sort of hesitant. But now that I know the importance of myself being confident, and confidence to the particular person that I am trying to sell something to, I have no qualms about speaking right out now, because I know not only is it going to benefit me but if there is anyone who I might be working for in this particular field it is gonna benefit them all, and by benefiting them I know it is gonna benefit me.
LW: So that all these sales presentations that people are making in class are useful?
Anthony: (. . .) Public speaking is. *I knew it had a definite importance or it wouldn't be offered in a college level* [my emphasis], but now I have become aware of what it can offer if you are gonna be in this particular field or any field. (a Business Administration student)

* * *

Jerome: [on a Salesmanship class]
No matter what attitude the instructor has, he is presenting some valid material. You can't fight it nowhere round the world. In the sense that he is giving it out wrong, that might be another thing, but the material *is* valid. There is a reason behind it; you

have to be very naive not to see it. (a Fashion Merchandising student)

* * *

James: One of my primary objectives is to write. A man like Mr ———, the English composition teacher, has helped me immensely in this regard. (. . .) Now I want to become a writer because I believe I have something to say and heretofore I have done the same thing that a writer would have to have, giving people advice, counseling them, that sort of thing. But today I would like to put it down on paper so that those who come after me will at least have certain guidelines whereas they can get around the pitfalls I have experience with. And I have had experience with some pitfalls. You can't be out there [the streets] for twenty years without running into these pitfalls and witnessing the effects of these pitfalls.
LW: So you feel that there are specific skills, like writing, that a school like this can give you. Are there other things beside writing?
James: Sure, the law. The law encompasses it all, that people, random people, ordinary people to and fro up and down the street they run afoul of the law because they have had no experience with the law. They haven't been taught or they haven't been trained in the legal aspects of living. I feel that if people did have a basic working knowledge of the law and how the law works, you would automatically have less crime because they would have learned to appreciate the law.
LW: You are saying something very interesting. You said that people don't know the law on the streets and you also said that if they did know the law there would be less crime. Why is that?
James: This is going to lower crime because if a person understands the legal machinery they can protect themselves better, but the law has heretofore been used to victimize certain people who don't know the law. But this other guy knows and you don't know, like you have a (. . .) relationship with the preponderance of the dominance resting with the people who have knowledge of the law and he can work the relationship the way he chooses. So you end up being used in your ignorance of the law, and I have seen this happen countless times. It hasn't happened to me, but I have seen it happen to others.
LW: So you want knowledge to be more evenly distributed?

> *James:* I want it to be universal, because you see, law, contemporary law, man-made law is with us from the cradle to the grave and it is incredulous to me that the system would deny basic legal education to its citizens if you are talking about making better citizens. You have crime because citizens, to a degree, do not want to obey the laws. Now spiraling crime keeps pace with inflation and just as inflation can go into a depression, spiraling crime can go into outright anarchy. All because they do not know; all because way down the line you had the tendency to cancel out respect for the law by keeping the knowledge away from ordinary people.

The point here is that students affirm rather than contradict legitimated knowledge. This goes well beyond merely viewing knowledge as legitimate; students see an immediacy and potency to knowledge and some, like James, argue that it should be shared. He wants to write "so that those who come after me will at least have certain guidelines whereas they can get around the pitfalls I have had experience with. And I have had experience with some pitfalls. You can't be out there [the streets; see chapter 1] for twenty years without running into these pitfalls and witnessing the effects of these pitfalls." For James, knowledge does not represent a commodity to be accumulated and exchanged solely on an individual basis; it is useful primarily in terms of the collectivity. This of course deviates from the middle class model where, as Jean Anyon argues, knowledge is seen as a "possession." In exchange for information, facts and dates, middle class students expect to obtain good grades, acceptance at college, and a good job.[10] While there is certainly some of this among lower class black students (due primarily to a dominant ideology which stresses individual accumulation and exchange), knowledge is also seen in relation to the collectivity.

Chronic absence

A second cultural element is related to class attendance. For Willis's working class lads, absenteeism signals their generally oppositional stance; their "struggle to win symbolic and physical space from the institution and its rules and to defeat its main perceived purpose: to make you 'work'."[11] Students are adept at managing the formal system and winning space for themselves. The core skill here is being able to get out of any given classroom, thus preserving personal mobility within the school. These actions do not contradict their perceptions of schooling and school authority. London also concludes that high absenteeism among white working class students follows more or less logically from perceptions of the institution.[12]

Urban College students, unlike those of the white working class as described in previous investigations, actively affirm knowledge and the idea of teachers. Criticism of the faculty centers around beliefs that they are not trying hard enough, are not meeting their contractual obligations (showing up to class), or are too impersonal. There is a sense on the part of Urban College students that faculty possess knowledge that is worthwhile. Despite this, the absentee rate at Urban College is exceptionally high. This coincides with the fact that one of the things that the institution attempts to extract from students is regular attendance and a sense of responsibility for such attendance.[13] There is a well-articulated attendance policy which is announced at the beginning of each semester in every class. Students are allowed a pre-determined number of cuts in any given class before their names are struck from class rolls. Attendance qua attendance *counts* and student names are removed from class lists if the maximum number of cuts is exceeded within the first three weeks of school. Students are given "W" or occasionally "F" grades if they exceed the maximum number of cuts during the remainder of the semester. If a student's name is dropped during the first three weeks of the term, he/she is not eligible for grant money that semester.[14] Grant checks amount to approximately $500.00 per term (tuition is also paid) and are distributed about two-thirds of the way through each semester.[15] It is possible for students to receive all "W" grades and still maintain grant eligibility. Over 90 per cent of students at the college receive financial aid of this sort.[16]

In spite of the attendance policy and the fact that, generally speaking, students do not overtly reject the nature of knowledge embedded within the institution, the absentee rate is extremely high. Students consistently register for classes, obtain grant money, are given "W" or "F" grades for excessive cuts, and register for these same courses next semester when the pattern is likely to repeat itself.[17] Data presented below for courses offered in the 1979

Fall semester provide some indication of the extent of absenteeism and associated dropout rates.

While these data do not measure absence from class *per se*, the "W" grade, in particular, provides an indication of such absence. Faculty generally give "W" grades to students who stop attending class, although some faculty fail these students. Since "F" and "W" grades are also given to students who attend class regularly but do

Table 2.1 Fail and withdraw in College Credit and Remedial classes, Fall 1979[a]

Courses	Fail		Withdraw	
	%	No.	%	No.
College Credit				
Mathematics[b]	14.5	12	36.1	30
Science[c]	8.4	34	26.8	109
English	13.0	65	27.3	150
Social Science	8.5	56	25.5	168
Health and Physical Science	3.1	4	30.5	39
Secretarial Science	25.8	86	27.3	91
Business Administration	4.7	32	33.5	227
Paralegal Assistant	7.5	14	21.3	40
Fashion Buying and Merchandising	—	—	28.4	25
General Studies	—	—	28.5	59
Criminal Justice	—	—	44.1	30
Child Care	6.6	11	22.9	38
Radiologic Technology[d]	4.2	1	4.2	1
Remedial[e]				
Mathematics	15.9	34	31.3	67
Business Administration	6.4	3	29.8	14
English[f]	16.0	66	31.2	129

[a] Figures were calculated on the basis of grade sheets turned in by instructors at the end of the term. All day classes are included in the tabulations. Data are presented for the combined male and female population. An analysis by gender revealed only slight differences. Figures refer to percent of total enrolled in all courses in each curriculum.

[b] Calculated by curriculum.

[c] Chemistry, Physics, Biology.

[d] This program has very few black students due to stringent entrance requirements.

[e] Students are placed in these courses on the basis of test scores on an examination in English and Mathematics. Many of these classes are graded on a Satisfactory (S)/Unsatisfactory (U) basis. The "F" and "U" grades are consolidated here.

[f] Over 21 per cent of all students enrolled in Remedial English classes received "incomplete."

not complete the course successfully, they must be interpreted with caution.

The high percentage of withdrawals is noteworthy. An average of 30 per cent of males and females end up with "W" grades in college courses. The failure rate is also high, and it is only a slight overstatement to argue that close to half the students do not successfully complete any given course (not including those who drop out in the first three weeks). It is only in the Radiologic Technology program, which is the only selective program on campus and is comprised overwhelmingly of white students (see Table 2.4 for estimates of enrollment in curriculum by student race) that this pattern does not occur.[18] Here the failure and withdrawal rates are each less than 5 per cent. This is in sharp contrast with mathematics, where 36 per cent of the students receive "W" grades in college credit courses and 15 per cent fail them. The data are similarly striking for remedial mathematics courses: 31 per cent of students receive "W" grades and 15 per cent fail.

Absenteeism is further clarified in Table 2.2. Faculty were asked to note the number of students attending their classes "regularly" on 14 January and 1 April 1980. Since the semester does not end officially until the middle of May, the data understate actual attrition per semester.

Data again suggest widespread absenteeism. In remedial courses, teachers estimate that 50 per cent of students attend regularly by 1 April, and the situation is only slightly better in college credit classes: 68 per cent attend regularly by the same date. My own in-class observations indicate even greater absenteeism than Tables 2.1 or 2.2 suggest. A class in Fashion Merchandising began with close to 35 students; by 14 December between seven and 12 students attended the course. Twelve of an original 32 students were attending Salesmanship by 17 November. Thirty-four students attended a Business Seminar (a remedial course) on 8 February; attendance dropped to between four and 11 by 5 May. *Actual attendance* is even lower than that suggested by data presented in Tables 2.1 or 2.2. It must be kept in mind that this is not simply a measure of class attendance: students who do not attend class do not receive credit for the course.

Chronic absence as well as stopping in and out are distinct elements of lived cultural form among students at Urban College. As the discussions below indicate, students comment negatively on

Table 2.2 Class attendance as reported by faculty, Spring 1980[a]

Courses	14 January	1 April	Percentage retained
College Credit			
English	386	230	59.6
Mathematics	109	74	67.8
Business Administration	532	324	60.9
Science	426	297	69.7
Social Science	275	204	74.2
Secretarial Science	115	82	71.3
Fashion Buying and Merchandising	64	41	64.1
Child Care	69	64	92.7
Radiologic Technology	24	21	87.5
Criminal Justice	78	67	85.9
Total	2078	1404	67.6
Remedial			
English	315	144	45.7
Mathematics	227	125	55.0
Business Administration	72	40	55.6
Total	614	309	50.3
Total College Credit and Remedial	2692	1713	63.3

a Faculty were asked to note the number of students who attend "regularly" in each class they teach. Data are presented by curriculum.

this practice and are quick, like the faculty and administration, to label it a "problem." At the same time, these students are part of the collective culture and engage in the very practices they criticize. Among the students interviewed below, only one (Diane) attends class regularly.[19] James was not allowed to register for courses the following semester because of the number of "W's" on his record. Jerome only occasionally attends class and has been enrolled in degree programs at Urban College and other local institutions on and off for over ten years.[20] Belinda has been at Urban College for over four years and has still not accumulated enough credits to graduate. The widespread nature of this practice contributes to an exceedingly low graduation rate per entering class. It has been estimated that of the 827 students admitted into degree programs in the Fall of 1977, only 93, or 11 per cent, graduated in May 1979. The figure is somewhat better for the following year: of 527 students admitted in Fall 1978, it has been estimated that 131, or 25 per cent, graduated in May 1980. Even assuming a three-year cycle, only 131 of the 827 (16 per cent) admitted in the Fall of 1977 graduated three years later.[21]

Jerome: The retention rate of the students is awful now, you know. Were you around in September? The campus was full, you know, you couldn't move around. Now it is like an isolated jungle.
LW: I've noticed that. (. . .) Why do people drop out?
Jerome: They lose interest in it. They lose interest in the school. Like what I am saying is, when you sit down and really weigh the advantage, you say now here I am, got two kids, I know I need a job bad but I don't have the skills to get this job. Now school can provide me with some of the skills that I need to obtain a job that will take me up off subsistence, but I don't have time to go to school. My time now has become so valuable that I have to use it wisely to more or less like make sure that everything stay correct at home. So you cannot study with all them problems on your head, you know, knowing where your rent gonna come from, your next food of mouth, not so much your mouth, it's the kids' mouth, making sure they stay warm and healthy, you know. This is the problem.

So, a lot of blacks are eliminated through a whole lot of social mis-errors, not only blacks I would imagine all people – white too (. . .) but it is more pronounced, you can see it better in the black community than you can see [it] in the white, where the average age of the teenage girl at 13, you know, five out of six, you know, got a baby already. You know, it's a lack of training, and definitely, it's no question, clear across the board that it is a lack of home training. Then you get into a deeper psychological sort of thing; people accept the attitude that they just got a position in life, their position is never having any importance into it. They are willing to accept that. (. . .) They just give up. (a Fashion Merchandising student)

* * *

Belinda: Before I came here I drove a cab. There were pimps waitin' on these girls [at Urban College]. I had one guy I drove him around for a whole year; four times a year when the BEOG checks came out. He registered, came to a couple of classes now and then, checks came out and he withdrew. (a Business Administration student)

* * *

LW: Do you get the impression that most of the students here are pretty serious about their work?
Diane: Well I find that it splits. I find that some are very serious and others, they could [not] care less. (. . .)
LW: Why do you think they're here if they're not serious?
Diane: Well I don't know. It's hard for me to understand. Like when grant checks come out classes all of a sudden get very small, and they also get smaller when the work gets difficult and they can't do it, so they drop. (a Secretarial Science student)

* * *

James: I feel that the attendance policy, as it is structured, it is unfair. But at the same time I feel that there are some people who go to the school who should be penalized because they are undertaking fraud, because when you register you sign a contract in order to get the BEOG grant, in that you will attend school etc. etc. Now if you go for a week or two and you don't go back anymore till they hand out the BEOG checks and you go pick up the check and you initiated this knowingly and intentionally, it's fraud and they should be dealt with accordingly.

Now the attendance policy, I think, has a tendency to penalize students who really want to come to class but due to their lifestyle or their problems, or the neighborhood where they live, or problems with children in the household that they [classes] sometimes are missed, and I believe a system could be worked out whereas all of these factors can be taken into consideration, whereas these outright wrongdoers can be penalized.

(. . .) I am almost out of Public Speaking. (. . .) I don't have children, I don't have a wife to go home to, but there are people over there who do and it works to an extreme detriment and it has a tendency to demoralize them and it will drive them off campus. I feel that they should adjust the attendance policy. There are classes that started out with 35–40 people and now they have got about 9 or 12 people. And that shouldn't be. (a Paralegal student)

While students are critical of this practice, they engage in the behavior they criticize. James admits that he is "almost out of Public Speaking," and Jerome rarely attends class, even when he is on campus. Students are far more critical when, as James puts it, "you go pick up the check and you initiated this knowingly and intentionally, it's fraud and (. . .) should be dealt with accordingly." If it is not intentionally fraudulent, students label absenteeism a "problem" but are less harsh in their judgment, locating the source of this problem in the home. Both James and Jerome clearly articulate this. Jerome refers specifically to the "lack of home training" and James argues that the attendance policy has a "tendency to penalize students who really want to come to class but due to *their* lifestyle [emphasis mine] or *their* problems, or the neighborhood where they live, or problems with children in the household that they [classes] sometimes are missed." Unlike that of the working class whites, the behavior depicted here is not *overtly* oppositional and is not linked totally to the institution. Students partially locate the source of this behavior in themselves. This is important, and, as I will argue in later chapters, must be linked to factors within the institution as well as the broader class/cultural context in which it operates, and the history of black resistance in the United States.

Arriving late to class

Even students who attend class often walk in late. They are marked "absent" or "present" depending on a given faculty member's policy with respect to lateness.[22] Some faculty consider a student absent after the first ten minutes of class, while others count a pre-determined number of late arrivals as one absence. Still others consider anyone "present" who comes to class at all, no matter how late. Individual faculty policy appears to exert little impact on this practice since the pattern described in the two classes below is rather common.

*Salesmanship class 17 September 1979**

10:00–10:50 a.m.

[*Professor takes roll at 10:00*]

[only ten people in class – over half the class is missing]

Mr Pierce: (. . .) Full consumption and full production means full employment. We are prosperous so long as goods are bought and sold. As long as goods are bought and sold, everybody is busy working.

[*10:10 two women walk in*]

(. . .) In a market economy employment is based on full production. This country depends on production and goods being sold. Salesmen are very important for this country. We need salesmen to keep the economy going.[23]

[*10:12 one man walks in*]

[*10:15 another man walks in*]

(. . .) In this country we depend on factories doing maximum production. To keep prosperity high, you have to be constantly selling goods. Goods have to be sold. When selling drops off, we go into a dangerous recession. You're all too young to have lived through the first depression. We're now coming into the second, but government takes over. Government hires people to work. Got to find a source of income for people. Government steps in and creates jobs for people. Government doesn't mind since roads are being built; parks are being cleaned up. In our economy which is based upon full production, goods have to be produced, things have to be sold. Keeps economy going.

[*10:20 one woman walks in*]

(. . .) Salesperson produces profit for self and company. I'm talking about the industrial professional salesperson, not the clerk at the counter; they usually make a fixed wage.
(. . .) A salesman who can build up a following of happy customers will do well and make a lot of money (. . .)

[*10:25 one woman walks in*]

[*10:30 one man walks in*]

*Business Organization 21 September, 1979**

9:00–9:50 a.m.

Mr Fitzgerald: Almost was going to forget attendance, can't do that, I'll have the administration after me.

[takes roll]
[many people absent]

[*9:05 one woman walks in*]

(. . .) We're going to do something different with respect to the quiz. I'll go over the quiz right after you take it.

[*9:06 one man walks in*]

(. . .) Take all your paper off your desk.

[*Quiz administered*]

[*9:35 one woman walks in*]

[*9:45 two women walk in*]

The practice of walking into class late is widespread. Unlike the case of white working class males, however, this cannot be understood as a deliberate attempt to win symbolic and physical space from the institution and to defeat its main perceived purpose – to make you work. Willis's lads, for example, developed to a fine art the practice of stopping in class before "waggin off," and Paul Corrigan's "smash street kids" behaved similarly.[24] Investigators suggest that among the white working class, absenting oneself from class or being late to class is deliberately and overtly oppositional. It is an overt attempt to gain space within the institution and live one's own culture in direct opposition to institutional culture. While arriving late to class at Urban College is, in the final analysis, an assault upon official notions of time, it does not constitute a direct assault, and, like absence from class, reflects different tensions in located cultural form. I will pursue this point in chapter 3.

Drugs

Cocaine, "horse"[25] and especially marijuana are obtained easily at Urban College. Drugs are an important part of campus life and students often "get high" between classes and attend class "stoned."[26] This is common particularly among men, although women engage in this practice as well. The point here is not that students smoke marijuana (this is exceptionally common among college students in the United States), but that many do so before and after each class and before examinations and quizzes.[27]

The interviews below suggest the frequency of drug-related activities on campus. It is significant that a number of white students resent these practices.

> *LW:* If you could make changes at Urban College, what changes would you make?
> *Mike:* (. . .) Well I think I'd tighten up security. You can get high in any one of the bathrooms and not really get caught.
> (. . .) The enthusiasm of the students is the pits. I doubt that any of them open a book. (. . .) The majority of the students get high, and just from my own experience if you get high during the early part of the day, the THC that's in the pot kind of depresses you and you are really not into homework. (a white student)

* * *

> *George:* People are stoned down here [Urban College] a lot. It's part of the culture. In fact, when you shake someone's hand, you often hand them a joint. That means "come out and have a smoke." It's part of everyday life; it's part of the way people socialize – every party, every day. (a Business Administration student)*

* * *

> [an informal discussion]
> *Caroline:* They [students] actually sit there and deal in front of everybody. (. . .) They think I'm a teacher since I wear skirts and stuff. I walk into the ladies' room and they yell "flush, teacher" and everything goes down.
> *Cynthia:* I wish there was some kind of fining, something like that. Like if they get caught smoking marijuana they'd get $50.00 taken out of their check. That's the only way you could hurt the students because they're all on BEOG and TAP monies. The only way to hurt them is to hit them in the pocketbook. (two white students)

* * *

> *Jay:* I have a good time [at Urban College]. Maybe it's the way I

> dress. Being white in an all black school. Maybe it's the way I dress that allows me to be friends with them. I've grown up in the [Italian] ghetto . . . the west side, lower _______ you know, the pits, and you kind of pick up the lingo, you know, it's really slang, "hey bro'," this and that, and I can talk to 'em on their level and I dress like 'em, I *dress*, you know. It's not so bad. I don't get my ass kicked in the bathroom every day.
>
> (. . .) I do smoke pot [marijuana,] that helps too in a sense just being with peers in the school (. . .) I feel comfortable. I don't know if I would go out to black bars with them; there's just certain limitations. (a white student)

Jay points out that it "helps" to "smoke pot" since students often share a joint (marijuana cigarette) between classes. This annoys many of the white students since they feel that this detracts from their education. As Cynthia argues, "I wish there was some kind of fining. Like if they get caught smoking marijuana they'd get $50.00 taken out of their check." Obviously this does not characterize all white students since, as Jay argues, smoking pot "helps (. . .) in a sense just being with peers in the school." Drugs are, however, symbolic of a larger struggle between blacks and whites in the institution.

While students engage mainly in the use of marijuana on campus, harder drugs are available and can be purchased with little difficulty.[28] Belinda, a Business Administration student, is employed in the bookstore and makes the following observation:

> "I know the game they [some of the students] play. I know the street game. We have pros here. A lot of junkies still. That's why my penny candy goes so well here [in the Urban College bookstore]. You get quick energy and those on heroin want sweets."

While drug use is widespread, only certain individuals sell drugs. An individual *deals drugs* on campus simply to make his or her own life more comfortable. Clifton, for example, a Business Administration student, buys and sells drugs for profit. He considers it a part-time job and visualizes Urban College at least partly as a marketplace – it is a place to sell his wares.

Clifton: [You have to do something] on the side to put away for a rainy day. (. . .) You have to do something . . . . If it was something very harsh you would go to jail because people talk and no way I would do that. It's just a little side hustle. I make fifty, sixty dollars a day. I do all right, better than the average student. I mean, you are a student, you don't have much money and you have to work on the side just to make ends meet, especially if you have an apartment.

The desire for an apartment of one's own and money to purchase consumer items such as clothes, stereos and records ensures a steady supply of drugs on campus.[29] Peddling drugs is simply a way of earning money.

That drugs are part of the very fabric of life at Urban College is further exemplified in the essay below written by a student in an Introduction to Sociology class. Students were asked to interview a person and write about "a typical day." A female student turned in the following essay.

The Nickel Bag Man[30]

Marijuana has become so prevalent in today's society to those users of this drug that it is now no longer a problem to find or buy. Marijuana is used by people of all ages. It has crossed all educational and economical barriers. I will look at a typical day for one seller of marijuana, who will be called C.B.

"I've been a hustler all my life, Baby. Coming from down south where nobody had anything. I soon learned that I had to hustle if I was going to have anything in life before I die. Ain't that what we all want to have, a nice crib [place to live], wear a suit, and have a bad ride [nice car]?"

"You want to know how my day goes don't you Baby?" I get up at 5 a.m. five days a week, and make my way to my slave [place of work] that's Chevy, you know. A man in my line of work has to have a straight slave. The man [police] is always watchin' you. Besides Chevy be a great place to sell my herb. The people on that damn line needs a break from all that bullshit them foremen hand out.

"I leave the plant at 10 o'clock every day to take care of the people who come to the crib to get their bags. At 11:30 I'm on my way back to ______ to work the rest of my shift.

"I'll sell to anybody. I got a few regulars who are about twelve and some are way up there in age. If they got the cash I sell. Most of them only want nickel or dime bags [five or ten dollar bags] though I don't mind that 'cause you make more money nickel and diming it. That's the name of the game make as much money as you can."

"My regulars they trust me, they know I only sell good shit. They can't get to the suburbs where the really good stuff is so they find old C.B. Now, I'm not saying my shit ain't good 'cause it is. But white folks still get the best. Same old story the white man seems to have the best of everything.

"About 7 o'clock I start hitting the spots. A man has got to show his face or he ain't trusted. You know how folks are, if you can't be seen you don't make sales.

"That's how a day goes, ain't nothin' to it. I've got what I need and so does my lady. She takes care of me so I take care of her."

While students do not spend all their time engaged in drug use at the college (although some do just that), drugs are part and parcel of day-to-day existence within the institution. Drug use serves to maintain the collectivity (it is not, for the most part, an individual act),[31] and also serves to distance students from the process that is education. We have here an example of a "lived contradiction": unlike working class white males, Urban College students, both male and female, affirm the idea of teachers and school knowledge. Elements of their own lived culture, however, are contradictory. Students embrace and reject schooling at one and the same time; they affirm the process that is education but drop in and out of school, arrive late to class, exert little effort, and engage in extensive drug use. What are the effects of this culture on student outcomes?

Urban College outcomes

I pointed out earlier that elements of student culture contribute to an exceedingly low graduation rate per entering class. It has been estimated that of the 827 students admitted into degree programs in the Fall of 1977, only 93, only 11 per cent, graduated in May 1979. Even assuming a three-year cycle, only 131 of the 827 (16 per cent) admitted in the Fall of 1977 graduated three years later.[32]

These data, while informative, represent an aggregate of black and white student attainment. While the graduation rates of 11 and 16 per cent are striking, such figures (which are not tabulated by race) cannot adequately portray success rates of black students relative to white students. Data presented in Table 2.3 represent estimates of Urban College graduates by race. These estimates are based on student residence upon graduation. Since the city in which Urban College is located has distinct black neighborhoods (like most American cities), it is possible to provide such estimates with a reasonable degree of accuracy.[33]

Over 70 per cent of Urban College students are black. While I cannot provide data on *actual* attrition by race within each curriculum (such data are not available), data presented in Table 2.3 are suggestive in this regard. Overall it can be estimated that 63 per cent of graduates from 1975–8 were white and 37 per cent were black. In all fields except two of the Liberal Arts areas (Social Sciences and Humanities) and General Studies,[34] the proportion of white graduates exceeds that of black graduates. This is despite the fact that the institution was designed specifically to serve racial minorities and that black students are in a clear majority in all classes except those associated with the Radiologic Technology program.[35]

Table 2.4 provides estimates of enrollment in curriculum by student race in Spring 1980. These data indicate an exceptionally high proportion of black students in all curricula except Radiologic Technology (17 per cent) and Paralegal (50 per cent). Business Administration, Child Care, Criminal Justice, General Studies, Liberal Arts and Secretarial Science are over 75 per cent black.[36] While it cannot be assumed that the proportion of white to black students was exactly the same in 1975–8 as in 1980, there is no reason to expect the 1975–8 figures to differ substantially from the 1980 figures. If anything, the college may have enrolled *more* whites relative to blacks in 1980 than during previous years.[37]

The data presented in Tables 2.3 and 2.4 suggest strongly that while black students constitute a clear majority in nearly all curricula, they make up a relatively small proportion of those who graduate. This must be linked, in the final moment, to the culture the students *themselves* produce within the institution. It is not simply a

Table 2.3 Estimates of Urban College graduates by curriculum and race, 1975–8 (Associate degree only)[a]

Courses	Black		White	
	%	No.	%	No.
Security Administration and Loss Control	22.2	2	77.8	7
Liberal Arts – Mathematics	0.0	0	100.0	2
Liberal Arts – Science	41.2	7	58.8	10
Liberal Arts – Social Science/ Human Services	50.0	23	50.0	23
Liberal Arts – English/Humanities	60.0	18	40.0	12
General Studies	57.1	12	42.8	9
Recreation Leadership	100.0	1	0.0	0
Radiologic Technology	2.6	1	97.4	38
Criminal Justice[b]	0.0	0	100.0	1
Child Care	25.0	12	75.0	36
Business Administration	42.7	35	57.3	47
Secretarial Science	30.8	8	69.2	18
Total	37.0	119	63.0	203

[a] Calculated on the basis of final graduation lists. Student race was estimated from place of residence.
[b] This is a new program at Urban College.

matter of the institution creating the outcomes.

The lived culture of students also serves to exacerbate tensions between blacks and whites. While there is little *overt* tension between the two groups (e.g. fighting, racial taunts), black and white students do not, for the most part, mix.[38] There is no question but that students (both black and white), given a generally racist society and a collective response to such racism on the part of blacks, are predisposed to this "apartness" before entering the institution. The culture that is created within the institution, however, serves to reinforce and reproduce these tensions and antagonisms. My goal here is to map culture as it is produced among urban blacks and discuss the response to such culture among white students at the college. This is not to imply that it is black culture that "determines" such outcomes. Clearly this is not the case, since whites produce their *own* located culture in the college which is

Table 2.4 Curriculum by student race, 1980[a]

Courses	Black %	Black No.	White %	White No.
Business Administration	75.0	39	25.0	13
Fashion Buying and Merchandising[b]	100.0	1	0.0	0
Retail Business Management[b]	100.0	3	0.0	0
Paralegal[b]	50.0	5	50.0	5
Security Administration and Loss Control	0.0	0	0.0	0
Child Care	81.0	17	19.0	4
Criminal Justice	75.0	6	25.0	2
Emergency Medical Technology	0.0	0	0.0	0
General Studies	77.3	34	22.7	10
Liberal Arts	86.1	31	13.9	5
Radiologic Technology	16.7	1	83.3	5
Science Laboratory Technology	66.7	8	33.3	4
Secretarial Science	85.7	12	14.3	2
Total	75.1	157	24.9	52

[a] Based on results obtained from a questionnaire administered to all day English classes in Spring 1980. Among other things, students were asked to state their curriculum and race. Data presented here do not distinguish between students enrolled in degree or certificate programs.

[b] These are new curricula at Urban College.

dialectically linked to both black culture and broader white working class cultural forms. In fact, the shape and form of white culture is somewhat different than that noted by previous investigators of the white working class.[39] Since I did not study white culture directly, however, my intention here is simply to highlight the response of white students to black culture as it is produced in the college, and explore the way in which this culture and white response to it may be linked to the reproduction of fundamental antagonisms. The comments of white students below are suggestive of this process. Students respond most fervently to the issue of absenteeism and dropping in and out.

> [an informal discussion]
> *Caroline:* (. . .) I don't like the kids who come to school, get their BEOG, and they don't show up. . . . You don't see them

until next semester.
Cynthia: (. . .) I don't think they should be accepted back into school next year. But I understand they have phony proof. That kids were collecting under phony names and stuff. I heard a rumor – you know the machine downstairs that takes pictures – that somebody came in and took a bunch of pictures, they stole them from the machines or something. So they had all this phony proof and came in and picked up [other students'] checks.

Whether that was true or not or whether that was rumor I don't know. But when you first go to school the classroom is completely filled. Now I'm lucky if I have twelve students in the class. My biggest class there's about twenty students. And if there's any kinds of money distributed, after that three-quarters of the class is gone.#

* * *

Jennifer: I was in a minority – I was paying for my education. A lot were getting EOP; a lot were getting BEOG (. . .) I *wanted* to be there. I cut my classes here and there but I would generally attend my classes. But there would be some classes where there would be six students in there once the money came in. (. . .) A lot of kids really came out well. They get tuition, spending money, textbooks and transportation, so they were really making money by going to school.

(. . .) You find a lot of people who go to school because it's worth their while. This creates a lot of problems because you get into some of the classes and they really don't give a darn; they don't really want to be there and it makes it really difficult for you sometimes because I was paying enough money where I didn't want to waste the time. But you can't really change something like that. (a Child Care graduate)#

* * *

Joannie: [I would change] the students themselves. They're here just for the money or they're here just to, you know, to be with their friends. (. . .) I think it's just a big joke with some of the people. They're not here for an education. I was doing some transcripts in General Studies [she is a work study student] (. . .) and there were people who took five courses and passed one. (. . .) One took six and failed all six. It was terrible. They're not here for an education. They're just here for the fun of it all.

LW: (. . .) In Child Care, do you feel this?
Joannie: Yeah, like we have a test, OK. Most of them don't show and then they have an option of taking a makeup. But they even miss the makeup day too. It doesn't bother them.

(. . .) I'm work study. The other students got their grants and I'm still waiting for money from work study (. . .) As soon as the BEOG and TAP come in, they leave. *They cheat me* [my emphasis]. I'm working for my money and it bothers me. (. . .) They're giving the school a bad reputation.

(. . .) My studies here are so easy for me. Child Care doesn't require much from students. It's nothing. I haven't had homework in the last three or four weeks. It's just like high school to me. (. . .) In math I just sit and do my homework in class. (a Child Care student)

Absenteeism is clearly a point of contention. While many black students complain about high absenteeism as well, they do not express the same bitterness as white students and, for the most part, do not feel that *they* are being cheated because of others' absence.[40] Students like James and Jerome, for example, engage in the very practice they criticize. It is significant that white students resent high absenteeism among blacks basically because they feel that it affects *their* education. Joannie argues that "(t)hey're giving the school a bad reputation" and that she hasn't had "homework in the last three or four weeks. It's just like high school." Jennifer states that many students don't "give a darn" and that she resents this "because I was paying enough money where I didn't want to waste the time." While black students often comment negatively on absenteeism as well, there is no comparable sense that others' absence affects *their* chance of success. This is felt very strongly by whites, particularly if they are not receiving money to attend school. The issue of money should not be overstated, however: the majority of white students at Urban College are also grant recipients.[41] As comments below suggest, white students also react negatively to the low level of academic skills and perceived level of effort among blacks.

Julie: There's one thing that really bothers me [about Urban College]. I'm very upset by it. I can't understand why they allow people that don't even know how to multiply 4 times 6 in the school. There's a girl that was in my class and one day I was sitting across from her and she asked me how much 4 times 6 was. I mean that was such a blow. I still can't understand why they let people come in that aren't ready. (a Fashion Merchandising student)

* * *

Barbara: That is the thing that stands out most in my mind – that the majority of people could not read – they just couldn't read. I was very shocked; I just couldn't believe it. (. . .) They couldn't read a page out of a book without it taking them an hour.
LW: (. . .) Did you know white students who couldn't read also?
Barbara: No – there was one girl that seemed to be having a hard time, but I don't know if it's that she just didn't understand what was going on.
LW: Did you feel that this slowed down the classes you were in?
Barbara: Yeah, it did. (. . .) The courses went very slowly, that's about what it came down to.
LW: (. . .) Were your friends black, white or both?
Barbara: The majority were white. I wasn't close with any of the black students.
LW: There wasn't much mixing between black and white students?
Barbara: Not really. (. . .) There wasn't any hostility; it was very casual. You're in your own little cliques. (a Secretarial Science graduate)#

* * *

John: In several cases I sat next to people who couldn't spell their name and they were working on their second year of an Associate's degree. (. . .) Most of the time you could walk through the halls without even seeing anybody. It was not an overcrowded school by any means. But two days out of the year (. . .) was what they called "EOP Day." You couldn't move in the school. You could not move because there were so many people swarming. (. . .) It was like somebody opened the doors and people started rushing in. It was certainly an absenteeism school where most of the people there were not there.

(. . .) I would have to say that in large part it was a big waste of taxpayers' money. I don't think that anybody should be paid to go to school if they're not going to go. (. . .) If you're going to go to college you should get *something* out of it and I don't think they did. (a Liberal Arts graduate)#

* * *

Jan: I found that I was one of the few people there that actually did any work. (. . .) The other students didn't bother to do the work. (. . .) The work had to be a lot slower. (a Business Administration graduate)#

* * *

Dick; The RT [Radiologic Technology] program was an advanced course; in fact you had to take four exams before you could even get into it.

(. . .) The other classes were mostly empty; in fact they were mostly scatterbrain type courses. (. . .) I think Urban College is a below standard school. I think that is because of the socioeconomic level of the community that is supporting the school – that is basically the black community here. (. . .) They lower their standards in order to accept most of the blacks.

(. . .) A lot of the students come from the south; I think they're getting a free ride. They go and they get all this money from BEOG and TAP and everything else. (a Radiologic Technology graduate)#

There is no question but that white students react negatively to elements of black student culture. Many feel that students are there "just for money," that they absent themselves from class after checks are distributed, and that they put little effort into school-related work. As Joannie puts it, they were "there for the money" or "to be with their friends." There is little sense on the part of white students that black students, as a group, are serious about school or that they are serious about trying to get ahead. Dick argues that a lot of the students come from the south and that "they're getting a free ride." He also states that "the American thing is sort of to move up and improve yourself. Basically from what I can see from the southern blacks, they don't care."[42]

White students also feel that many black students do not have adequate basic skills and that this lowers standards. Courses have to proceed more slowly due to high absenteeism, low level of effort and lack of basic skills among blacks. As Dick states, "the other classes [outside the Radiologic Technology program] were mostly scatterbrain type courses." There is a distinct sense not only that students are "getting a free ride," but that, as Jan notes, "students didn't bother to do the work" and "the work [in classes] had to be a lot slower." An important point here is that white students resent black student culture primarily because they feel that it hurts their own personal chance of success within the institution and in the broader society. There is a strong sense on the part of whites that classes are not as rigorous as they might be and they hold blacks responsible for lowering standards.

This tension is exacerbated by the amount of drug use on campus. As Caroline states, "they actually sit there and deal in front of everybody." Cynthia adds that there should be "some kind of fining. (. . .) Like if they get caught smoking marijuana they'd get $50.00 taken out of their check." White students articulate strong antagonism toward blacks and feel that they suffer in the institution *because* of blacks.

Unquestionably the United States is a racist society and many white students enter Urban College with well-developed prejudices through which their perceptions of blacks are filtered. White students are, none the less, responding to actual elements of black student culture as produced within the institution. While whites may exaggerate these elements to some extent given their own prejudices, it *is* true that many blacks drop in and out of class, arrive late to class, exert little effort in school, and engage in activities that otherwise serve to slow the pace of learning.[43] White students are not simply reacting to black students on the basis of long-standing prejudice and stereotypes. Elements of culture are *created* within Urban College and it is these elements that help reproduce and maintain broader race and class antagonisms. Larger antagonisms are not simply "lived out" in Urban College – they are re-created and experienced anew in this particular site. It is this very production of culture (which is, after all, a highly human activity) that serves to polarize further (or at least reinforce existing polarization) blacks and whites. Barbara states "there wasn't any hostility; it was very casual. You're in your own little cliques." In the final analysis, however, despite the lack of overt hostility, deeply rooted antagonisms are re-created within the institution and blacks and whites interact very little.[44]

I have argued in this chapter that the lived culture of black students contributes to low "success" rates in traditional academic terms. I have also suggested that black culture, in concert with white culture, reproduces existing antagonisms in the larger society. Given that the lived culture of black students is in itself contradictory (students embrace and reject schooling at one and the same time), how does it arise? What factors, both within and outside the institution, "determine" the shape and form of student culture? I will explore these issues in the remaining chapters.

3
"Thirty years old and I'm allowed to be late!"

I have, thus far, described elements of black student culture at Urban College. While student cultural form must be seen in relation to broader class and race logics (which I will discuss fully in chapters 6 and 7), it is also the case that the internal workings of the school contribute to the production of culture in some rather profound ways.[1] This chapter focuses on the hidden curriculum and explores the relationship between this curriculum and student culture.[2] I will argue that the hidden curriculum affects the shape and form of student culture but it does not "determine" student cultural form in any simple sense.[3] Rather, the hidden curriculum and student culture emerge *in relation* to one another, creating aspects of the other, and neither can be discussed or analyzed separately.[4] My discussion of the hidden curriculum is not meant to be exhaustive. Rather, I will highlight two elements that emerge as exceptionally significant to those who live and work within the institution: (1) messages embedded within staffing patterns; and (2) those associated with the college attendance policy. The latter is particularly revealing and constitutes one of the elected grounds of struggle between both students and faculty and, as described in chapter 2, black and white students. The way in which these elements combine in a concrete culture will also be discussed.

Staffing patterns

One of the most striking elements of the hidden curriculum at Urban College relates to faculty race and gender. Since students experience faculty on a daily basis, it is important not only *what*

Table 3.1 Urban College faculty by race and sex, 1979–80[a]

	Field										
	Science	Business	Secretarial Science	Child Care	Radiologic Technology	Mathe-matics	English	Social Sciences	Music	Physical Education	Total
White											
Male	100.0(6)	87.5(7)	0.0(0)	0.0(0)	50.0(1)	66.7(2)	62.5(5)	20.0(1)	0.0(0)	0.0(0)	55.0(22)
Female	0.0(0)	0.0(0)	0.0(0)	33.3(1)	50.0(1)	33.3(1)	25.0(2)	0.0(0)	0.0(0)	0.0(0)	12.5(5)
Black											
Male	0.0(0)	12.5(1)	0.0(0)	0.0(0)	0.0(0)	0.0(0)	12.5(1)	20.0(1)	100.0(1)b	100.0(1)	12.5(5)
Female	0.0(0)	0.0(0)	100.0(3)	66.7(2)	0.0(0)	0.0(0)	0.0(0)	60.0(3)	0.0(0)	0.0(0)	20.0(8)
Total	100.0(6)	100.0(8)	100.0(3)	100.0(3)	100.0(2)	100.0(3)	100.0(8)	100.0(5)	100.0(1)	100.0(1)	100.0(40)

[a] Data refer only to full-time faculty except where otherwise noted. Data were obtained from the 1979–80 Urban College Catalog. Newly hired faculty, although not in the catalog, are included in the above table.

[b] This person has part-time status although he teaches a full load. This is due to his lack of a BA degree.

faculty teach, but who they are. What kinds of individuals possess and transmit the knowledge, skills and demeanor that, for the most part, students consider worthwhile? Given that it is a largely black college, the racial breakdown of faculty is particularly important. Table 3.1 provides these data by faculty academic field.

The striking point here is the high percentage of white faculty (close to 70 per cent) in an institution that serves lower class black students. It is particularly striking that the faculty at a college whose expressed mission is to "serve the community" is, by and large, white. Urban College does, however, exhibit a higher proportion of minority faculty than is the norm for two-year colleges. There is some evidence to suggest that, overall, blacks account for approximately 4–5 per cent of all teaching faculty in the two-year sector.[5]

While Urban College may be above the norm for two-year colleges in terms of minority hiring, the effects of this hiring in an institution that serves primarily lower class black students are likely to be profound. This is even more the case when hiring patterns are scrutinized more carefully. When blacks are hired at Urban College, in which fields do they obtain positions?

Data presented in Table 3.1 are quite revealing here. While blacks constitute 33 per cent of faculty, they are employed primarily in three fields: Secretarial Science, Child Care and Social Sciences. The prestigious academic fields such as Science, English, Mathematics, and Business Administration are staffed overwhelmingly by whites, with Science and Mathematics 100 per cent white. Faculty members in Physical Education and Music are black, reflective of a recent ghettoization of blacks in these areas.

It is also noteworthy that black faculty dominate in those areas that are traditionally female, and therefore less prestigious. With the exception of Social Sciences, all the academic areas are dominated by white males.[6] Black males tend to be hired one at a time in select academic fields. There is, for example, one black male in the English department and one in Business Administration. Black males are a lone exception in predominantly white male academic areas. While black females have fared proportionally better, they are, with the exception of the Social Sciences, concentrated in traditional "female" areas.[7] This serves to communicate to students that college knowledge, especially of the most prestigious sort, is possessed most "naturally" by white men. It is only the exceptional black male who possesses comparable knowledge. Areas that are open to minorities in a more sustained fashion are traditionally female and less prestigious.

The position of female faculty irrespective of race is also important here. Females, when hired, tend to be concentrated in particular fields and there are *no* females in Science or Business – two traditionally male enclaves. Even in the English department, where some representation by gender has been achieved, females teach reading whereas male faculty teach writing and literature courses.[8] It must also be noted that white females are proportionally less well represented relative to white males than black females are to black males. Nineteen per cent of white faculty at Urban College are female compared with a full 62 per cent of black faculty. This is not unlike the case nationally. In tertiary level education, in general, white female faculty percentages are less than white male faculty percentages where black female faculty percentages surpass those of black males. This disparity characterizes the two-year sector, in particular, where data suggest that the rate of black female appointees is three times that of black male appointees.[9] The messages embedded within the hidden curriculum of faculty hiring are quite clear here: prestigious knowledge is the purview of white males with both minorities and females being seriously underrepresented in prestigious fields. It is the lone black male that is hired among white males in high-status academic areas. Significantly, he is by himself. Minorities have achieved greater *collective* representation only in those areas that are traditionally female.[10]

While in many ways not surprising, given general racism and sexism in American society, the effects of these messages are likely to be anything but shallow. It is particularly significant that only *one or two minority males* have established themselves within "true" college knowledge areas and that they have done so *by themselves*. In other words, college (white) knowledge is realized only by the lone black male rather than the collective. At least symbolically, it is only those minority males who break with the collective culture that obtain these positions. In contrast, this is not the case for minority females. Minority females are embedded within "female" areas and they are not alone amidst whites. The minority female can, by embracing a *certain* type of college knowledge (Secretarial Science, Child Care), remain a part of the collectivity. Thus symbolically, college knowledge as used by minority women does not signify an extreme break with the collective black experience.

"Thirty years old and I'm allowed to be late!"

The messages embedded within staffing patterns at Urban College exert a profound effect on the shape and form of student culture. This is even more the case when such messages co-exist with other elements of the hidden curriculum. In the next sections I focus on messages regarding time and its appropriate use. I will return to the interaction of these elements in a concrete culture toward the end of the chapter.

Time and its use

Without question one of the elected grounds of struggle within Urban College is time. At least two of the themes embedded within student cultural form relate to time and its appropriate use. Students attend class inconsistently, arrive late, and exhibit a pattern of dropping in-and-out semester after semester despite tuition remission and grant money attached to college attendance.[11] Even drug use on campus can be seen as a "waste of time" – as time "not properly spent." Thus elements of student culture may be seen as constituting a set of oppositional cultural practices in that they signify an assault upon official notions of time. That opposition takes a somewhat different form from that of the white working class (it is less direct, for example) should not be surprising: opposition will *always* be coded by class, race and gender.

While all schools distribute dominant forms of time in that courses are divided into arbitrary time units and bells signal the beginning and end of class, post-secondary institutions rarely enforce official time. There are no bells or mandatory study halls in college, and students, while expected to attend class, are not generally subject to compulsory attendance regulations. If students "waste time" by not attending class or not studying, they simply fail the course. Students can, by borrowing another student's notes, even pass a course without ever attending a class. The point here is that students, by the time they get to college, are expected to be responsible for their own time and institutions rarely respond with regulations enforcing its proper use.

It is within this context that messages regarding time at Urban College become important. Urban College does, in fact, attempt to regulate student use of time quite directly. Students, in turn, act in opposition to official time – they miss class frequently and arrive late; they "waste time" by smoking marijuana and attending class "stoned" instead of studying or paying attention to classroom activity. These impulses must be seen in relation to both lived realities within and outside the institution. It is these very same impulses that, in turn, act partially to create aspects of the hidden curriculum. These points will be clarified through a careful look at the college attendance policy.

Urban College attendance policy

In mid-October 1979 rumors circulated through the college that BEOG checks would be delayed because, as one student put it, "the government is trying to keep people in their classes and prevent dropouts as soon as the checks arrive." While in reality grant checks were delayed due to a shortage in personnel, a group of vocal students called for a boycott of classes to pressure the administration into releasing the money. Cries of "boycott classes – no class tomorrow – if we don't show the teachers can't get paid and then they'll make sure that we're paid" rang through the halls.[12]

On Friday, October 19 an assembly was held in the gymnasium in response to the frenzy over the late BEOG checks. The group of students who advocated the boycott agreed to the assembly.

The assembly began with free coffee and donuts. The gymnasium was soon crowded and additional chairs had to be brought in. Classes were cancelled for the day and attendance was ostensibly mandatory. Key students were circulating through the audience asking others to put their questions on three by five cards so that the assembly would be orderly. While numerous questions related to the late BEOG checks, many others, such as that reported below, relate directly to the attendance policy:

> *Question:* What is the attendance policy?
> *Academic Dean:* You are allowed two cuts per credit hour. That's six cuts for a three credit class. Also, if you come to us with a good excuse, you were very ill, somebody died, or something else that is sound, we do make exceptions. Just bring in the doctor's excuse, the obituary, or what have you and we do make exceptions to the rule. If you cannot keep your hours then we tell you that you are not ready to be in school this semester

and come back next semester. You are just not ready to be in school.

The Vice-President (the chief administrative officer at the campus) added that this is an Urban College policy since "there is about 5 per cent of the student body who come to school to get their check and then disappear. They are not serious about school and we all know that. It is unfortunate that this 5 per cent makes it difficult for all the rest of the student body. The 95 per cent are serious."[13] The policy was repeated several times during the course of the assembly and the humane nature of the college when it comes to *real* student problems was stressed.[14]

The attendance policy and changes therein received more attention at Urban College than any other single item of business. Almost every issue of the student newspaper had one story devoted to the policy. Two-thirds of all issues produced in 1979–80 contained major pieces on the subject.[15] The item was consistently on agendas for faculty meetings, and numerous memos were sent to faculty outlining and explaining the policy. On the first day of all Fall and Spring classes observed as part of this study the policy was distributed to students in mimeographed form or read aloud by the faculty member.[16] It is constantly being discussed, modified, and enforced.

During the first semester 1979–80 Urban College allowed two hours of absence for each hour of course credit. In a course that met three hours a week (three credits), for example, six absences were allowed. During first semester, instructors were encouraged to make allowances in the case of individual students. If an instructor felt that a student could academically handle a few more absences, he or she made exceptions to the rule. If a student exceeded the number of allowable absences and the instructor felt that these absences were hurting the student's academic status, the student was reported to an Attendance Review Board. At the same time the student's social security number and course number were posted in the Academic Building to inform the student that he or she had excessive absences. Students so named were required to appear before an attendance hearing committee, after which time they were either dismissed from a course or reinstated with a limited number of additional absences.[17]

By second semester the policy was changed, and the college no longer recognized *any* excuse as valid for missing more than a pre-specified number of classes. The new policy, as originally proposed and later adopted, is quite lengthy and was published in total in a December issue of the student newspaper. It was also mimeographed and circulated to all faculty members. In February 1980 a simplified version of the adopted policy appeared as follows:

Urban College attendance policy[18]

(1) In courses which meet two or more times a week, students who fail to attend at least two meetings before the end of the third week of the semester will be dropped from the course.
(2) In courses which meet only once a week, students who fail to attend at least one meeting before the end of the third week of the semester will be dropped from the course.
(3) There is no appeal for students dropped for reasons 1 and/or 2.
(4) Students will be dropped from classes in which the absences from class are four times the number of times the class meets each week.
(5) Academic units may make point 4 more stringent for specific courses, but they may not make point 4 less stringent.[19]
(6) There is no appeal for students dropped for reasons 4 and 5.
(7) The Academic Dean's Office must be informed of all Special Unit stipulations concerning specific courses.
(8) Teachers have the prerogative of establishing their individual policy as to tardiness provided that policy is made known to students and is approved by the Dean's Office.
(9) Attendance should be computed starting the first day of class.
(10) The procedure for dropping a student from class for reasons of non-attendance is to strike the student's name from the blue book and inform the student, the Academic Dean's Office, and Mr ______ [Coordinator of Student Services].

"Thirty years old and I'm allowed to be late!"

The most fundamental difference between the attendance policy of semester one and semester two is that "there is no appeal on the grounds of having an excuse for being absent or late." A second difference is that students who do not attend class at least twice during the first three weeks will be stricken from the roster. Being stricken from a class roster has two meanings: (1) if dropped during the first three weeks, the student does not receive a BEOG grant check for that semester;[20] and (2) if a student receives a "W" or "X" grade it slows their progress toward a diploma or degree in that credit is not obtained for the course.

The second semester policy is an attempt to further control and regularize student use of time. While the attendance policy, in general, must be understood as an attempt to control student time, the policy second semester represents increased effort in this direction. The first semester policy did not result in the desired outcome – students still attended class intermittently and dropped in and out of school. The institution's response to elements of student culture was to make the policy more rigorous, with greater negative sanctions applied to offenders. The message here is clear: students *must* learn to take time seriously and work within official conceptions of time. As John Horton observes, "the diversity of time perspectives can be understood intellectually – but it is rarely tolerated socially. A dominant group reifies and objectifies its time; it views all other conceptions of time as subversive – as indeed they are."[21]

The attendance policy is aimed primarily at ensuring class attendance. This must be seen as a direct response to chronic absence – a distinct element of student culture. In response to a second element of student culture – tardiness – a "lateness clause" is attached to the second semester policy. Individual faculty are free to enforce attendance even more vigorously in that they may develop "lateness" policies subject to the approval of the Academic Dean. One faculty member considers a student "absent" if he or she is ten minutes late, for example, while others count a pre-specified number of late arrivals (or early departures) as one absence. Faculty are free to exercise their own discretion in this area.

Student time is thus carefully and specifically regulated and it is done so ostensibly for the student's own "good." The second semester policy rests on the assumption that "for an attendance policy to be effective, its sole objective must be to stipulate academic achievement and not to police grants." Portions of the rather lengthy justification for the policy are reproduced below:

> That there is a correlation between a student's class attendance and his [sic] academic achievement cannot be seriously questioned. It is our concern that the relationship is such that our institution's concern for academic excellence and quality education mandates the adoption of an attendance policy, compliance with which is enforced by predetermined sanctions.
>
> We have been operating under what appears on its face to be a strict attendance policy [referring to the first semester policy]. However, it has not been effective in curing the identified problem [class attendance]. In our judgement its lack in this regard lies in its primary thrust; the policing of the financial aid system. As a consequence, its enforcement has been tempered by compassion for the reason of absence, rather than realistic and just concern for the educational effect and impact thereof upon the truant student as well as his non-truant classmate. The net result is that the academic objectives of attendance have not only not been fostered, they have been obscured.[22]

While the attendance policy is justified in terms of "academic achievement," grant money, grades, diplomas and degrees are dependent *directly* upon one's appropriate response to the subject of attendance. Unlike most tertiary level institutions (including most community colleges), students at Urban College *cannot* receive institutional rewards (money, grades, degrees) if they do not use time in a manner defined as appropriate by the college. As I will argue later, this represents an attempt to impose the dominant notion of time upon students from a subculture which embodies oppositional cultural practices.

This is not to suggest an absence of debate about the attendance policy nor to suggest that the college is wholly conscious of the fact that it is imposing dominant time upon a group with distinct cultural practices in this area. In fact, as indicated above, the attendance policy is justified primarily in terms of academic achievement. While this is the official reason for the policy, the actual reasons are rather more complex.

"Thirty years old and I'm allowed to be late!"

The attendance policy: faculty perspectives and practice

Despite official pronouncements, it is clear from discussion at faculty meetings and informal discussion with and among faculty that the *raison d'être* of the attendance policy is not primarily academic achievement. The attendance policy is in large part an institutional response to elements of student culture, specifically those regarding time and its appropriate use. The non-academic nature of the debate surrounding the attendance policy is clear from interaction at faculty meetings as reported below.

*Faculty meeting, February 27, 1980**

> The attendance policy was brought up. The Acting Academic Dean outlined it once again and there were still questions. It is being differentially enforced and this is causing a lot of problems. Ralph [a Business Administration instructor] said that he is accused of being 'hard-nosed' because he actually enforces the attendance policy whereas others don't. This makes him the "bad guy" and he doesn't like it.
>
> Percy [an English instructor] said that "students respond to the particular teacher. If they respect the teacher they show it and nothing we do other than that is going to make a difference."
>
> Ralph responded with the problem of 'lateness.' Some faculty count 'lates' as absences after a certain period of time and others don't. He said that this was very confusing and that students find it confusing.
>
> The Acting Dean's response was "faculty members have the right to do with lateness as they please. There is an attendance policy. If you want to count lateness as absences, do so, if not, don't. That is at faculty discretion."
>
> Ralph suggested that we have a 'lateness policy' and Percy groaned. So did Phil [a Mathematics instructor] who was sitting next to me. Alex [the Acting Dean] moved that we table this until the next faculty meeting. It was so done.

The underlying debate over policy is further clarified at the May 6 meeting.

*Faculty Meeting, May 6** [on the attendance policy]

Percy: Move to abolish it.
Jim [an English instructor]: It has not been in force long enough. We need to test its effects. We'll have higher drop out rates.
Jerry [Coordinator of Administration]: What is the attendance policy? I'm not a faculty member but I know one who is and doesn't know what it is either. [laughter]
Alex repeats it [re-states the attendance policy aloud].
Val [an English instructor]: It helps faculty deal with disruptive students who don't know how to behave in class. Some of these students can't behave. They are not college material. In my personal opinion they disrupt the educational process and should not be here.
Jim [an English instructor]: It gives faculty the opportunity to get rid of students who are not serious rather than deal with them all semester.
Glen [a part-time Social Sciences instructor]: This is an interesting discussion because all we're asking is how the attendance policy helps the faculty. If it helps the students, then we should keep it, if not, drop it.
(. . .)
Percy: Call the question.
Alex: Those in favor of abolishing the policy?
(. . .)
Fourteen to twelve. Motion defeated.[23]

The important point here is that a majority of faculty support the policy because it makes their lives more manageable. As Val states, "[the attendance policy] helps faculty deal with disruptive students." Jim reinforces this by arguing that "(i)t gives faculty the opportunity to get rid of students who are not serious rather than deal with them all semester." It is only Glen, a part-time instructor, who points out that the policy is being considered in light of its effect on faculty rather than students. As he states, "(i)f it helps the students, then we should keep it, if not, drop it." Glen's position, however, is not shared. Faculty, due to their own lived realities in the institution (which I will pursue further in chapter 4), have developed a substantially different set of perspectives.

Despite some division within the faculty as to the appropriateness or necessity of the attendance policy, the policy exists and faculty by and large adhere to it. At a very minimum they adhere to it in so far as they must record student attendance for each class period and submit these data to the Academic Dean at the end of the semester. Class attendance data must also be submitted to the Financial Aid Office at specified points during each term.[24] Some faculty take the policy exceptionally seriously and many welcome it as a means of dealing with disruptive students. Whether faculty support the policy or not, however, its very existence ensures that the institution's conception of time is communicated to students. At the very least, faculty take attendance and students are continually assaulted with the official notion of time. This is clarified in classroom observations below.

*Salesmanship, September 21, 1979**

Hank: When it comes to grades, if you're absent about 25 per cent of the time, you get a 'C' at best.
Male student: You base grade on attendance?
Hank: Yes, I call that participation.
[He takes roll and tells them their attendance rate thus far.]

*Salesmanship, December 10**

Hank: Attendance is important. Wednesday is a tape; Friday is a record. Both are on the final. Attendance is very important here. You are allowed six cuts [referring to the first semester policy]. I give you ten. With ten cuts you can't get above a 'C'. I count attendance. I may drop you with ten cuts, maybe not.

*Criminal Justice, September 5**

Dave: [Introduces himself] I look strict but I'm really not. Strictest on attendance. If you miss four times, you lose one letter grade. After four cuts, it's up to me whether you stay in class or not. For people who have a tough time attending class, drop the class.
(. . .) Perfect attendance gets you an extra letter grade. (. . .) If you have an attack of appendicitis, call me, I'll call the hospital

and verify. That's how strict I am on attendance. (. . .) Twenty-five per cent of the grade is attendance.

*Business Seminar, March 12 1980**

Rick: OK. We will finish these problems and then I will give you your absences so you know how many classes you've missed already. If you miss twelve then you're automatically given an "X" [referring to the second semester policy].

*Business Seminar, April 23**

The instructor offers "two class sessions" or an "A" to be averaged into a student's grade if the student attends the political debates between Bess Meyerson, John Lindsay and Liz Holtzman [senate candidates] at ______ high school on Saturday. Proof of attendance is a bumper sticker, literature or the instructor seeing you there.[25]

*Public Speaking, September 7**

[several students walk in late]

Bill: Class starts at 1:00. At ten after 1:00 you are considered late. After ten after 1:00 you are considered absent. If I am ten minutes late, you are free to leave. If you are a serious student, even if you are late, you will come anyway. I am not keeping you out of the classroom. The attendance policy has taken *me* [emphasis mine] a number of years to evolve.

The classroom excerpts make clear the continual bombardment of messages regarding time. They also suggest the rather arbitrary nature of actual practice. Whereas one faculty member (Dave) allows only four absences, another (Hank) allows ten. Hank suggests that he may or may not drop a student with ten cuts, and Dave adds that "after four cuts it's up to me whether you stay in class or not." This is even more the case with respect to tardiness. As Alex, the Acting Dean, states, "faculty have the right to do with lateness as they please. (. . .) If you want to count lateness as absences, do so; if not, don't." At this point it must be asked, what is the reaction of students? To what extent do they accept these messages?

Student reaction to the attendance policy

Students, for the most part, resent messages regarding the appropriate use of time. Students not only react to the fact that the institution defines time for them, but they also respond to what many consider the arbitrary exercise of faculty power.

Most feel that the policy is demeaning and some, like Anthony and Belinda, argue that the college ought to exercise greater initial care in the selection of students.[26] If this was done, they argue, there would be no need for an attendance policy since only "serious" students would attend. Others state that the policy is simply racist. As comments below indicate, students complain loudly about the general thrust of the policy as well as the use faculty make of it.

> *Clyde:* Some teachers don't go by school policy. We have eight absences and we go before a review board [referring to the first semester policy].[27] Some teachers are very strict. One teacher (. . .) has a credit criteria. If you miss one day you're docked two credits. If you miss two days you're docked four credits. By the time you miss your fifth day you're pretty much out of the class. At the end he's a little fair; he will tell you you have no chance of passing this class or you have a chance of passing this class. Just by following his own criteria. (a Criminal Justice student)
>
> * * *
>
> *Belinda:* I think the attendance policy is totally ridiculous from this standpoint. Because if the school was together it would not be necessary. Because even though you have students you are still dealing with adults. The students resent it. If a student is paying, whether he is on grants, TAP is paying his tuition or whether you are paying the tuition yourself, that if you choose to mess up your thing, they should not be forced into going to class because of the attendance policy. It is ridiculous because nothing else is in order around here so why should they be so adamant about that point. Dumb is what it is.
>
> If you have a student that comes here two, three and four semesters and has poor attendance and drops out of class after the BEOG checks, why let him back in? After a person has done this one semester, then let him back on probation. Then he does it again – then goodbye! If you are going to do that then put an

attendance policy. I pay my money and if I have an illness – an excuse – I am out of the class? I think it's ridiculous. (a Business Administration student)

Students resent the policy and feel that they are adult enough to know when to attend class. As one student said in response to a statement from another student that she was late to class: "You bet I am. Thirty years old and I'm *allowed* to be late!" (emphasis in original).[28] Students do, however, note the high drop out rate and some, like Belinda, hold the school at least partially responsible for admitting students who have a history of this practice. As she states, "Why let him back in?" Anthony, a Business Administration student, argues that the institution should be more selective and that institutional personnel should be able to judge who will "make it" and who will not. He articulates this position below.

Anthony: Except the only drawback [with the school] is the screening process. I don't know what it is but I've seen quite a few drop outs at Urban College as compared to other schools judging from the number of people in the class. Overall, I would say that drop out rate is 50 per cent or greater in all classes.
LW: And you think it has something to do with the screening process?
Anthony: Yes. I feel that they could be more selective in the persons they let into the school. (. . .) I feel that the administration could be more selective, like there might be cases where the student would come and they knowingly know that this particular student might not be able to measure up to the curriculum itself and, just for the sake of having a minimum enrollment or whatever the county requires for student participation, they will more or less just pick the student knowing that I know they are not going to make it.
LW: You told me about two months ago that if I wanted to start talking to people and if I wanted to catch those people that are going to leave that I had better start now, and I did notice that enrollment dropped off. Did the people that you thought would leave in fact leave?
Anthony: Ninety-five per cent of them. (. . .) Just from listening to conversations around campus and various people that I did have in my class, I'm quite sure that someone in administration

> would see the same things that I saw. (. . .) Because they have been exposed to this kind of thing much more so than I have, so what I am saying is that they should have the knowledge that is greater than I have as far as school and people go. And if I could see it in 95 per cent of the people that I thought were going to drop out, but never knowing them before and never having the experience of screening people, I think they could be a little more selective.[29]
>
> I guess you heard about the demonstration [referring to the assembly discussed earlier] – well not demonstration – the conference with the faculty and other members of the school hierarchy – a lot of complaints.
>
> *LW:* I was there.
>
> *Anthony:* Now they were stressing the point that 5 per cent of the students enrolled here at Urban College were hurting [it] for the other 95 per cent. That's why I'm saying that a little more selective screening would be to the benefit not only to the college but the students also.

An important point here is that students, Anthony in particular, have partially seen through official justification for the attendance policy. While the policy is justified in terms of "student good," there are, in fact, other more important reasons for its existence. Faculty admit, for example, that it enables them to control disruptive students and make their lives easier. This suggests that the traditional means of controlling students (grades, expectations for the future) are not, at least from the point of view of faculty, terribly effective in this context.

The state also centers conflict in this area through grants and institutional reporting attached to such grants. As the president of the college expressed at the October assembly, "Urban College *has* to keep attendance due to the amount of state and federal funds that are in the campus. Urban College has no choice; they *must* [emphasis in original] keep hours for the students or they simply will not receive any more financial aid from the state. [The larger college unit] and Urban College cannot afford to lose that money."

While there is, as the president notes, external pressure on the college to report and thus keep attendance data, this does not explain fully the policy itself. The policy is not a simple response to demands from the state. It can be argued that the state, in an attempt to legitimize (or eventually cut back) massive spending in this area, "requires" such data in order to argue that money is being "well spent" (or "not well spent"). Again, however, the "needs" of the state cannot totally explain the internal workings of an educational institution (see chapter 1). It is here where the interaction between students and institutional agents becomes so important. The discussion below with a Fashion Merchandising instructor is very illuminating.

*After Paul's Fashion Buying class, November 2 1979**

> When I walked in Paul stated that he had just had a big problem in his class. A woman, normally bright and articulate, had challenged the entire Urban College attendance policy. The issue had come up since he is taking the Buying class to New York City to visit markets, the Fashion Institute of Technology, and various other places, and he can only take five students since he is using a "company car" and "company gas." They have to drive and only five will fit in the car. He has to find a way of sorting those who go from those who don't. He decided to use class attendance as a major indicator of who is to go and who is not to go.
>
> This was challenged by a woman in the class. She said that the whole attendance policy is "racist and that other schools do not have [such] a policy." I said [to Paul] that other schools probably do not have an attendance policy, but that I understood that Urban College had to have one because of the amount of federal and state aid attached to the school. Paul told me that "the state only requires that we report attendance, it does not require us to have an attendance policy. At Urban College we have an attendance *policy* [emphasis in original] and that is doing much more than the state requires."
>
> He pointed out that the attendance policy is used to order students out of classes after excessive cuts, grading and so forth. He said that faculty use the policy differently, but that the policy gives faculty leeway to do as they wish. "Very few students are dismissed from school, but attendance is used to determine grades as well as who stays and goes in particular classes."

Paul's comments substantiate my argument. The faculty play a key mediating role here in that they, for their own reasons, support the existence of a policy. This is linked to: (1) control of students as discussed above; and (2) demands from the state. Faculty (and other institutional personnel) are well aware that continually high drop out rates could adversely affect the amount of money the state, county and federal government are willing to provide, thus jeopardizing the existence of the college itself.[30] Since faculty and staff jobs are dependent in the final analysis on such funding, it is in the best interests of institutional personnel to ensure continuously high enrollment and low drop out rates. If this is not done, attendance data may be used to appropriate less and less money to the college since it may not be considered "cost effective." The attempt on the part of the college to control student use of time is in part an attempt to secure the future of the institution and, more specifically, faculty and staff jobs. The contradictory nature of the policy should be obvious here: while it is designed to maximize attendance, it is difficult to dismiss students from school given the need to maintain high enrollments. As Paul states, "(v)ery few students are dismissed from school, but attendance is used to determine grades as well as who stays and goes in particular classes." Anthony has at least partially understood this. He argues that "just for the sake of having a minimum enrollment or whatever the county requires for student participation, they will more or less just pick the student knowing that (. . .) they are not going to make it." It is, in fact, not easy for the college to be "selective" or say "goodbye" in the way that Anthony and Belinda desire.[31]

Without question a student's career at Urban College depends far more on his or her regular attendance and adherence to official time than it does on test grades, homework or subject mastery in general. Even if a student passes all tests, he or she will fail or receive a "W" grade if time is not used appropriately. More than any single factor then, time and its use determine success or failure at Urban College. That students resent the policy reflects an understanding, albeit partial, that the policy does not work primarily in their interest, official justification notwithstanding. This is precisely the way in which oppositional forms of time emerged historically; they arise partially from an understanding that dominant forms of time serve to benefit primarily those in power.[32]

The dialectic of the hidden curriculum

Most activities in modern life, argues Hareven, "are governed by specific and often rigidly enforced schedules, whether they result from personal relationships or other kinds of social communication. Being early, late or on time, juggling complicated schedules, and fulfilling a series of conflicting roles within time slots have been essential characteristics of modern society, the product of urban, industrial living."[33] Time in industrial society is, as Horton notes, clock time. "It seems to be an external, objective regulator of human activities."[34]

Numerous scholars have suggested that variations in time exist within contemporary black American culture. Horton, for example, argues that "keeping cool and out of trouble, hustling bread [money], and looking for something interesting and exciting to do (creates) the structure of time on the street" for lower class black males.[35] He states that

> On the set [the peer group and the places it hangs out] yesterday merges into today, and tomorrow is an emptiness to be filled in through the pursuit of bread and excitement. (. . .) The rhythm of time – of the day and of the week – is patterned by the flow of money and people.
>
> (. . .) Time is "dead" when money is tight, when people are occupied elsewhere – working or in school. Time is dead when one is in jail. (. . .) Time is alive when there is action. It picks up in the evening when everyone moves on the street. (. . .) On the street, time has a personal meaning only when something is happening.[36]

Street time differs radically from dominant industrial clock time. It is, in fact, "built around the irrelevance of clock-time, white man's time, and the relevance of street values and activities."[37] It is significant that watches are for pawning and not for telling time. When worn, they are simply ornaments of status. The street clock is informal and personal; it cannot be easily synchronized to other clocks. In short, it is not standard. Within this context, it is meaningless to be "on time," and being late is the norm. Large areas of life run on late time, and events run indefinitely rather than being terminated at a pre-specified time.[38]

This is, as Horton notes, a class phenomenon, rather than a trait of black Americans *per se*. Middle class blacks, for example, often refer to a lack of standard time sense as "CPT" – colored people's time.[39] It is important to note that time, as expressed in street activity and associated ghetto culture, is not simply a deficient use of dominant time. It is, in fact, oppositional in that it represents "a positive adaptation to generations of living whenever and wherever possible outside of the sound and control of the white man's clock."[40] Street time is, without question, embedded within the broader class/race subculture from which students at Urban College come. They are part and parcel of the community which created and re-created it since black Americans were first enslaved.

The hidden curriculum at Urban College must be situated within this context. The institution takes its role as distributor of dominant meanings very seriously and, for a variety of reasons discussed earlier, particularly those associated with time. While it is less than useful to see student cultural form as a simple extension of lower class black culture (students do, after all, come back semester after semester attempting to change aspects of their own culture), student culture does embody oppositional practices, some of which are embedded within the broader race/class subculture. While such practices are available within the broader class culture and certainly can be drawn upon, students do not simply "act on" them when they begin college. Students begin the semester with new hopes; it is only after a period of time within the institution that they forge a lived culture that embodies the practices outlined in chapter 2. They initially attend class regularly and arrive promptly. As the semester progresses, however, students exhibit chronic absence, drop in and out, engage in extensive drug use and arrive late to class. Nevertheless, these elements co-exist with another element of culture – the sense that college knowledge is in fact worthwhile. How is the hidden curriculum related to these contradictory elements?

From the moment they enter the institution students are bombarded with messages regarding the appropriate use of time. More specifically, they are bombarded with dominant time; a concept of time that differs radically from their own street time. This is, by far, the most powerful message distributed through the college and it is reinforced daily. In response to this element of the hidden curriculum (which students, over time, partially understand as not being primarily in their interest), students act on and emphasize *certain* aspects of a highly contradictory culture. While students affirm both the content of school knowledge and the idea of teachers (which is also embedded in the broader race/class subculture, see chapter 7), they do drop out, arrive late to class, spend little time studying, and engage in drug use. In other words, they "waste time" and contradict regulations which demand attendance and attention to "correct" arrival and departure times. Given the context in which Urban College rests (attendance must be reported to the state and faculty/staff positions are dependent upon enrollment) as well as a generalized commitment to dominant values on the part of institutional agents (faculty also use attendance as a means of control), the institution responds by re-affirming its position on attendance and the proper use of time. In practice this means strengthening the policy. Thus, the policy emerged dialectically in relation to both student culture and demands from the state, as well as the way in which these demands are mediated by institutional personnel. The policy itself, however, further encourages students (as a group) to act on oppositional impulses already present in the larger class/race subculture. Thus aspects of the hidden curriculum and student culture emerge in relation to one another, each creating and re-creating aspects of the other.

The fact that college knowledge is the purview of whites becomes exceptionally important here. It is important also that student affirmation of knowledge is in itself contradictory. Although college knowledge is valued, it can at the same time be perceived as "not ours" – it is white, not black (see chapter 4). The fact that faculty in the academic areas are overwhelmingly white only serves to reinforce this.

The *interaction* of hidden curricular elements is apt to be quite profound. As the college emphasizes and rigidifies its position on the need to operate within dominant forms of time, students as a collectivity live their own time (which is embedded in the broader class/race logic) in opposition to dominant time. Since students are reminded daily that college culture is "not theirs" simply by virtue of staffing patterns (this co-exists with a generally positive attitude toward such knowledge and culture), they live and strengthen the collectivity (and their *own* cultural practices) in opposition to the college and ultimately mainstream culture. It must be clear, however, that this process is not necessarily conscious.

"Thirty years old and I'm allowed to be late!"

That the student culture serves to maintain and strengthen the black collectivity becomes clearer from an examination of student response to black faculty in the academic areas. While some students certainly appreciate "role models," many are critical of black faculty members, arguing that they are unnecessarily demanding and that they are too individualistic. Clifton, for example, suggests that black faculty are too "difficult" in the interview below.

> *Clifton:* I noticed that about a few black teachers here, Mr _______ , Ms _______ at times too, they try to be more hard on you, try to make the course more difficult.
> *LW:* (. . .) Why do you think that is?
> *Clifton:* Well I think the simple reason is that they feel they are trying to bring up the education to a better level, but I think they shouldn't be difficult, that difficult. I can deal with that, but not that difficult as far as making the corrections, but having to type it, you know. I'm not no great typewriter [sic]. I have to pay somebody. You just make the course difficult, that what's a pain in the butt.
>
> We had workbooks for Ms _______ , never use them, but we're going to pay our money. That's stupid, but I feel that the black teachers they don't understand it or something – and really disheartening you know.
> *LW:* What about the white teachers?
> *Clifton:* Yeah, they teach on a smoother level, because they, how they outline their course, it's simple, you can grasp it. (a Business Administration student)

While many students express some generalized resentment toward black faculty for being "too hard," George, a former Business Administration student, takes a different position. He criticizes black faculty for being too individualistic – for divorcing themselves from the collectivity. The tension between the black collective experience and social mobility as represented by Urban College is very apparent here (see chapter 5). George is, by his own admission, closely aligned to what he calls the "village [ghetto] economy."[41] He is very critical of the "black educators" [intellectuals] who "don't care about people cut from the cloth – like me, I'm cut from the cloth. The black educators don't care for their people.

They want to stay comfortable." He expands this point in the rather lengthy interview below:

> "I went to a party at _______ 's home last nite, and all the bourgies were there sipping wine and eating cheese and crackers, not even out there fighting for their people. Seeing *Birth of a Nation* at _______ 's house. Before I walked in, nobody was even smoking – I mean cigarettes! I lit one up and then one or two others came sneaking out. (. . .) I almost let a "mother fucker" or two slip out but I caught myself.
>
> (. . .) Black people are on their way to being slaves and the black educators – the intellectuals – are not doing shit about it. They have their nice homes and their wine and cheese, and that's enough for them.
>
> (. . .) The black intelligentsia aren't even making themselves a future and you'd think they'd have enough abstract [thinking] to understand that. They're not even making *themselves* a future! God damn! That's hustling backwards! Every street hustler, the successful ones on the corner even know how to make themselves a future! Shit, I don't understand it.
>
> (. . .) Look, the community is really going downhill. People fighting gas bills every winter, trying to go to school, fighting welfare cases, you know. You just don't see any of the education in sociology, in urban planning, education in history that blacks have been able to acquire, you just don't see very much of it being spent in the village. Like to me, if you don't make a contribution to your bottom half, your top half is bound to fall."

While the majority of students are not as articulate as George, it is possible that they also feel that black faculty have deserted the collectivity – that they are no longer part and parcel of the collective black experience. Since this understanding is only partial, it is expressed in terms of black faculty demanding too much, not being sensitive enough to student needs and so forth. In fact, black faculty do carry the dominant culture. While they may be "bi-cultural," they live and distribute dominant culture in their role as faculty and act on this culture within the institution. Thus, as far as students are concerned, they *have* left the collectivity in terms of cultural style (language, notions of time, dress). Since, as noted earlier, black faculty are essentially alone in the academic areas, their "apartness" from the community is highlighted. While students express some generalized resentment toward such faculty, their resentment may, on an unconscious level, represent a limited defeat of individualism.

I have argued in this chapter that the hidden curriculum plays a key role in producing aspects of student cultural form. Student cultural form in turn produces aspects of the hidden curriculum. Thus each produces and reproduces the other, and neither can be discussed or analyzed separately. In the final analysis, student lived culture at Urban College strengthens the collectivity and reinforces aspects of a collective black experience, ultimately reproducing and deepening class/race antagonisms that lie at the very heart of American society. In the next chapter I will examine the role that faculty play in the production of student consciousness.

4
The role of faculty

> "When you're up to your ass in alligators
> It's hard to remember that your initial goal
> was to drain the swamp."
> (Placard in a faculty office)

It is often argued that community college faculty look upon themselves as "second class" – that they actively desire to obtain positions in four-year colleges and universities. London articulates this position clearly in his ethnography of a white working class community college in the United States.[1] Many of the liberal arts faculty at "City Community College" see themselves as too intellectual, too abstract, for their present position. A majority resent the fact that they are teaching on the community college level. To what extent does this characterize faculty at Urban College?

At stake here is the role that faculty perspectives play in the production of the lived culture of students. If, for example, faculty at Urban College resent their present positions as seems to be the case for many of the Liberal Arts faculty in London's study, it might be argued that faculty culture serves substantially to *produce* student cultural form. In other words, if a large proportion of the faculty feel that they ought to be elsewhere – that they are teaching on a level below where they should be – it is possible that elements of student culture could be a simple response to faculty attitudes. In this sense then, faculty perspectives might be said to "determine" located cultural form among students.

While it is tempting to so argue, the actual processes through which student culture is produced at Urban College are far more complex, as is the production of faculty culture itself and the linkage between faculty and student culture. While faculty perspectives, like elements of the hidden curriculum, are tied to the production of student culture in some rather important ways, they do not "determine" such culture. Faculty, like students, produce their own lived culture and it is dialectically linked to student culture.[2] As I argue below, faculty at Urban College do not, by and large, wish they were elsewhere. They are, for the most part, quite satisfied with their position and most do not desire positions at four-year institutions. The reasons for this are rather complex, however, and again are linked to the production of student cultural form.

Faculty views toward the college

An appreciable number of faculty at Urban College possess MA and PhD degrees from well-established state institutions such as Pennsylvania State University and Ohio State University, and a smaller number possess degrees from elite institutions such as the University of Pennsylvania, Brandeis University, Johns Hopkins University and Harvard. As Table 4.1 indicates, while the institution requires only a BA to teach, few faculty members possess only this degree. Over 26 per cent of all faculty possess doctorates or the Juris Doctorate and over 65 per cent possess Master's degrees.

Although the vast majority of faculty have obtained at least a Master's, faculty are not disappointed with their responsibilities at Urban College and would not prefer to teach in a four-year institution. While they may not have initially envisioned themselves at a community college, most have come to terms with their position and actively embrace their career. It is this very *coming to terms* with their position in the particular site in which they work that constitutes a major component of their own lived culture. It must be understood that elements of faculty culture did not emerge full-blown. Faculty culture, like student culture, is dynamic and best understood as the product of collective human praxis.

As the interviews below suggest, faculty were initially struck by the exceedingly low level of student academic skills. The lack of basic skills coupled with the fact that faculty could view their predominantly ghetto student population as "other" than themselves contributed to a rising antagonism on the part of faculty and students. This antagonism took on a distinctively race form, re-

Table 4.1 Faculty academic credentials by teaching field (reported as percentage of total faculty; N = 37)[a]

	Doctorate	Juris Doctor	Master's	Other[b]
Field				
Science	13.5(5)	—	2.7(1)	—
Business	—	5.4(2)	13.5(5)	2.7(1)
Secretarial Science	—	—	8.1(3)	—
Child Care	—	—	8.1(3)	—
Radiologic Technology	—	—	—	2.7(1)
Mathematics	2.7(1)	—	5.4(2)	—
English	5.4(2)	—	16.2(6)	—
Social Sciences	—	—	13.5(5)	—
Music	—	—	—	—
Physical Eduction	—	—	—	—
Total	21.6(8)	5.4(2)	67.6(25)	5.4(2)

[a] Data refer to full-time faculty only.
[b] BA or less.

creating and reinforcing a fundamental antagonism in American society. While this antagonism is not necessarily vicious or even overt within the college itself, the very fact that faculty (the majority of whom are white) increasingly see students as fundamentally "different" from themselves serves to reproduce racial antagonisms which lie at the very heart of society. Where faculty feel comfortable with those "other" than themselves, it is generally due to the fact that they lived in the ghetto at one time (as college students, for example) or had other previous contact with ghettoized minorities. The tendency to see students as "others" does not diminish under these circumstances. I have chosen to quote at length here in order to allow faculty to speak for themselves.[3] The discussions below are with white faculty: the views of black faculty will be considered separately.

Phil: I'd like to talk about Urban College and my various stages of growth or whatever in dealing with the urban student. I went through several shocks in dealing with the students. First of all, the general lifestyle and then what they didn't know so far as the basic simple ideas of mathematics.
LW: Such as?

Phil: Well, not being able to deal with decimals or fractions and then my wondering how they are able to purchase a television set on credit or how they are able to deal with consumer-type problems, and I've since found out that they don't. They just let "the man" so to speak, decide those things for them and make those decisions. So that if a new car costs $150.00 a month that's what it is and there's no real feel for how much interest they're paying or anything else.
LW: When you say people don't have basic concepts in mathematics, what about addition, subtraction, multiplication and division?
Phil: It's really a conceptual problem in fractions and decimals. In adding and subtracting there's no real problem. In multiplication there's a problem because they don't know the times table, and of course I'm talking about the majority, there's some who can. But when it comes to division, that is a terrible problem. I don't think they *ever* learned division – *ever*.

(. . .) So they can add and subtract, some can multiply and very few can divide a two-digit number into a three-digit number. And then it gets worse from there because no one really knows what a half means or what is a third. There's no light that flashes in their mind. (a Mathematics instructor)

* * *

LW: When you first came here did you have any problems orienting yourself?
Hugh: That's right. As bad as I thought it would be, student intelligence-wise, it was worse. I just couldn't believe some of the things students couldn't understand. But I'm very patient. I didn't get angry or mad. But I wondered if it was possible for these students to learn. (. . .) For example, not knowing that two-dash-three [2/3] means two divided by three. I tried to understand this and finally came to the realization that what the students didn't know was that the word *increase* means get bigger. Without exaggeration! So the problem is that you're teaching in English and they don't understand English. So all of a sudden that hits you. I was very disillusioned when I first came. Even though I imagined that the students were not that good, they were absolutely non-students for a long time.

(. . .) You probably heard the story about how quickly we opened one year and how we had practically no students, not even in August. So we delayed opening until October. In the meantime _______ was hired to be Dean of Students and he went around advertising through the inner city saying that students could receive a thousand dollars to come to Urban College and not have to pay for books. With a bullhorn! This hurt my ivy league sensitivities [laughter].

(. . .) I have found a level that I'm quite satisfied with. Students are not always so satisfied with it. I think it's the right thing to do. I'm satisfied in my mind. What happens is that I suffer a lot of attrition in my courses. I also have decided that I don't mind attrition at this level.

(. . .) I certainly expect these problems now [lack of basic skills] whereas I didn't expect them at first. So when I want to do a certain thing that requires knowledge of mathematics, I now forget that certain thing and teach mathematics. Having decided to do this now, I'm not going to accept *less than*, you know what I mean?

(. . .) The material is covered. For example, I might take a topic that I cover in one week and delay it by covering it in two or three weeks. That's the difference between ten years ago [when I first began teaching here] and today.

(. . .) I think it's OK to take twenty people and graduate five. (a Science instructor)

* * *

LW: When you first came here did you have any difficulties orienting yourself to this school?

Dennis: Yes, academically. I was very surprised how poor the students were. Reading comprehension and especially writing – I couldn't believe how bad it was. (. . .) Even now when I give exams I give almost totally objective exams. Almost totally objective. (. . .) The English teachers are going to have to handle the comprehension and the writing.

(. . .) I've got students who are graduating in May and I look at their exams and it takes me twenty minutes to figure out what they're trying to say. (. . .) I'll have fill-ins. Every once in a while I'll slip one in. Even when I'll need five words it'll be unbelievable. (a Criminal Justice instructor)[4]

* * *

LW: When you first came to Urban College did you have any difficulty orienting yourself?

Jim: No. I had lived in [a large Eastern city] for three years. I lived in what was then, well it was called "the gut." (. . .) My neighbors and the people I worked with while I was going to school were the economically disadvantaged, were the minorities, were the poor, so I had a great deal of experience dealing with the people that are very similar to students here.[5]

(. . .) [But] occasionally the students would go to the department and say [I am] a racist and they said that about most of the white faculty at one time or another, and periodically over the last ten years I've been accused of that. (. . .) That's part of working here, especially if you're going to have fairly strict standards and you're going to demand a great deal from the students. There's always going to be a certain group that are not making it and have to find some excuse for not making it and [calling the faculty member] a racist is a good way.

(. . .) I have been keeping track in my records over the years because I'm concerned. I don't want to somehow without knowing it have become a racist and so I look at grades from one semester to the next and so far I've seen no grade indication that it has anything to do with race, sex, age or anything else. It has to do with their performance in the course.

I've also learned to set up course requirements, exams and so forth, so that the accusation can't be made. (. . .) I structure my tests so that they are more or less objective. Wherever possible I ask objective kinds of things and (. . .) in the essays I ask for a very specific kind of response. (. . .) [Also] by curving the exams it allows the students to really compete against each other using my exam, and that way it's done much more objectively and it eliminates any accusation of favoritism, etc.

LW: (. . .) How do you define success in your teaching?

Jim: [Laughter] Depending on my frame of mind in the semester it can be one student in a class who all of a sudden really has it together. Like I've got one student that I can think of offhand this semester that throughout the semester thus far has been doing passing work but not really outstanding work but now he's shown me the beginning of his last paper and it's such an *incredible* improvement. So well organized and thought out. Well researched. That kind of thing is thrilling very honestly here and I think you've got to take your successes where you find them. You don't have a lot of success. (. . .) I feel good when I see progress and sometimes it's only one student in a semester. (an English instructor)

As is obvious, faculty were initially disappointed with the quality of their students, particularly the low level of academic skills. Most admit that they responded by teaching concepts that they had expected students to already know, and by relying increasingly on objective examinations which require little or no writing.[6] Hugh, for example, suggests that "when I want to do a certain thing that requires knowledge of mathematics, I now forget that certain thing and teach mathematics," and Dennis points out that he gives almost "totally objective exams. (. . .) The English teachers are going to have to handle the comprehension and the writing." Thus curricular form and content at Urban College developed over time and in relation to a dynamic student culture.[7] It is not a question, then, of community college faculty *imposing* a particular curricular form on their largely black student clientele, thereby reproducing inequalities in the larger society. The form and content of the curriculum is in large part the result of ongoing interaction between faculty and students at the level of their own lived culture. In so arguing I am not attempting to suggest that faculty consciousness develops *only* in relation to students, nor that curricular form and content develop *only* in relation to faculty consciousness. As noted in chapter 1, education is a state institution and subject to contradictory pressures within this sphere as well as among political, economic and ideological spheres. While both faculty consciousness and curricular form are arguably the product of more than the interaction between students and faculty, student consciousness exerts a powerful effect on the development of both.[8] The form and content of curriculum cannot be understood as the *simple* imposition of a form of control applied to particular groups. This is especially true at the tertiary level where faculty exert substantial control over the curriculum.[9] The way in which faculty "choice" over curricular matters may serve to reproduce existing social inequalities despite the good intentions of faculty becomes quite important here.

The data also suggest that faculty, over time, begin to define success as reaching one or two students per term, and many admit that they expect attrition and no longer mind it. Hugh states that he "doesn't mind attrition at this level" and Bill, an English instructor, argues similarly below.

> *Bill:* Sometimes we have an attrition rate problem (. . .); that is the nature of the beast. We do have a high attrition rate and we do come to accept that. Since we are a full opportunity program college, we cannot by law turn anyone away, but as is obvious, everyone is not qualified to go on to higher education but at least we have to give them the opportunity. (. . .) I have a lot of high attrition, there's no doubt about that. (. . .) I consider it a weeding out area. The weeding out comes in the classroom.

Faculty thus focus increasingly on the one or two who "make it" and devote less energy to the vast numbers who do not. They define high attrition as "normal" at the same time that they define success in terms of one or two. This collectively held set of attitudes must be seen in relation to students. It emerged in its present form (and appears structural) only through years of collective interaction and struggle within this site.

It is also important that faculty, despite initial disappointment in the quality of students, have, overall, a very positive attitude toward the school. Faculty enjoy the institution and do not, for the most part, wish they were elsewhere. At the same time, with few exceptions, faculty do not pinpoint students as a reason for enjoying their jobs. Given that the *raison d'être* of the community college is teaching, what then accounts for their positive outlook? How does this relate to the production of student cultural form? The discussions with Alex, Jim and Hugh below shed light on these issues.

> *Alex:* I never thought of myself as a community college teacher. I was caught up in the notion of teaching at a prestigious university, with graduate students and majors, but at a period of time when I had a physical injury – I smashed my pelvis in an automobile accident – I was being removed from the job for political reasons and blacklisted as I have evidence to show, documentary evidence, I had a difficult time getting a job so for me, teaching at a community college meant putting bread on the table. (. . .) I saw a newspaper story saying that this campus was opening up so then I applied and got the job. That was ten years ago. It was not ideological, just the need to have a job.
> *LW:* (. . .) Do you see yourself staying here, or would you like to move on?
> *Alex:* Well, I don't think I have any job mobility (. . .) but on the other hand this is a good place to end up, so I have accepted

my final placement at this institution and don't see it as a stepping stone to anything but as a world unto itself. So I think that I lack the desire but I also lack the means to move in the current climate. (. . .) On the other hand, I am very well positioned here so it isn't like we [sic] want to leave a bad situation. I have very good personal relationships with people here. There is no alienation from this institution. I don't have to hide in my classroom. I can relate to the affairs of the school. I have a lot of informal input and a lot of informal influence through persuasion in my position. So it is a good position; it is enviable from many points of view.

Now I do sometimes think of my former classmates like ———, a full professor at Harvard, publishing books and I get twinges of jealousy. On the other hand, I think I am quite happy here, and I am just prepared to grow old and retire and be given a testimonial dinner. This is my career, without any sense of failure. (an English instructor)[10]

* * *

Jim: I don't think I'm going to enjoy teaching anyplace else as much as here. Part of the problem here is that I work with a group of people that I think are phenomenal. They are just beautiful people and they're great to work with, and I don't think there are very many places in the world where you can get that sense of community camaraderie and I appreciate that much more than I do necessarily the title or the prestige of the institution. I think that predominantly life is something to be experienced and lived, not necessarily to make marks someplace, and I really enjoy the day-to-day (. . .) gut-level experiences you get here.

(. . .) I don't see going on to another institution. For a number of reasons. I don't see the teaching profession allowing you a great deal of bouncing around, especially with the job market the way it is. I am now at the point in my career where I can no longer afford to change [jobs].

(. . .) There is a good interaction between faculty and administration which again, doesn't happen in a lot of places. (. . .) I like to be in a place where you've got to fight – one of the things I really like about this campus is that it is the poor cousin out of the three [in the county system] – I enjoy a good fight! (an English instructor)

* * *

LW: What is it that you like about being here?
Hugh: Well, I like teaching. From the day I started teaching as a teaching assistant in graduate school, I liked it. It's a great way to make a living and I would sacrifice money if it came to that. What I like about teaching is that it is so diversified. Every day is different, every year is different. (. . .) In addition to that, here I'm into so many things. Heading a whole department which is perfect for me. (. . .) And I have here the head coaching job for the baseball team. One of the reasons I came here to begin with is that they told me that I could have the baseball team at this campus. (. . .) So the baseball aspect here takes up many, many more hours than the other part. It's just like I'm two different people. Six out of seven days a week I'm involved in baseball, either playing or coaching in the summer.

(. . .) That is why I really feel unique and why I like this place so much. Also, I find the administrators here to be absolutely super. They're either very poor and don't know what to do, or they have enough sense to let certain people run their own show. I've always been able to do pretty much what I wanted. Not that I've ever wanted to do anything improper, but the kind of teaching that I've wanted to do, the courses I've wanted to run, the kind of courses I've wanted to teach; I've pretty much had my way, which contributes to the good feeling I've had here.

(. . .) I think that this campus is unique. It opened at the time when there was very high unemployment among professionals. There were a lot of very talented people who were out of jobs, or who were looking for jobs – people who were eminently talented and lost jobs. They all convened here. They looked at it and said, "I'm so good and this job is so bad" that they said "I can do this job so easily, the salary is good (. . .) I like it here." (. . .) It made it kind of an arrogant, very, very confident place. (. . .) The uniqueness of it is the faculty. (a Science instructor)

It is apparent that faculty not only alter curricula in response to students, but they define other aspects of their job as more intrinsically satisfying. This is particularly striking since students are the *raison d'être* of the community college and faculty are paid to *teach*, not to produce knowledge as is arguably the case at the university. It is, therefore, particularly interesting that, in the absence of an alternative mission such as universities have, faculty locate the primary source of their satisfaction in relations with colleagues, "community camaraderie," positive experiences with administrators, sports and, as one faculty member put it, "a good fight" (referring to the political position of Urban College *vis-à-vis* the county). This is not to suggest that these factors are unrelated to one's classroom teaching. Indeed at least some of them are related in some rather powerful ways. It is nevertheless telling that faculty discuss these factors without *ever* mentioning their student clientele. It is only after I asked faculty what constitutes success in their teaching that students were mentioned at all.[11] As I noted earlier, faculty tend to define success in terms of the one or two students who do well in a course.

Despite the ability of faculty to define their experience in the college positively in terms other than students, faculty must continually clarify, if only to themselves, why it is that student behavior is as it is. Why, in particular, do students exhibit so little success in traditional academic terms? Why is the graduation rate persistently so low? This is exceptionally important since faculty, despite their collective ability to create a positive climate for themselves, must nevertheless confront students daily in five courses per week.[12] Significantly this must be done on an individual rather than a collective level.

Faculty views of the student culture

Despite their generally positive feelings about the school, faculty are forced to grapple with why the student culture takes the form it does. Faculty must confront on a daily basis increasingly empty classes and low "success" rates in traditional academic terms. Faculty, therefore, at the level of their own culture, attempt to explain student behavior, which in turn has an impact on their own classroom practice. Basically these attempts take one of two forms: (1) students are just there for the grant money and never *were* serious about education;[13] or (2) while students may be serious about education and genuinely desire upward mobility, problems associated with lower class ghetto life make the pursuit of education exceedingly difficult.

It is significant that faculty, in an attempt to explain and respond to student culture, focus almost exclusively on those elements associated with time, particularly the pattern of dropping in and out. The other elements of culture (affirmation of knowledge, in particular) are, by and large, not acknowledged. The first set of interviews below reflects the perception that students attend the college simply for the grant money; the second set reflects an attempt to situate the pattern of dropping in and out within a broader class cultural context.

> *Tim:* Dislikes? I get ticked off sometimes at the immaturity of the students. "Written homework – who me, are you crazy?"
> *LW:* Why do people [students] come here?
> *Tim:* Well there's no doubt in my mind but that some people are here for the money. My classes have gone down about 25 per cent. But see, it's not just the quick-buck artist that hit us once. People come here because they have nothing else to do in a shitty, pardon my expression, economy. People will say, "Well, I'll try it." They get paid a little bit for it and they're not getting paid that much. It's not worth their time, but people say "heck, I get paid for it and I might as well do something." I think people get into it after they get here. There is also the feeling, "hey, I just did fifteen hours, let's try another one." But some come here for Paralegal or Radiologic Technology – they come here with definite career goals in mind. It's a small percentage though. (a Business Administration instructor)
>
> * * *
>
> *Dave:* Well, I think there's a lot of abuse here in most of the financial aid programs. I've been here two terms and I see students come – stay for two or three weeks – get their money and leave, and then come back again [the following semester]. I have one student – a good student, capable of getting probably straight As in all her courses – she was in about halfway last term, she was in about halfway this term, and now she's gone, and I'm sure she's going to be here next Fall. Hey, what the hell, you can continue doing that probably forever. And we are talking about a good student – a student who could probably get straight As. It looks to me like she's abusing the system. There are people with lesser intellectual ability that are doing the same thing. I think it's widespread.
> *LW:* Why do you think these students are here?

Dave: Well, again, I have to suspect there's money motivation here. I used every penny I had coming to me under VA [Veterans'] benefits and I encouraged my brother to do likewise, not to mention other friends I've talked with. I think a person is foolish if they *don't* take advantage of federal programs where they can get government help in getting an education. The point is, if we're going to take the government's money to get ourselves an education then by God we ought to apply ourselves and get that education, not just take the money and disappear.
LW: You see that as a real problem?
Dave: I see abuse. I've seen more abuse here (. . .) than I've seen anyplace else.

(. . .) This term (. . .) I've seen several repeat students who were here last year come and do the same thing this year. (. . .) I have a feeling from advisement that some of these students have been around here for quite some time. Not just one or two years, not just one or two semesters, but *several* years. Again, you can get that kind of information from teachers who have been here the past six to eight years.

(. . .) Incidentally if I come across on this interview as having quarrels with financial aid, I don't – I think it's wonderful. What I think is that everybody who is coming here – financial aid or otherwise – ought to be applying themselves a little bit more. And I see some people who are coming here just taking advantage of the system. (a Business Administration instructor)

Dave and Tim emphasize the idea that students are *simply* there for the money. The pattern of dropping in and out is seen as a con – as a way of "ripping off" the system for monetary gain. Faculty below tend to emphasize the constraints imposed by lower class life. Faculty in both categories, however, focus on a single element of student culture – the pattern of dropping in and out – and neither consider the effects that the school itself might have (including faculty) on the production of student culture. With the exception of Phil (the first faculty member below), faculty by and large focus on only this one element of culture and define it as a "student problem." This categorization not only loses the contradictory nature of the culture but its relational quality as well.

LW: The attrition rate is high in your classes [mathematics].

Why do you think that is?
Phil: Well I would say that the attrition rate is high, one, because we have no support services to really speak of, that is, no active support services, and then we're probably not starting at the place where we should be starting in our math sequence. In other words, we say that arithmetic is the lowest you can go, and then we try to do a lot in one semester. We try to go through arithmetic and include a bit of algebra. We stick to that schedule so that when the attrition rate begins to climb we don't let up; we just continue to do it.
LW: Do you think it's just the frustration of failure?
Phil: I think there's a lot that goes on in their outside life that causes them to miss. For example, I saw the name of two of my students last semester in the paper as being picked up for being prostitutes. Another student in my class – we were talking about budget a few weeks ago – told me that she made $100.00 a night, you know [as a prostitute], and that she was amazed that it added up the way it did because she didn't get all that money, her boyfriend did.

So there's really a variety of factors that cause attrition, and I'm not sure how many of them are school-related and how many are related to their outside work. (a Mathematics instructor)

* * *

LW: What prevents you from being as successful [in teaching] as you would like?
Bill: That's a tough question. Maybe something that I have no control over, and that is outside influences on the student. Pressures on them, not scholastic pressures, but economic pressures, community pressures, social pressures.
LW: Can you give an example of what you mean?
Bill: Someone who has to walk to school and can't make it all the time. I've had people like that. Someone who has trouble heating their home during the winter, feeding their kids the way they should be fed, feeding themselves properly. I think we have a higher incidence of sickness at Urban College during the winter because I think that some of our people have problems heating, feeding and clothing themselves properly. For a number of reasons – economics is one of them. Background – not having been taught how to keep themselves properly. (an

English instructor)

The point here is not only that faculty miss the contradictory nature of student culture, but that they see this culture as a simple extension of lower class black culture. Student culture is seen simply as "hustling" or, less negatively, a response to problems associated with lower class life. Faculty miss the way in which their own located culture in part *creates* the very culture they are attempting to understand. Student culture is at least partially a response to collectively held faculty perspectives and subsequent behavior, whether rooted in a "liberal" or "conservative" mode.[14]

Perceptions of black faculty

The perceptions of black faculty must, by necessity, be treated separately. Black faculty, by virtue of their experiences, warrant distinct analysis. It is indeed important, for example, that of the four faculty members interviewed below, three have a firmer grasp of the contradictory nature of student culture than white faculty. Significantly, the fourth black faculty member grew up in West Africa and is not rooted in the Afro-American experience.[15] It is also noteworthy that of all the faculty interviewed, it is only black faculty who cite students as a reason for enjoying the institution. The relationship between black faculty and the institution is not an easy one, however, and minority faculty are often put in positions *vis-à-vis* students that white faculty are not. In addition, as I noted in chapter 3, there is some generalized resentment toward black faculty on the part of students. This tension is clarified in this chapter. The position of minority faculty *vis-à-vis* students is articulated most clearly by Percy, whose comments are reproduced at some length.

> *Vivian:* Right now I'm into teaching. I enjoy it. I get a lot of satisfaction out of the interaction with the students. (. . .) I think a good part of my being here and enjoying it a lot is because I'm black and the vast majority of students I'm associated with are the black students and I get a lot of pleasure and intense enjoyment out of thinking, not knowing, that I provide a little bit more pleasure and enjoyment to someone who is also black and striving to get somewhere.
>
> In one of my classes the females had decided (. . .) that if I

could make it and stand up in front of the class and teach and show a bit of success in my life, that they could too. They had decided that I was someone that they could use as a model which makes you feel good. There's a lot of politics [at Urban College], a lot of involvement – sometimes I'm amazed at some of the things that happen around here – but still, all in all, it's a fantastic environment. I thoroughly enjoy being here. I prefer being at this campus. In part because I'm black and enjoy being around a good number of black students.

(. . .) I think our young people need to see that there are successful, in quotes, black people. That they can see that one of them has made it and you can do it too. I don't think there are enough people like that around and involved with some of our students. I really don't. I think the more of them we have the more we can instill to go on and on and move up and on. (a Social Sciences instructor)

Not all black faculty share Vivian's perspective. While there are points of similarity, there are also points of distinct difference as Percy's comments indicate.

Percy: [On first teaching at Urban College] People kind of assume that because you're black or minority that you can relate instantly to minority people. I *could* relate on different levels, but educationally it was very difficult. They [students] didn't have the skills I thought they should have. (. . .) I just assumed certain things even though I was teaching some remedial type of courses in composition here.
LW: What did you assume?
Percy: I assumed that they could at least write sentences, that students had some idea of grammar. I assumed [that they knew something about their own history]. I would say, you know, Martin Luther King or Malcolm X. They would look at you like who's that?

(. . .) The matter of being scholars too. I guess I'm somewhat of a scholar and I guess I try to project that on to my students – to be excellent in what they do. In fact that is what I always say the first day of class – that you will be excellent and you will do very good in this class. I didn't realize that some of these students had no orientation in studying or in being a scholar or

being intellectually curious. That's sort of disheartening.
LW: Do you still find that people assume that because you're black you have some kind of understanding?
Percy: Yes, [and] obviously I do have a link. Having been born in the south and grew up on the east side of ______ of course I have it. But I also have other kinds of training and background.

(. . .) Students get the impression that you are not *supposed* to know or do that [appreciate Mozart, enjoy caviar]. You know, "you're like us and why can't you give us a break?" (. . .) They look for the break in terms of "don't be so hard on us because you understand that we come from this poor background and we are so destitute" and so on.

I tell them "bull." "Don't tell me about poor backgrounds; don't tell me about walking the streets; don't tell me about drugs and all that kind of stuff. I've seen it and I've been there. You don't *know* prejudice. I know prejudice. I knew prejudice in the 40s and the 50s – I'll tell you about prejudice. You have to make it on your own. You are really responsible for yourself and you *can* learn."
LW: What is the response to that?
Percy: "Yeah, but you made it." Yeah, and I'll tell you *how* I made it. My mother scrubbed other people's floors while I took care of the other three kids and she went out to the suburbs and scrubbed floors. I washed dishes in the city's restaurants for about two years; every summer I worked in a drug store, paid my tuition to [State College] myself, so don't talk about that. I don't want to hear about that.
LW: (. . .) When you were talking about – "hey you're just like us, give us a break" – is that a reaction of men or women or both?
Percy: The men more than the women and I find black men unfortunately have an attitude of give it to me. (. . .) "Man, I'm trying to make it and this world is terrible, especially on black men." I've worked it out somewhat. The kinds of societal pressures on black men as we know in America, in their wanting to *make* it, but more than that, their (. . .) feeling of wanting gratification *now*. They don't think in terms of deferred gratification because we have been taught as black men that tomorrow is not promised; you gotta do this *now*. The men are more apt to want to do it now, try to get it now, therefore

they're more inclined to want me to give them a break now, slide them through now because they had a jail record or that sort of thing, and that's not stereotypic because a lot of black men do have jail records. They come from the ghetto. (an English instructor)

Percy argues that black students, particularly males, expect him, as a black faculty member, to "understand" their background and "give them a break" – to slide them through because they have jail records, for example. Percy's response to this is " 'bull.' – Don't tell me about poor backgrounds; don't tell me about walking the streets; don't tell me about drugs and all that kind of stuff. I've seen it and I've been there. (. . .) You have to make it on your own. You are really responsible for yourself and you *can* learn." Percy's remarks embody a spirit of individualism in that he argues that the individual can always "make it" if only he or she is willing to try hard enough. This is not to say that Percy is unaware of structural barriers for blacks. Any black American knows full well the extent of racial prejudice in the United States. The individual, nevertheless, *can* escape the urban underclass, and this is what Percy stresses. Percy resents the fact that he is "hustled" by black students and responds by being even more rigorous than many white faculty.[16] There is, therefore, some truth to the accusation on the part of black students that black faculty make it "more difficult" for them. Faculty like Percy respond negatively to the expectation that they should "understand" students and therefore pass them whether they meet course requirements or not. Students do not, in contrast, expect this same "understanding" from white faculty.[17] While Percy may respond negatively to what he perceives as a "hustle," he nevertheless understands the contradictory nature of student culture to a far greater extent than white faculty. This is clear from the discussion below.

Percy: Academia is very scary. It's foreign and a lot of black students see it as a white world. A lot of them feel that it is completely foreign to them.
LW: Why?
Percy: How it was presented to them before (. . .) attitude on the part of other teachers, administrators, people for whom they have worked. The kind of orientation that America gives us.

You get a feeling (. . .) from seeing the companies or advertisements white-oriented and so on [and the fact] that larger universities have white students, and (. . .) the kinds of things they learned in school are white-oriented.

(. . .) When I say [to students] "you're going to be excellent," that's (. . .) hard to take, because I'm imposing on them another value that is foreign in many ways, that I don't think should be foreign. I think excellence should be across the board, but to them often times excellence means being kind of white.

LW: Is that negative?

Percy: Yeah, it's negative sometimes. That kind of excellence is negative here.

LW: But yet, what are people doing here?

Percy: They don't know often times. They can get money to come here – some – so it's a ticket to getting a new stereo. They can get some extra money perhaps their husband, boyfriend, or father of their child isn't giving them. That's one of the reasons.

(. . .) It's also style. [Like a guy] I see around here all the time whom I know is not in class, but he dresses to a "t." He wears a suit – you have probably seen him – very tall person, wears glasses, in his own way fashionable, and I don't think he is [ever in] a class. He was in my class for a while, but he was kind of a pretty boy who'd come in and I flattened his conceits one day and I never saw him again. (. . .) He would come in so the girls could see him walk in, a mirror of fashion.

LW: So in part you think it's prestige?

Percy: Oh, definitely so. To say "I'm a college student. (. . .) I got a 'D' average but I go to [State College]." (an English instructor)

Percy is quite critical of many aspects of student culture, and, while he links student behavior to the position of blacks in the American class structure, he is nevertheless highly critical of it. At the same time, however, he acknowledges the contradictory nature of the culture, which is not true for white faculty. Percy understands the contradictions with respect to education embedded within the black American experience.[18] He notes, for example, that "excellence means being kind of white" and therefore excellence is perceived negatively by many black students. He also suggests that "academia is very scary. It's foreign and a lot of black students see it as a white world. A lot of them feel that it is completely foreign to them."

At least on one level, then, Percy argues that college knowledge is perceived as "not ours" – it is white, not black. At the same time, he pinpoints the contradictory attitude toward education by suggesting that many students at Urban College attend the school for reasons of "style." Being a college student also carries some prestige in the culture – it is a matter of style. As Percy puts it, "To say I'm a college student (. . .) I got a 'D' average but I go to [State College]." Thus Percy is intimately aware of the contradictions surrounding education that are rooted within the black experience. While Percy admits that some students are there for "a new stereo, (. . .) some extra money perhaps their husband, boyfriend, or father of their child isn't giving them," he also recognizes the contradictory nature of these impulses. On the one hand, education *is* valued (even by those who are there for a new stereo); on the other hand, education is not part of *our* culture – it is white and therefore must be contradicted. This could explain why students adopt the *form* of college attendance without engaging in its substance. Again, however, this does not mean that college knowledge is totally rejected either consciously or unconsciously. The point here is that it is both embraced *and* rejected at one and the same time.

The position of Eboe, a Social Science instructor who grew up in West Africa, contrasts sharply with that of both Percy and Vivian. Eboe's position on student culture more closely resembles that of white faculty. This suggests that those rooted in the Afro-American experience have a clearer understanding of student culture than those outside the experience, whether black or white.

> *Eboe:* One of the biggest problems at Urban College is that there is a lot of con people – slick people – those who would use their disadvantage that they have as an excuse not to do their work. It took me a long time to learn that.
>
> (. . .) I ask them, "Don't you know that things are rougher out there now than ever before? You have to work harder."
>
> "Yes, yes brother, we see that." "Then why don't you work harder?" [The student] laughs. That is strange and it is disheartening.

LW: When you say that the men are busy being slick, what do you mean by that?
Eboe: Well if there's a test tomorrow they would rather go to a party. Many girls [sic] would say no, "I'm going to sit down and study." Many of the guys think that having a good time now is more important than postponing it for some time.
LW: Where does that come from?
Eboe: It might come from the fact that some of the guys have had to take money or make things the illegal way, the only way he knows. Therefore he thinks that if I don't get it I can cheat, I can do this, he always thinks everything is going to come easy or the illegal way.
LW: But why are the men here?
Eboe: For the money. It's like a job to certain people. To a big degree [it characterizes] most of the men [here], especially those that you don't find in class after the checks are given out. Some people stay because they know that if they don't stay they might get Fs and next semester they will not be able to come back to pick up those checks. So they stay and do mediocre work until the semester is over.

The faculty member below offers a unique set of insights since he was a student at the college and now teaches part-time.[19] George's insights are particularly valuable and highlight the role of dominant ideology in shaping aspects of student culture.

LW: Why do students come one semester, maybe six weeks later drop out, then come back the following semester, then maybe drop out again, do you see what I mean?
George: In my judgment (. . .) there is a search for the light. There is a search for some light but when they come there [Urban College] and they look around the rooms and the foyers and learning centers they do not find much light, you know. So they retreat, and when they retreat they're bombarded from every angle of their perceptions, of their objective observations, they're confronted with the idea that education *somehow* is the answer – *somehow* is the key. They got posters – Urban College is the key – and there will be the keys. One key says "brighter future," another says something else. Somehow or another they feel that maybe they missed the boat. Maybe it's not the school,

maybe it's them. They become more negative in their self-opinion but conflicted by the contradiction that they become positive in their search for the light again. "Well, I didn't see it *that* time, it must have been me" – blame themself – but "God damn it, I'm going to find it," and they come back again.
LW: So there is a sense that it's there and if they don't see it, it's because they're wrong?
George: Right.
LW: Do people think that maybe it's the school?
George: Some. When the negative self-opinion gets too intense they have to blame somebody besides themselves. So a lot of the time you hear them bitching about the school *loud* – "This school ain't shit! This is the most disorganized place!" They'll bitch about the school very loud because they blamed themselves a number of times and have no answer for the problems so they've got to start blaming the school now. You know, because it can't be the fact that somehow the light's not around, it's just not *here*, so, they've got to get through here to some other school to find the light to get the answer – to get the keys to a brighter future.
(. . .) Although they [white kids] don't get an education [either] enough of the education serves them. It influences their misconceptions. It continues a series of seemingly positive transactions. I say seemingly positive because a lot of white kids come up and find out that they were holding something empty. The ones in the 1960s said, "hey, this is really very empty." (a part-time Music instructor)

George's comments once again reinforce the fact that students attend school in all seriousness; it is not, as Eboe puts it, simply a matter of "con people – slick people" making money quasi-legally.[20]

Most faculty miss the contradictions embedded within student culture. Even if they recognize these contradictions (for example, Percy), faculty, on a day-to-day basis, must interact with student culture, and the pattern of dropping in and out assumes primary importance. This *is* the aspect of culture that faculty truly live – that they come into contact with day after day, year after year. It is within this context (in addition to demands from the state, see chapter 3) that faculty support for the attendance policy must be understood.

Students, on the other hand, interact on a day-to-day basis with faculty who see student culture largely in terms of chronic absence. It is *the interaction between student and faculty cultures that produce and reinforce aspects of the lived culture of each*, drawing out and emphasizing particular elements of respective cultural form. It is these very interactions on a day-to-day basis that in part produce and ultimately reproduce aspects of dominant ideology and structure. This is not to deny the impact of dominant ideology on these emerging forms. Certainly aspects of faculty and student culture (or at least a tendency toward certain forms) existed prior to their shared community college experience. At the same time, both faculty and students are actively involved in shaping their own reality.

Student and faculty cultures

I have argued that faculty, in response to both the low level of student academic skills and what they see as the non-serious nature of the student body, turn their attention away from students and begin to define enjoyment in their work more and more as lying *outside* of students. In addition, they increasingly define success in terms of one or two who will "make it," while at the same time minimizing their labor in the classroom. Many faculty admit, for example, to the fact that they rely more on tapes, filmstrips, and other pre-packaged material than ever before. Many also use worksheets in class and have students exchange papers and correct them before class is over. Actual *teaching* and preparation time is thus minimized. An increased reliance on multiple-choice tests rather than essay questions reflects this same tendency. Not only do objective tests take less time to correct, but such tests can easily be corrected by others. Several faculty mentioned that their children correct examinations by using a "key." These practices all serve to minimize teacher labor. Significantly, most faculty did not start out using these materials and practices – they began using them only over time in this particular site.[21] Faculty perspectives and important aspects of practice are therefore shaped in large part by the student culture itself. In particular they are shaped by faculty perceptions of this culture. In the final analysis, faculty adopt a set of classroom practices that are increasingly routinized and simplified. It is here that faculty culture embodies its own contradictions. In response to student culture, faculty focus increasingly on one or two students who will succeed and define their own success in terms of such students. At the same time, they provide these one or two students with a less demanding curriculum (more objective tests, relatively simple concepts that students "ought to know") due to a second, contradictory response to the group logic. Thus, while faculty see themselves as teaching to only a few, they are, in fact, working from a curriculum that they designed in response to the group.

It is here that dominant ideology plays a critical role. Racial antagonisms and stereotypes are deeply rooted in American culture. When faculty and student cultures polarize as they do in this particular site, faculty can draw upon already existing antagonisms to support their own perceptions and subsequent practice.[22] Thus faculty are able to withdraw increasingly from students and gain support for such action by an ideology which emphasizes "equality of opportunity," an ideology which ultimately serves to justify racial inequalities. They are thus able to minimize their labor to some extent within the classroom and distance themselves from students and the educational process, thus enabling them to place their efforts elsewhere (for example "a good fight").[23] For the faculty, then, the *raison d'être* of the college is defined more and more in terms other than direct involvement with students. Interestingly enough, dominant ideology plays two roles here: it sustains the urban community college (and faculty jobs) in that the college offers "equal educational opportunity" at one and the same time that it enables faculty to distance themselves from students. Its effects, then, are inherently contradictory.

Faculty consciousness, in turn, affects student cultural form. While students affirm both the idea of teachers and the content of school knowledge, they are critical of faculty in so far as they do not, as I suggested in chapter 2, encourage a *fair* transaction. Where negativity is expressed, it is in terms of faculty not caring enough, or not working hard enough, to ensure that students learn.

> *James:* There may be some [faculty] who don't have what I consider a dedication, they are just there to get the money. They

are not unlike the students themselves. They are there to get paid and they are going to do as less they can. (. . .) I feel that the ones who are not dedicated should be held to performance within the scope of their employment. If they cannot perform, then it's about standing aside and allowing someone to assume the position who can. (. . .) I want my teachers to be dedicated in teaching me, not just there to get the dollar.

* * *

Johnnie: As far as the professors, I'd attempt to keep their attendance in line (. . .) because the professors at Urban College tend to just take for granted the students in this school.

(. . .) There's a lot of good instructors there but *they don't apply themselves* [emphasis mine]. I know the students don't either and that has the instructor's motivation drops somewhat. (. . .) I can understand that, but that is their job.

* * *

Jerome: So you know that with that knowledge that most instructors up there have, they are still around there with the Harvard School attitude and that's not Harvard. "I'm going to do my job and fail three-quarters of them and the two/three good ones can just slip through," you know.

Students, then, *correctly* perceive that faculty minimize their labor in the classroom and they have seen through a widely held acceptance of high attrition rates and a definition of success that rests on two or three students. They understand that faculty do not, for the most part, define success in terms of the group. As I suggested in chapter 3, students have also seen through the institution's emphasis on attendance. They have partially understood that appropriate use of time is an end in and of itself rather than a means to academic achievement.

At the same time, however, students take some responsibility for faculty practice. As Johnnie states, "I know the students don't [apply themselves] either and that has the instructor's motivation drop somewhat," and James argues that "they [faculty] are just there to get the money (. . .) not unlike the students themselves." Faculty, on the other hand, do not perceive their own collective role in the creation of student culture. It is seen, solely, as "a student problem." In response to collective faculty consciousness (which they partially see through), students once again emphasize particular aspects of their already contradictory culture. They drop out, arrive late, exert little effort, and engage in drug-taking. While there is a genuine affirmation of learning within the culture as well, this affirmation is in itself contradictory (although knowledge is respected, it is nevertheless white). Faculty consciousness and practice encourage students to act on *certain* aspects of a highly contradictory set of cultural elements. The school is not neutral here. Faculty culture, like aspects of the hidden curriculum (which they help shape), plays an important role in the form that student culture ultimately takes within the institution. As noted earlier, it is this very student culture that in part gives rise to faculty culture to begin with.

That faculty tend not to see their role in this process is linked, once again, to a dominant ideology which stresses the usefulness of education and the fact that "if you fail, it is your fault." Thus dominant ideology plays a role here, but it is truly recreated at the lived cultural level; it is not simply imposed. It is also noteworthy that while students may blame faculty, in the final analysis, they also blame themselves. Thus students not only reassert their "otherness" in an institution designed to break down such "otherness," but they also take some responsibility for their own position in a highly stratified class structure.

One last point needs to be stressed here: tensions *within* the black community are also reproduced through faculty/student interaction. Black students often resent black faculty for demanding too much, and conversely, black faculty come to resent underclass students. Carl, a physical education instructor, takes a position similar to that of Percy, whose comments were reproduced earlier.

> "One thing that drives me crazy is women who bring their kids to class. Why don't they have a babysitter or put them in a day care center? (. . .)[24] The students here just aren't motivated. They don't *want* to learn – if you really want to advance you can. They play 'jive man' in high school and don't get basic skills."

Both Percy and Carl express some hostility toward students. They themselves are now part of the black middle class and feel that students are unwilling to put enough effort into getting there themselves. They simply want to "slide through." They want someone to "give them a break." Black faculty see this as a "hustle" and resent the fact that students expect them to "understand" – "understanding" which they do not expect from white faculty. As Carl argues, "they don't *want* to learn – if you really want to advance you can."

Criticism goes both ways, however. After the October assembly about the late BEOG checks (see chapter 3), George had the following comment:

> "I smoked a joint before I went into that assembly this morning. You know what these students wanted? They wanted to know how they're supposed to pay their light bill, how they're supposed to feed their kids, and how they're supposed to keep from getting their heat turned off in the middle of winter! This meeting didn't tell them shit. The black educators don't care about people cut from the cloth – like me – I'm cut from the cloth. The black educators don't care for their people. They want to stay comfortable."

The above comments suggest that tensions *within* the black community are reproduced within the urban community college. Thus not only are race/class antagonisms reproduced in terms of white faculty versus black students, but tensions internal to the black community are reproduced by virtue of interaction between black faculty and black students. As I argued in chapter 2, race/class antagonisms are also reproduced in relation to white and black students. Thus tensions that exist within the broader society are truly lived out and recreated within the site of the urban community college.

5
The individual versus the collective: "success" at Urban College

"It's like no different than say, someone from France coming here and having to learn to speak English." (an Urban College graduate)

I have argued throughout that student cultural form, as it is lived and partially produced within the institution, embodies oppositional tendencies. Such tendencies can be seen as an assault upon official notions of time as well as a partial defeat of individualism. Given that the collective culture encourages low "success" rates in traditional academic terms, the question must be asked, who succeeds within the institution? What are the characteristics of those students who graduate? While my primary goal here is to detail student culture and explore the way in which this culture is produced and may be related to ongoing inequalities and antagonisms, I interviewed a number of graduates in order to gain insight into those who "succeed," thus further illuminating the collectivity which "fails."

Unquestionably Urban College students exhibit characteristics which destine them to become part of a permanently trapped population of poor people – the industrial underclass. Students are aware of this and view Urban College as a mediator between two worlds – the ghetto "streets" and the cultural mainstream.[1] As Anthony, a Business Administration student, puts it, "In the black community it [attending Urban College] is an attempt to identify with another group of people and still do what we call 'hang' – you know, 'be in.' The community puts a lot of pressure on you. By going back to school, believe me, I have lost friends in the community." George reinforces this point as follows:

"[Ghetto kids] are always looking out of a window; looking for money and power and not really knowing where to get it. (. . .) At a very young age these kids are faced with a choice; they can go the easy way as a pimp, numbers dealer, prostitute, or, they can try to make it another way – through the schools. [Urban College] represents a way back for those who took the left fork first and became disillusioned."*

Students perceive that the world of the ghetto and that of the cultural mainstream are vastly different: they necessitate different forms of knowing and acting. Students enter Urban College with a desire to escape ghetto poverty. Within the institution, however, they create a collective culture that ensures that the vast majority of them will remain on the streets. In order to understand this and understand those who "succeed," we must look carefully at ghetto life.

The collective nature of ghetto life

Carol Stack's work on urban poverty and the domestic strategies of urban-born black Americans is useful.[2] Like Urban College students, residents of the Flats have limited employment opportunities. Employment available to those hopeful of breaking out of poverty consists of low paying seasonal and temporary jobs. In response to this, the urban poor form extensive networks of kin and friends who support and reinforce each other – constructing schemes for self-help, strategies for survival in a community of severe economic deprivation. Stack illustrates the collective adaptions to poverty of men, women and children within the sociocultural network of the urban black family. She documents the alliances of individuals trading and exchanging goods, resources and the care of children, and the intensity of their acts of domestic cooperation. As Flats residents would say, "You have to have help from everybody and anybody," and, "The poorer you are, the more likely you are to pay back."[3] There is a powerful obligation to exchange goods and services when one has them, rather than accumulate them for one's own later use as is the norm in the middle class.

Within domestic networks, women and men maintain strong loyalties to their kin, and kin exert powerful internal sanctions upon one another to further strengthen the bond. Kin often attempt to thwart marriage plans, for example, in order to keep an individual within the network of obligation and exchange. Attempted social mobility involves a precarious risk in contrast with the relative security provided by the kin network. One's day-to-day survival demands the sacrifice of upward mobility. To be upwardly mobile means that one has to amass a certain amount of capital – capital that could otherwise be distributed through the kin network. An individual attempts upward social mobility only if he or she is certain of success.

Stack's portrait reveals extensive cooperation among urban ghetto residents. Unlike the middle class, and, in the United States the stable working class, where individuals can live *as if they are independent*, the poor harbor no such illusions. They *know* they must depend upon one another and an attempt to break out of these networks is made only after careful appraisal of one's chances.[4] This is not meant to be a romantic portrayal of cooperation in the ghetto. Such networks exist as a response to harsh urban poverty – people simply could not survive on a day-to-day basis without them.

It can be assumed that Urban College students, the vast majority of whom live in the urban ghetto, are enmeshed within similar cooperative arrangements. Female students, for example, allude to the fact that their mother, sister, aunt or other member of the kin network takes care of their children a good part of the day, thus enabling them to attend school. There is also evidence of a cooperative spirit within the institution itself. The most important example here centers around the fact that women bring small children to class when their regular system of child care breaks down.[5] It is not uncommon for two or more children under the age of 4 to be in each classroom. While this is indeed distracting at times (children are often left to wander about the room), the majority of students voice no complaint about this practice; significantly, it is white students who object. Comments such as that of a white female below are not uncommon.

> "I'd like them [the administration and faculty] to enforce [no] smoking in classes, food eating, the pot smoking. And bringing children to class I find extremely annoying. Because somebody has a hardship and has to bring their child [to class] it shouldn't be *my* misfortune [emphasis in original]."[6]

The point here is that the vast majority of students are willing to share the misfortune. They understand only too well that tomorrow *they* might have to bring their children to class for similar reasons. Male students, while not the primary caretakers of children, know that their nieces, nephews, sons, daughters or children of friends may also be there. This brings to mind the comments of the Flats residents: "You have to have help from everybody and anybody," and "The poorer you are the more likely you are to pay back." Thus while children are often disruptive in the classroom, students do not complain. It is only white students, who are not part of the collectivity, who raise any objection.

As I suggested in chapter 2, white students are far more likely to argue that *their* education suffers because of the behavior of others. The issue of children in the classroom serves to polarize further black and white cultures on campus.[7]

Jim, an English instructor, discusses the collective orientation of students below.

> Jim was telling me that students really support each other in class and that they don't exhibit the competitive ethic that one finds at [State University] or elsewhere. He said this was probably not racially linked, but rather a characteristic of the poor in America. Susan [another English instructor] also told him a story about her Public Speaking class that reinforces this. Apparently one man was really "out of it" and he got up to give a speech and literally just stood there for three minutes. The student said a couple of things but really had nothing to say. The other students then "jumped in" to help the man reorganize his talk and were giving him pointers on how he could do it better next time. They were saying that he should have an introduction, etc., all the things they were taught in class. The students were really supporting one another and did not see each other competitively. Susan had been surprised about this and told the story with a great deal of surprise. Jim likes this [the cooperative spirit] and said that he has noticed that such networks exist outside of class as well. He has often overheard students telling each other problems and working them out jointly. This refers to money, child care, and the like. He has noticed this as a pattern over the years and attributes it to being poor: "People have learned that they have to stick together or they just won't make it."*

Jim's perception is, by and large, correct. Students are part and parcel of the urban black community – a community which is, by its very nature, collective. As Stack and others point out, it *has* to be if individuals are to live with even minimal security. Anthony and Jerome discuss the relationship between Urban College and the community below.

> *Anthony:* [I knew] quite a few [of the students] before I came to Urban College. I know them from the neighborhood, from the community.
> *LW:* When you say community, what do you mean? Just surrounding Urban College or –
> *Anthony:* No, the black _______ side as a whole. Quite a few students I know personally. Some of them I know all my life and some I have known for quite a few years just from being in the community. That college represents just what it says – a community college – because where it is located and the majority of the people that attend the school are from the community. As you can tell, it is predominantly black. The majority of the people that is in Urban College is from the community. That college represents just what it says – a community college. I've known Randy for seven years and Jerome all my life.[8]
> *LW:* People seem to know each other well. It is not my imagination?
> *Anthony:* No, it's not at all. Some of us been going to grammar school, high school, junior high together – that's how long some of us been knowing one another. We know brothers, sisters, mothers, fathers, aunts, uncles, cousins – the whole family.
>
> * * *
>
> *Jerome:* Actually the reason that most people is here [Urban College] is a word of mouth situation. So your friend tells another friend that such and such is going there – OK, I think I'll go there too. And this is the type of thing it is. I don't think too much is happening on advertising or anything like that,[9] but just the simple fact that somebody else had sanctioned it that the school is cool for the moment. But after people get up there and see what's happening, they tend to drift away.
> *LW:* Do most of the students know one another?
> *Jerome:* Sure. Well how could you not expect most blacks, if you

> was all congregated on one side of town, you would have to touch bases at some time or other. You know, one thing I have to say about [the city in which Urban College is located] is that there are a lot of different families here. So most families know each other through association through brothers or some kind of way. Like I say, personal – social – you would have met that person at one point in time or another in your life. See now I am in school now and that's a reinforcement of "I must be doing something right, say wow – here's a friend that I haven't seen in a long time and they're trying to make that effort too."

While the urban black community has few resources, residents share available resources and services. Unlike middle class students, students at Urban College do not enter the institution embodying a spirit of possessive individualism. On the contrary, they live within and survive because of a lived ethic of cooperation. It is only white students (and black and white faculty) in the college who exhibit an individualistic ethic.[10]

Given the cooperative nature of the broader race/class culture and the fact that student cultural form as it is produced within the college ensures that the vast majority of students will return to the ghetto streets, who "succeeds" within the institution?

Those who succeed

Interview data suggest rather striking differences between students who succeed and those who are embedded within the collective student culture.[11] Certain individuals are not part of the cultural dynamic outlined in chapters 2, 3 and 4. The question is, who are they and how are they different?[12]

To begin with, those who succeed have a generally positive view of Urban College faculty and the community college in general. While this may seem mundane on the surface, it is not so mundane given that the larger student culture embodies oppositional impulses. Students criticize faculty in so far as they do not encourage what students consider a fair transaction. They argue that faculty do not care enough or work hard enough to ensure that students learn. They correctly perceive that faculty minimize their labor in the classroom, and have seen through a widely held acceptance of high attrition rates and a definition of success that rests on one or two students. They have also seen through the emphasis on attendance. Those that succeed, on the other hand, argue that faculty are willing to help them, and they do not voice any objection to faculty practice. They are not, in other words, attached to the collective culture which affirms knowledge and teachers, and criticizes Urban College teachers at one and the same time. The three interviews below clarify this point. The first is with Leonard, a 1977 graduate in Business Administration. Leonard is currently completing his BA degree at (State University). His remarks below suggest a strong identification with faculty.

> *Leonard:* As far as individual teaching capacity, I found that Urban College might be a little bit better [than State University] in a sense. (. . .) At Urban College, classrooms have started to enlarge to a degree but they're still basically small compared to [State University]. The teacher has more time for individual instruction, plus there's a certain social atmosphere too because we all party together, not only at school but at places nearby. Teachers get to know the individuals not only academically, but socially too, which helps in a lot of cases. So I feel in a way the atmosphere is better.
> *LW:* Most of the professors at Urban College now – and I suppose when you were there too – were white, right?
> *Leonard:* Yeah, but I never found that to be a problem because as I said we also get together socially so really to a point most of the time you never really (. . .) think about a color difference. It's really not a problem. (. . .) The instructors that are there whether they be white, black, green or purple, are there because they actually *want* to teach – they want to get the message across – and therefore as far as any racial incidents and things like this, they are close to non-existent.
> *LW:* (. . .) Looking back at the time you were at Urban College, what did you particularly like about the school?
> *Leonard:* I liked the close contact I had with my professors because I was able to get into one-to-one conversations about whatever we were studying – macroeconomics, business management, or some aspect of law – and they would sometimes converse with you fifteen, twenty minutes, to half an hour, before or after class or maybe during lunch.
> *LW:* (. . .) If you could make changes in Urban College, what

would you change?
Leonard: Well I wouldn't make any changes in the administration or the teaching staff at all. I would, if I had the power to do so, I would make some adjustments as far as the students.
LW: What kind of adjustments?
Leonard: I'd try to make them understand that an education is important and the more technical it is the more important it is. With America really going into high technology and computers, if you don't have some kind of scientific technical background in another ten years you'll be lost. Even humanities are being pushed aside for high technology. That's the one thing I would impress upon them – to get a good education and to never stop.#

Leonard argues strongly that faculty are there to help and that he had a close relationship with them. He also stresses the point that racism is not a problem at Urban College. The brief interviews below reinforce these points. Evonne, the first woman, is a black female in her late fifties. She graduated from Child Care in 1978. Carla, the second woman, is also a Child Care graduate. She is in her late forties. Evonne is presently taking courses part-time at (State College) and is director of a summer day-care program. Carla is a secretary.

Evonne: I thought the faculty was marvelous because they was always willing to help. At [State College] they don't really have the time. You had to make an appointment there. At Urban College they said "come on in and let's talk about it."
LW: (. . .) Looking back at Urban College, what did you like about the place?
Evonne: The people. A lot of the students would have parties and we were invited. (. . .) I just found that it was a nice warm friendly place – like families. If you wanted to find someone to talk to, you could talk.#

* * *

Carla: One thing I really like about [Urban College] was the instructors. You felt like you really belonged to the school. At Urban College the instructors would call you by your name and they seem to be a little more patient with you.

> (. . .) At Urban College the instructors would take time and help you with your problems, even if they had to help you on the weekends. Everything was really brought down to basics and you could really understand. #

This suggests strongly that students who succeed view the faculty positively. While it is arguably the case that such students are positive toward faculty only *after* they graduate, it is unlikely that they exhibited the same spirit expressed by Jerome below while they attended the college. There is, in fact, a substantial difference in tone, one that cannot easily be attributed to success alone. Jerome's comments are in sharp contrast with those of Leonard, in particular.

> *Jerome:* [about Urban College] To me it's that lack of anyone who really cares. (. . .) I think the status quo on the campus is a little too thick for most of the students to deal with.
>
> (. . .) Like in most schools, you find that students and teachers, I mean students and instructors, they do have some communication other than the formal classrooms and other than one-to-one basis as far as going to his office. That's still a cold and impersonal approach, but yet instead it should be a little more close-knitted.
>
> At Urban College everybody is more or less segregated from each other. The instructors gather off with the instructors and then they're cliqued off into a little certain clique; the students are cliqued off, there's a lot of false information being given out. No one is even trying to monitor that type of thing with the students. You got a big gap there. I would strictly say there needs to be a more steadier flow of communications between the administrations [sic], professors and students.

Jerome's statement contrasts sharply with those of Evonne, Carla and Leonard. While the latter experience the faculty–student relationship as warm, and some describe it as "like family," Jerome finds no one "who really cares," and argues that the status quo on campus is a "bit thick." He also suggests that there is a lack of communication between students, faculty and the administration. While Evonne, Carla and Leonard discuss their *close* out of classroom contact with faculty, Jerome talks about the "cliques," and suggests that there is no communication with faculty, outside of formal instruction. He explicitly states that the campus needs to be "a little more close-knitted." The "close-knitted" nature of the campus is exactly what Evonne, Carla and Leonard see as its most positive feature. Jerome further notes:

> "People get frustrated [at Urban College]. You don't feel like you're getting nowhere. To me I think that people just have to get a little more personally involved. You [faculty] got to more or less show that you really want to see these people learn."

There is a distinct difference with respect to perceptions of faculty between those who succeed and students who are part of the collectivity, such as Jerome. Jerome states that he never sees faculty outside of formal instruction and urges faculty to "get a little more personally involved." Leonard, on the other hand, saw faculty socially (partying at local bars, for example). In this respect then, the successful individual is at odds with the collective. I will return to this point toward the end of the chapter.

Adopting mainstream culture

Those who succeed not only experience a closeness with faculty, but they are also willing to change aspects of their own culture. It is the students who *act* on the desire to embrace mainstream values and learn associated skills, for example, who succeed. Such students operate outside of the contradictory cultural code outlined in chapter 2. Leonard is a particularly good example here. While his class background is no different from any of the other students at Urban College (he is from the ghetto and has roots in the broader class/race subculture), he stresses the importance of learning mainstream values and, more importantly, is able and willing to act on this belief. He articulates this position as follows:

> *Leonard:* You have to remember also that as far as blacks, they haven't been exposed to the mainstream and therefore the level of conversation, comprehension, things like this, are not on that [high] level, and when they get to Urban College naturally most of the instructors are on this level and they're [the faculty] trying

> to get them [the students] to understand that, "hey, if you want to make it out here in the world, in the mainstream, you have to be able not only to understand it but to speak it." It's like no different than, say, someone from France coming here and having to learn to speak English.
> *LW:* (. . .) Did you find that there was a kind of cultural gap [between faculty and students]?
> *Leonard:* No.
> *LW:* Maybe not between you in particular, but between some students and the professors?
> *Leonard:* Well, like I said, that's gonna be typical. (. . .) Most inner-city high schools are next to non-existent as far as teaching skills and awareness levels – so that no matter what happens, yes, there is going to be a certain amount of cultural inferiority. There's no way to escape that at the present. And I feel the only way we can alleviate that problem is to upgrade the central public school system.
> But I don't feel that it really causes a problem between students and teachers at Urban College because any student who really wants to go there to learn eventually will understand that this is a problem that exists and it's up to him to achieve that level and if possible overcome it, to you know, bring *himself* up with the help of these teachers. Because the majority [of teachers] don't look down their nose at you – most of them are really there trying to help.

Leonard's statement is important. He suggests that students at Urban College must learn the dominant culture as if they were "someone from France coming here and having to learn to speak English." This implies that the individual has to adopt a totally new culture from that which he or she knows. The cultures are as different, he argues, as the English and French languages. This can be accomplished, according to Leonard, in Urban College. The individual can "bring *himself* up with the help of these teachers." It must be stressed here that the form the collective culture takes in the college works against this. Success therefore involves a break from the collectivity, and a willingness and ability to adopt a new cultural style. While the majority of students may enter the institution *as individuals* with this goal in mind, it is only a very few who remain outside the collective culture that is produced in the college and accomplish this end. It is *these* individuals who have access to a disproportionate share of faculty time in that they are defined by the faculty as the "one or two who will make it." As I argued in the last chapter, faculty define their own success in terms of these very students. Thus the sense among the graduates that faculty spend a great deal of time with them is not incorrect. Faculty do devote a disproportionate amount of time and energy to those that stand to succeed. The converse of this is obviously true as well; faculty tend not to devote time to the group as a whole.

While I argued in chapter 3 that students must adhere to dominant conceptions of time if they are to succeed in the college, they must absorb dominant culture in other forms as well. The most obvious example here is speaking, reading and writing standard English. Students enter the college with few skills in this area and they *must* conform if they are to succeed. Here Leonard's observation is particularly appropriate in that he uses the analogy of a French person having to learn English. To Leonard, having to learn standard English is obviously similar. Jim articulates the institution's position in the interview below:

> *Jim:* The only thing that happened was that in 1971 [when I was first hired at Urban College] that was the year when the attitude was "let me do my own thing; how can you, white man, tell me what's right and wrong?" And I said, "As far as making it in the big white establishment of the university there are certain things that you're going to have to learn."
>
> Where I really ran into that was in the writing course because *black English is different from white English* [my emphasis]. A lot of students here have not had any writing skills, or very little writing skills, or at least they didn't have adequate writing skills, and I was saying in a Harry Truman way, "The buck stops here," and demanding that they conform to what is considered acceptable college writing.
>
> (. . .) I think that what students need to learn is that they need to become language chameleons. They need to start using language depending on the situation. (. . .) There's going to be prejudice against language the same way there's going to be prejudice against other things. The person who can handle language to fit the situation is going to be much more able to make it in the society than the student who can't.

> (. . .) The college composition course is one of the most difficult to pass. If there's a sentence fragment or a comma splice or a run-on sentence in a paper, they fail, because we feel that the mechanics are important, especially if you look at it from the point of view of that big white world outside that is *definitely* going to be prejudiced against somebody who has not written standard English. Consequently, we have a high drop out rate in the college composition course. I have one section this semester that started out with thirty-one and has nine people left in it.

The college *demands* conformity with aspects of dominant culture. Students must operate within the dominant conception of time, and, as Jim suggests, students must be fluent in standard English. Success is thus linked to the degree to which individuals are able and willing to operate within dominant cultural categories.[13] Since students at Urban College exist within a broader race/class subculture that embodies oppositional elements (language *and* time are both good examples here), they must learn a new culture. Since the collective culture as it is produced within the college embodies oppositional impulses as well, it is only those students who break from the collective that ultimately succeed within the institution, thus availing themselves of the opportunity to escape the underclass.

It must be pointed out again that students do not articulate opposition to mainstream knowledge or culture.[14] While there is some understanding on the part of students that it is "not theirs," they do not oppose it directly in the way that working class whites do. On one level, students at Urban College *do* perceive college knowledge as valid, and they genuinely wish to obtain it. It is only their actions which reflect the contradictory nature of these impulses. For this reason it is highly unusual for students to articulate negative feelings about knowledge itself. While those that succeed can articulate the fact that they had to learn a new culture, those that do not succeed do not verbally reject dominant culture. In fact, they affirm at least parts of it. Jerome is an exception here. While he also embraces college knowledge at a general level, he pinpoints areas that he does not embrace – areas that suggest to him that college knowledge is "not his" and therefore would be difficult to obtain. The interview below clarifies this point. It must be kept in mind, however, that Jerome is the only student interviewed who articulates this position. It must also be noted that, generally speaking, Jerome is as supportive of college knowledge as are others currently enrolled in Urban College.

> *Jerome:* See like Mr _______ , teaching Fashion History. It's pretty cool that you went back and showed about the Renaissance time and the Greek periods, but how you going to tell somebody who can't hardly buy a pair of jeans about some designer jeans?[15] Yves Saint Laurent and Halston! Man, I'm never going to be able to put this on. So you are creating that separation again [between students and faculty]. That little type of understanding about where you are at can be the difference. That's the big difference; you have got to know what audience to run that role in. And you see right away I can't get into Calvin Klein – my pockets ain't into Calvin Klein. I don't want to hear nothing about what he's making this year, or next year neither, 'cuz I'm not going to buy nonc of that. This is cold-blooded stop and gap right there. People say Calvin Klein, but if I had an outlet to put some of them Calvin Klein on, then I would be more inclined to listen to him.
>
> (. . .) That was another area I was thinking into [Africa]. (. . .) See, if you had it broken down into a more various type of international type of existence, where fashion really originated from, you know, it would cut some of that stereotypeness off. Because most people think that most Africans never wore no clothes, but I know you [LW] went to Africa, I have read and seen so much, and talked to so many Africans, a whole lot of Africans ain't never had none of that stuff on that the stereotype of the African is, so, African art and things like that should have been a part of that course [Fashion History]. [It] would have made it more interesting too, and then you got something for somebody to identify with. If I can identify and it's a learning process, then I will be more into it.

Jerome suggests that knowledge itself may be biased in that Africa is omitted and his "pockets ain't into Calvin Klein."[16] He has partially understood the fact that since college knowledge is "not his," it is difficult to identify with and therefore obtain. While Jerome's position is not shared by students, the cultural form itself represents an "unconscious" understanding of these realities.

Success and dominant categories

I have argued in this chapter that it is those individuals who break with the collectivity and are willing and able to operate within dominant cultural categories who succeed in Urban College. It is not simply that the most "intelligent" students succeed. Here I concur with Willis that the occupational/class structure must be conceived in terms of radical breaks represented by the interface of cultural forms.[17] "Success" rates in Urban College, then, cannot be predicted simply on the basis of the undialectical notion of measured intelligence. It is more closely tied to the form that student culture takes within the institution, and the nature of the risk involved when individuals break with the collective.

On the basis of research conducted in a secondary school in England, Keddie has argued that pupils who are perceived as most able, and who in a streamed school reach the top streams, are those who have access to or are willing to take over the teacher's definition of the situation.[18] The behavior of students in top streams is generally judged "appropriate," as is their handling of what is presented as knowledge. Appropriate behavior is defined in terms of student ability to do a subject. As she argues, "this is not necessarily a question of the ability to move to higher levels of generalization and abstraction so much as an ability to move into an alternative system of thought from that of his everyday knowledge." Ultimately this means being able to work within the categories and framework that the teacher constructs. "A" stream pupils suggest a willingness to take over the teachers' definition of what is to constitute the problem and what is to count as legitimate knowledge. This may require pupils to regard as irrelevant or inappropriate what they might see as problems in a context of everyday meaning. While it is likely that all pupils can move between "common sense" and "finite provinces of meaning," the particular shifts that the school requires and legitimates are based on a social organization of knowledge that is most likely to be achieved by the middle class.[19] In other words it is middle class students who are most likely to have access to teacher categories, thus ensuring their relative success in school.

Students at Urban College are the failures of the public school system in the United States – the students who could not or would not work within teacher categories. It is also the case that such students received a less valuable education than students in the suburbs, for example,[20] and the level of basic skills possessed by Urban College students is exceedingly low.[21] These students were not in "college preparatory" tracks, and they did not work within teacher-imposed categories. In short, they did not absorb whatever mainstream culture was distributed through elementary and secondary school. They nevertheless return to college with the intention of gaining whatever skills are necessary to operate within the cultural mainstream. The culture as it is produced within the institution ensures that most will return to the streets. A small proportion of this group, however, *does* make it. Keddie's analysis is very helpful here. It is those students who are willing and able to operate within faculty-imposed categories that ultimately "succeed." Students who operate outside the group logic are defined as "good" students. Those students who are not willing to accept the teachers' definition of the situation simply fail.[22] Students who cannot or will not learn standard English, for example, cannot possibly succeed at Urban College.

It must be stressed here that an inability to remain outside the group logic does not represent a simple lack of individual will; it is materially based. The ethic of cooperation is deeply rooted among the urban poor, and individuals do not break these ties easily. While individualism may be a desired goal, it may be impossible to live out in a context of scarce resources. It must also be stressed that the desire for dominant culture embodies its own contradictions: while dominant culture may be desired on one level, it is white, not black. Given that student cultural form at Urban College acts largely to reproduce the urban underclass, success in school represents a severe break with the underclass community. Since the collective offers the only security students have, the individual must carefully weigh his or her chances for success against the loss of security that the community provides. Stack's comment on the risk of social mobility is very important here. This is especially true given the tension that exists between underclass and middle class blacks. As I pointed out in chapter 4, this tension is partially reproduced within the college itself.

There is one group that does not fit into this pattern – women who have raised their families and are returning to school. Many such individuals opt for traditional female fields such as Secretarial Science and Child Care, and the success rate in these fields is relatively high. It is possible to earn an Associate's degree in either area and still obtain employment in the city in which Urban College is located. Such jobs are low-paying, do not normally provide benefits, and would not allow an individual to even consider striking out on their own. A woman can remain a part of the collective and succeed at Urban College if she chooses one of these options. Wages would simply augment money already available in the kin network. Such curricula do not signify a break with the community in the same way that other choices do. The pattern of faculty hiring only serves to reinforce this point.[23] While younger women also elect these fields, it is older women who exist distinctly outside the student culture, thereby exhibiting a far greater success rate. Since success in these areas does not signify a break with the community, there is less risk. While younger women can also pursue these fields and remain part of the collective, most desire to escape the ghetto and elaborate the contradictory cultural code outlined throughout.

It must be clear that when an individual breaks with the collective he or she is breaking with a *certain* segment of the black community – the urban poor. Paradoxically the individual must place himself or herself outside of networks that enable survival in order to attempt survival in the cultural mainstream. This is indeed a risk, especially since the chances of "making it" in the current economy are slim. While "success" means leaving one's immediate community, Leonard argues that it does not necessarily mean abandoning the black community as a whole:

> *Leonard:* What I try to tell them [other students at Urban College] is concentrate on getting that schooling down, get the paper [degree], you know, maybe go into a four-year institution or go into the service, get some practical experience to go along with it, get some more education while you're in the service, "hey, you'll be cool," you know.
>
> (. . .) What I tell them is even with the college diploma it's not guaranteed that you'll get anything, but what will happen is that you can understand at times *why* you're not allowed to have things and you also may find ways to counteract it. Hopefully that will be in a non-violent kind of way, but if it ever gets to be

> in a violent type of way, you will have the knowledge and the intelligence and the awareness that you can (. . .) put that in a proper level, because no revolution [has] been successful without a middle class – an intelligent educated class that is backing it to begin with, and we have to [develop] that in our own black community.

Leonard is not suggesting that those who succeed must abandon the black struggle. He is suggesting, instead, that the struggle needs leaders, and that such leaders can be drawn only from among the educated. The successful have an important role to play in the betterment of the community. While this is certainly a powerful argument in some ways (and also historically accurate), class fraction tensions *within* the black community make this somewhat problematic. Underclass students resent those who "make it" at one and the same time that they wish to "make it" themselves. Leonard is well on his way to becoming middle class. While he sees a distinct role for middle class individuals in the black struggle, those still trapped in the underclass are not totally convinced. As George said earlier, "(y)ou just don't see any of the education in sociology, in urban planning, education in history that blacks have been able to acquire, you just don't see very much of it being spent in the village." It is not clear to those left behind that "success" does not imply leaving the community forever. On the contrary: tensions which are reproduced within the college suggest that it does. While Leonard can "look back" at the urban existence and see a role for himself, he sees this role only after the fact. The negativity toward middle class blacks which is elaborated in student cultural form makes it all the more difficult for individuals to attempt social mobility through the school.

6
Analysis of culture—I

"I have some friends who got married. One, he just got laid off from work and she's working and they are getting into fights and they have bought new things and they are stuck, you know. He had a really nice job, and they are going to be in trouble. They have a new car. . . . See, even now you can't count on a job, and if you buy all this stuff, they might give you a line of credit and you buy all that stuff, it's got to be paid; if you don't pay, it's going to fold. And that's what they did; they didn't put anything away, credit cards and this and that – really messed them up. (. . .) These are difficult times. Hey, the 1970s you had to tighten the belt, and the 80s you're going to have to tighten it more. The 90s, I don't know, it might be possible. I don't know." (a Business Administration student)

This chapter and chapter 7 analyze the inner meaning, rationality, and dynamic of the cultural processes outlined in chapters 1 through 5. Student cultural form at Urban College can be seen on one level as an assault upon official notions of time and as a partial defeat of individualism. The question remains, how does this happen? In chapters 3 and 4 I suggested that aspects of the institution contribute to the production of student cultural form in some rather fundamental ways. But is this all? Is student culture a response simply to interactions and practices within the institution itself? At best, this constitutes only a partial answer since practices within the college must themselves be seen in relation to student culture. Both faculty perspectives and practice and aspects of the hidden curriculum, for example, arise at least partially in response to students. Neither "determine" student culture in any simple sense.[1] While factors within the institution contribute to the production of student culture in some rather significant ways, student culture is, in the final analysis, firmly rooted in larger structural realities. Our task here must be to uncover the basic determinants of the cultural form whose tensions, contradictions and final outcomes we have explored in chapters 1 through 5.[2] What are these basic determinants?

Willis argues that an answer to this question can only be found below the surface of ethnography in a more interpretive mode. His concepts "penetration" and "limitation" are useful in this context. "Penetration" describes those instances where students have developed responses to school and work that show an awareness of the unequal reality they face.[3] In *Learning to Labour*, for example, the lads' rejection of so much of the form and content of schooling stems from an unconscious realization that while working class youth can succeed as individuals, schooling will not work for the working class as a whole. "Penetration" thus designates "impulses within a cultural form towards the penetration of the conditions of existence of its members and their position within the social whole but in a way that is not centred, essentialist, or individualist."[4] "Limitation" refers to those "blocks, diversions and ideological effects which confuse and impede the full development and expression of these impulses."[5] The "rather clumsy but strictly accurate term 'partial penetration' designates the interaction of these two terms in a concrete culture."[6] It must be stressed here that while ethnographic investigations can detail the terrain in which insights and limitations play themselves out, such investigations cannot show them separately. This is because they truly do combine in a concrete culture; the task of isolating them must be ours. This can only be done on a theoretical level. It is also the case that since cultural production is not "conscious," no amount of direct questioning will elicit a detailed explanation of these processes from its participants. *Culture truly is lived*; it is created and re-created on a daily basis and the elements of culture combine in ways unbeknown to its creators.

Willis's analysis of the lads' culture is helpful in theorizing student culture at Urban College. The distinctions made and acted upon by working class white males at the level of their own culture provide an important element in the re-creation of the ideological hegemony of the dominant classes. Braverman and others have argued at length that one of the principles guiding the articulation of capitalist social relations is the progressive divorce of mental from physical labor. Planning is separated from execution at every point in production, so that each process is standardized and controlled.[7] When the lads reject schooling and affirm application and manual labor in the way that they do, they embrace a distinction that lies at the very heart of a capitalist economy. Most importantly, they are experiencing a *necessary* division as a kind of cultural autonomy and freedom; they are living it as if they create it.[8] Paradoxically, insights that the lads make on the cultural level are "bound back finally into the structure they are uncovering in complex ways by internal and external limitations. There is ultimately a guilty and unrecognized – precisely a 'partial' – relationship of these penetrations to that which they seem to be independent from and see into."[9] Insights are thus deprived of their independence in two ways: (1) existing social and economic structures act partially to shape them; and (2) they are bound back finally into the very structures they are uncovering. The terrain in which such understandings occur, then, is the terrain of the existing system.[10] While the cultural level is never totally determined by existing economic and social arrangements, it is also never independent from such arrangements.[11] Willis's points on the relationship between culture and the economy are important here. He argues that

> (t)he counter-school culture and its processes [referring specifically to the lads' culture] arise from definite circumstances in a specific historical relation and are in no sense accidentally produced. The recognition of determination does not, however, dismiss creativity. Two qualifications must be insisted upon immediately however. Creativity is in no individual act, no one particular head, and is not the result of conscious intention. Its logic could only occur (. . .) at the *group* level. Secondly creativity cannot be pictured as a unique capacity or one able to produce limitless outcomes. Nor can it be considered in any sense as mastery – over the future or the present. (. . .)
>
> Having entered these caveats however, it must also be insisted that this cultural form is not produced by simple outside determination. It is produced also from the activities and struggles of each new generation. We are dealing with the collective, if not consciously directed, will and action as they overlay, and themselves take up "creative" positions with

> respect to finally reproduce what we call "outside determinations". It is these cultural and subjective processes, and actions which flow from them, which actually produce and reproduce aspects of structure. It is only by passing through this moment that determinations are made effective in the social world at all.[12]

It must be stressed again that insights made and lived out on the cultural level are not limitless. They *necessarily* "run along certain lines whose basic determinants lie outside the individual, the group or class."[13] In this context, then, it is not surprising that students in different schools and geographic locations "see through" and "live out" the same determining conditions, thus producing similar cultural forms which enable them to create and maintain class cultural bonds.[14] While the ethnography is obviously limited to a description of the field of play in one or two institutions, the cultural processes in these institutions are more or less generalizable to institutions which serve a similar clientele. These are *class* processes and, as such, not limited to action within one or two schools. While it is theoretically possible, of course, for select institutions to intervene in some fashion in order to arrest these processes, the processes themselves will unfold in particular ways and must be met head-on if institutions are to "succeed" with "problem" groups.[15] The point here is that we are dealing with fundamental class dynamics, and so-called micro investigations of cultural production ought not be considered idiosyncratic.

The shape and form of student culture will necessarily differ by class, race and gender (although I do not deal directly with gender here).[16] While the *basic* cultural processes described by Willis are at work in Urban College, for example, the lived cultural form of students is different from that of either Willis's lads or London's students in the United States. This is not surprising given that race has its *own* dynamic in the United States and that the economic position of white workers (whether in the US or England) and black workers is different. John Ogbu's point that blacks constitute a *caste-like minority* in America is very important here. The term caste-like is used as a methodological tool to emphasize the structural legacy of subordination rather than in the classical Hindu sense. As he argues,

> One may distinguish between three kinds of minority groups – autonomous, immigrant, and caste-like. This distinction is made on the basis of minority groups' relationships with the dominant group and the minority groups' perceptions of and responses to schooling. Among other things, caste-like minorities are distinguished from the other types in three important respects. Caste-like minorities have often been incorporated into existing societies or nations rather involuntarily and permanently. As a result, they occupy a more or less permanent place in society from which they can escape only through passing (that is, by secretly assuming the identities of dominant-group members) or emigration, routes which are not always open. Also, their members face a *job ceiling* – that is, highly consistent pressures and obstacles selectively assign minorities to jobs at the lowest level of status, power, dignity, and income, allowing members of the dominant group to compete more easily for more desirable jobs above that ceiling.[17]

The fact that blacks constitute a caste-like group in American society means that student culture will automatically take a somewhat different shape and form from that of the white working class. In particular, Urban College students are more aware of their own structured subordination than either Willis's or London's students. I will return to this point later in the chapter.

Student cultural form is also affected by the nature of historic struggle for particular groups. The black struggle in the United States has, by necessity, taken a different form than the struggle for a better life among working class whites. Unlike the white working class, blacks have, until recently, engaged in what Gramsci calls a "war of maneuver." This refers to a situation in which subordinated groups seek to defend their territory from assault and develop their own society as an alternative to the existing system – a system in which they are relegated to the lowest possible status. As Omi and Winant argue, "(t)he absence of democratic rights, of property, of political *space* within civil society forced racially defined opposition both outward and inward, away from the public sphere."[18] They further note that blacks (as well as other subordinated groups in the United States),

> having been driven out of the dominant political framework and

> relegated to a supposedly inferior sociocultural status, were forced inward on themselves as individuals, families, and communities. The tremendous cultural resources nurtured among such communities, the enormous labors required under such conditions to survive and still further to develop elements of an alternative society, can best be understood as combining with the continuous violent resistance (riots, etc.) which characterized these periods to constitute a racial *war of maneuver*.[19]

Even at its most oppressive, the American racial order was unable to produce "racial subjects." While the reign of terror on blacks in the United States served, until recently, to mute most forms of *overt* resistance to the regime, what historians call day-to-day resistance (which is, of course, part of what Gramsci refers to as a "war of maneuver") has its roots in slavery and persists today. Black slaves, for example, developed cultures of resistance based on music, religion, African traditions and family ties through which they sustained a committment to liberation.[20]

While such resistance does not constitute a frontal challenge to an existing order, it can set limits to that order and allow people to live with a minimum of decency in a society that would deny them this right. Because it is by its very nature collective, day-to-day resistance can also impart a sense of community and teach the rudiments of organization. It is this very day-to-day resistance which prepared blacks to make sustained interventions into the mainstream political process after World War II. Based on the strength gained through a "war of maneuver," black Americans were able to mount a subsequent "war of position" – a strategy which has sought "to transform the dominant racial ideology in the United States, to rearticulate its elements in a more egalitarian and democratic discourse."[21] As I argued in chapter 1, the major site for this subsequent "war" has been the state.

As Eugene Genovese points out, however, the effect of day-to-day resistance can be contradictory. Such resistance can imply accommodation to a regime, in contrast to insurrection. Resistance and accommodation thus developed as a single pattern in the black community and is reflected on the cultural level in language, notions of time and work rhythms.[22] These oppositional practices have been lived out and elaborated upon over the years and constitute core cultural elements in the urban black community today.

While there is certainly day-to-day resistance among working class whites, the white working class was never forced into a comparable "war of maneuver." Working class whites could and did struggle overtly in the public sphere.[23] They were never forced to develop elements of an alternative society in the face of complete absence of democratic rights, property and political space. The tradition of struggle is, therefore, quite different. Blacks were forced far more upon *themselves* than whites ever were. This, of course, is related to the position of blacks as a caste-like group. Both the fact that blacks constitute a caste-like minority in the United States and the particular form that struggle had to take in the black community exert an impact on the shape and form of student culture. I will return to the latter point in chapter 7.

What the culture uncovers

While working class white students overtly reject much of the form and content of schooling and act on this rejection within educational institutions, black student opposition will be coded differently given my points above. Like working class whites, however, blacks at Urban College have understood the unequal reality they face. While they do not overtly reject the form and content of schooling, their own lived culture reveals these impulses: students realize to some extent the value of education at this level for urban blacks. *The pattern of dropping in and out, arriving late to class and extensive drug use on campus must be seen as an impulse in the culture towards a true understanding of the position of the group within the social whole.* As with Willis's lads, this constitutes a rather realistic assessment of what schooling will do for them.

Karabel and others have argued persuasively that the community college in the United States, "generally viewed as the leading edge of an open and egalitarian system of higher education, is in reality a prime contemporary expression of the dual historical patterns of class-based tracking and educational inflation."[24] The success of community colleges has been linked to two phenomenon: (1) a change in the structure of the economy which necessitates a demand for personnel in such areas as data processing and the health semi-professions;[25] and (2) an American ideology regarding equality of opportunity through education.[26] Given racial contest in the state, the second reason has been instrumental in ensuring the success of the movement. In response to widespread demands in the 1960s for higher education from previously excluded groups in the population, large-scale expansion has occurred at the tertiary level. Rather than serving to broaden the base of recruitment in four-year colleges and universities, however, this led to increased differentiation within higher education itself. Two-year public colleges, whose mission differed from that of their four-year counterparts, were created specifically to absorb previously excluded groups.[27] "Herein," argues Karabel, "lies the genius of the community college movement: it seemingly fulfills the traditional American quest for *equality of opportunity* without sacrificing the principle of *achievement*."[28] Karabel further notes that

> (t)he latent ideology of the community college thus suggests that everyone should have an opportunity to attain elite status, but that once they have had a chance to prove themselves, an unequal distribution of rewards is acceptable. By their ideology, by their position in the implicit tracking system of higher education – indeed, by their very relationship to the larger class structure – the community colleges lend affirmation to the merit principle which, while facilitating individual upward mobility, diverts attention from underlying questions of distributive justice.[29]

Recent research by Olneck and others is also relevant here. Studies demonstrate that rates of return to schooling for blacks and whites are not the same. "The cost of being black" in the United States is that whites get greater rewards for any given amount of schooling than non-whites. This is particularly true for elementary and secondary education; it is only upon completion of the Bachelor's degree that the expected status advantage is larger for non-whites than whites. Non-whites with four-year college degrees are relatively less disadvantaged in terms of the job market than non-whites who do not possess such degrees. Completion of the BA appears critical in terms of black social mobility.[30]

These findings are important in light of student lived cultural form at Urban College. Elements of culture represent an impulse toward a full understanding of the conditions of existence of its members *vis-à-vis* the educational system, and the position of the community college in the status hierarchy. Students have seen through the ideology of the community college – they understand that the type of education offered them in response to the struggle of the 1960s is "second best." This, of course, has a historical referent for blacks in the United States since blacks have always had to struggle for the right to be productive citizens on a par with whites. Along these same lines, student cultural form unmasks an ideology which offers everyone an opportunity to attain elite status while simultaneously justifying an unequal distribution of rewards. Students unconsciously understand that the community college works fundamentally to divert attention from underlying questions of distributive justice – questions that have provided the central focus for the black struggle in the United States.

In so understanding, student cultural form makes a discernment of the difference between individual and group logics. Again, Willis is helpful here. He suggests that

> (t)he essence of the cultural penetration concerning the school – made unselfconsciously within the cultural milieu with its own practices and objects but determining all the same an inherently collective perspective – is that the logic of class or group interests is different from the logic of individual interests. To the *individual* working class person mobility in this society may mean something. Some working class persons do "make it" and any particular individual may hope to be one of them. To the class or group at its own proper level, however, mobility means nothing at all. The only true mobility at this level would be the destruction of the whole class society.[31]

This is true for Urban College students as well. While the individual may succeed in the college and may ultimately escape the urban underclass, the group can never follow. The college cannot possibly work for blacks as a collectivity. The issue of the collectivity is particularly critical here. In the case of the urban poor, the collective enables survival, and it offers literally the only form of security the urban poor have. While transfer payments such as welfare may appear to provide a stable income, not only can families not live on these meager allotments, but there is constant threat of being cut from the welfare rolls. The urban poor can, in the final analysis, count only on one another. This has been true for blacks historically. As noted earlier, it is only the community that has enabled black Americans to live with some decency in the face of a white nation which would deny them this right. For both material and spiritual reasons, then, it is not a community from which the individual separates easily.[32] Student cultural form reflects insight into the difference between individual and group logics and their ideological confusion in relation to education. It is only the individual who escapes the underclass via the college. The college does not herald the destruction of a class society; it simply offers a possible "way out" for those who are willing and able to break with the collective. Given generalized racism in the United States, breaking with the collectivity and obtaining dominant cultural capital may lead to very little.

A further point needs to be raised here. Karabel, Pincus and others have suggested a trend toward increased vocationalization of the curriculum. Such vocationalization, they argue, represents further class-based tracking, thus ensuring the reproduction of social inequality.[33] Rather than offer students the opportunity to participate in college parallel programs, community colleges serve increasingly to track working class students into vocational programs from which there is no escape. Thus working class students are channeled, so the argument goes, into working class jobs.

While on the surface this may explain the role of the community college in the reproduction of the class structure (and indeed, it partially does), there are, in fact, very few vocational programs at Urban College. This is unlike the situation at the nearby suburban colleges where, among other subjects, students may study Dental Hygiene, Automotive Technology, Computer Technology, Nursing and Data Processing. While it can be argued that such curricula serve to channel working class students into jobs where they execute rather than conceptualize labor processes, it is also the case that such curricula, if offered at Urban College, might provide students with the opportunity to obtain stable employment, thereby enabling them to escape the ghetto.[34] Paradoxically, what Karabel sees as ensuring class-based tracking might make it possible for Urban College students to escape the underclass. This, of course, would not alter the class structure *per se*, but it might make social mobility a reality for a few more individuals.

Finally, Urban College students have seen through the role of educational institutions in general *vis-à-vis* the class structure. Bourdieu and Passeron argue that it is "cultural capital – knowledge and skill in the symbolic manipulation of language and figures" – of the dominant groups in society which ensures the success of their children. Education serves to reproduce class position and privilege, they argue, since success in school is dependent upon knowledge of those skills that cultural capital provides.[35] As Young argues, "there is a dialectical relationship between access to power and the opportunity to legitimate dominant categories, and the processes by which the availability of such categories to some groups enable them to assert power and control over others."[36] What counts as appropriate knowledge reflects the interests and culture of the group or groups who have the power to distribute and thus legitimate their world view through educational institutions.[37] Those who have access to these categories to begin with will, quite simply, perform better.[38] This is exceptionally clear with respect to standard English in Urban College. While the system works primarily to benefit those with privilege, it appears neutral in that success is dependent upon an ostensibly meritocratic, neutral testing process. Since tests tap the cultural capital of the dominant classes, the system works to their benefit.

Student cultural form at Urban College makes sense within this context. Legitimate knowledge acts not primarily to "push people up – as in the official account – but to maintain those who are already on top."[39] Students must alter their *own* culture if they are to succeed within the college. Since they possess the wrong decoders to begin with, they will have a more difficult time than students who carry the dominant culture. In the case of blacks, since racism has its own dynamic in the United States, even possessing the "correct" cultural capital hardly ensures success. Student cultural form, then, represents a discernment of both the role of educational institutions in maintaining the class structure and the cross-cutting effects of racism.

It must be pointed out here that part of "what the culture uncovers" is consciously understood by blacks. Unlike working class whites, black students can, at times, articulate the fact that their education is "second best," for example. This is related to

Ogbu's point that blacks constitute a caste-like minority in the United States. As he argues,

> (c)lass and caste differ in their *cognitive orientations*. Caste-like minorities do not accept their low social, political, and occupational status as legitimate outcomes of their individual failures and misfortunes as lower-class people tend to do. Black Americans, for example, see racial barriers in employment, education, housing, and other areas of life as the primary causes of their low status. Most black Americans "blame the system" rather than themselves for failure to get ahead, an orientation which underlies their collective struggle for equal opportunities in employment, education, and the like.[40]

There is, therefore, a greater conscious understanding among blacks than whites of at least some of the discernments lived out on the cultural level. This is tied to the perception that whatever blacks get is not as valuable as what whites get. Gloria, for example, a Social Science graduate, makes the following point about Urban College:

> *Gloria:* I figure that what they did was put the school right in our community – they said "we'll give them this and this may satisfy them." (. . .) This was (. . .) convenient, but we were shortchanged as far as the education itself was concerned.
>
> I think they teach Optics out there at [the suburban campus]. (. . .) We're definitely cheated. I think what they're doing is "let's give the blacks a place in their own neighborhood, then we can give them as little as possible and maybe they'll be satisfied with it. (. . .) We'll give them as much as we can and they'll keep their mouths shut."
>
> For me, for an older person who's set in their job [she is a teacher aide] and about ready for retirement, it was fine. I took Liberal Arts courses. For young people you have to think what type of work am I going to do when I complete my college, you know. Why should I go take Liberal Arts and I'm not qualified to do anything once I get out?

Gloria's perception is not necessarily shared among Urban College students. Most are genuinely pleased with the quality of their education (see chapter 2) and they are not as familiar as she is with the suburban campuses. There is, nevertheless, a sense among blacks that whatever whites give them is bound to be inferior in some way – it is a historically rooted sense of subordination. As "The Nickel Bag Man" states (chapter 2).

> "Now, I'm not saying my shit [drugs] ain't good 'cause it is. But white folks still get the best. Same old story the white man seems to have the best of everything."

In this sense, then, there is a distinct difference between blacks and working class whites. Student cultural form represents an understanding in both cases of the unequal reality they face. This understanding is largely unconscious. In the case of black students, however, there are *moments of true conscious understanding* of these processes. The way in which this understanding is limited will be discussed in chapter 7.

Blacks in the United States economy

At this point we must consider carefully the position of blacks in the United States economy. Only then will we be able to gain a clearer understanding of the grounds that make the cultural sensible. In what context are cultural actions reasonable? To what does the cultural level respond? How, ultimately, may lived culture serve to reproduce the very structures which act partially to shape it?

In chapter 1, I argued that racial inequality persists in the economic area despite major changes that have taken place for blacks in other areas. Since 1945 most racial barriers to equal political and civil rights have been torn down; the sharecropping system in the south that served to maintain blacks at a level little better than slavery for so many decades has been largely dismantled. Most blacks now reside in metropolitan areas and work for a wage or salary. The provision of education is more equal now than ever before. Yet inequality by race persists. Why is this the case?[41]

Richard Edwards's analysis is helpful here. He argues persuasively that capitalist development in the twentieth century is characterized by distinct and enduring "class fractions." Unlike American capitalism in the nineteenth century, where an attempt was made to reshape a highly diversified labor force into an increasingly homogeneous class, capitalism in the twentieth century has attempted to institutionalize rather than erode divisions within the working class. Three distinct labor markets exist within the United States economy. These market segments – the secondary market, the subordinate primary market, and the independent primary market – differ in terms of form of control in the workplace, worker pay (both amount and form), and effects of education and seniority on wage or salary.[42] Studies by Gordon, Piore and others suggest not only that market outcomes differ by segment, but that market processes differ substantially as well.[43]

For the most part, blacks are rooted in the secondary labor market, and this goes a long way toward explaining income inequality. Jobs in the secondary sector are marked by the casual nature of the employment and the fact that work almost never requires previous training or education beyond basic literacy. In contrast to those in the primary market, such jobs provide virtually no job security and movement in and out of them is common. Most importantly, such work is not regular, and intermittent unemployment among individuals in the secondary market is widespread. *Thus a persistent feature of this class fraction is pervasive wagelessness.*

Blacks entered the wage labor force during a time of labor force segmentation. Blacks are poor relative to whites because they are, by and large, trapped in the secondary labor market; increasingly they constitute an underclass. Blacks are thus members of what might be called the "idle working class" due to lack of stable employment.

While this explains racial inequality to some extent, it must also be noted that racial minorities (like women) constitute a class fraction in and of themselves.[44] Racial inequality is not *simply* a matter of market segmentation as it relates to the capitalist accumulation process. Blacks do not increasingly constitute an urban underclass simply because they obtained wage labor during a time of market segmentation rather than homogenization. Race has its own dialectic in the United States and the relation between race and the process of market segmentation is in itself important. While race parallels market segments to some extent, racial distinctions also cross-cut segments in the sense that discrimination occurs *within* market segments as well.[45] Thus blacks in the secondary and primary markets share certain interests, and racism in and of itself explains income inequalities to some extent. In other words, while much racial income inequality can be explained in terms of class fractions, racial inequality also cuts across these fractions. Blacks, then, constitute a further fraction of the working class. As Reich notes, "slavery, sharecropping, Watts, the South Side, and other ghettoes – that is, the historical legacy and everyday manifestations of racism – shape a separate consciousness."[46] The United States is left with a highly fractionalized working class, and racism is linked to these fractions in more than one way.

An important point here is that working class fractions are most beneficial to the capitalist class. Industry has, for example, capitalized on racism in American society to break strikes, and many northern industries initially employed blacks under these conditions.[47] The continuing divisions by race in the United States have prevented the formation of a broadly based working class movement. Racial inequality and antagonisms have inhibited both union bargaining strength and militancy historically, thereby serving to reduce worker share of industrial profit. Since the working class is highly fractionalized, struggles become class fraction struggles rather than class struggles *per se*. The Traditional Proletariat, for example, as represented by unions, bargains for job security, pensions and higher pay. In the 1960s, what Edwards calls the Working Poor struggled for medicaid, public housing, food stamps and higher welfare benefits.[48] These are, however, class fraction struggles – they do not represent class-wide concerns. As Edwards notes, capitalist hegemony has remained largely intact because the working class has been unable to mount a single struggle. Each fraction has pursued different immediate interests in the political arena at the expense of fundamental class interests.[49] As Edwards states, "the result has been the demise of 'class' issues and the rise of 'fraction' issues."[50] In the final analysis, both black and white workers are hurt by racism to the benefit of capitalists and high-income whites. Reich provides impressive historical and econometric evidence to suggest that this is the case.[51]

We must be careful, however, not to assume that *all* forms of racial discrimination and market segmentation are unequivocally functional for the capitalist class.[52] As Erik Olin Wright has recently argued, capitalism undermines and reproduces racism at one and the same time. The notion of racism as a divide and conquer strategy which benefits the capitalist class is, without question, a central theme in marxist analyses. What is generally not acknowledged is a contradictory theme: the fact that "the more labor power becomes a pure commodity regulated by pure market principles unfettered by personal ties and ascriptive barriers, the more rapidly can capitalism expand."[53] The capitalist accumulation process tends to *erode* distinctions between categories of labor at the same time that it needs and exploits these divisions for its own reproduction. Thus labor market segmentation and enduring class fractions evident in twentieth-century American capitalist development *is simultaneously reproductive and non-reproductive*. Capitalism is inherently contradictory and it is these very contradictions that are linked to the production of worker consciousness. While a highly fractionalized working class may be reproductive at the present time, the contradictory nature of such fractions as they relate to the capitalist accumulation process should not be forgotten. The tendency for capitalism to transform all labor into a pure commodity means that on one level at least, there is a tendency to treat black labor power like white labor power, and one class fraction like any other. This, of course, contradicts enduring divisions by race that are historically rooted in the United States. While such antagonisms may be "functional" for the capitalist class at present, it cannot be assumed that this will always be the case. Enduring divisions by race are not as smoothly linked to the maintenance of capitalism as many analysts have implied.

I have argued in this chapter that student cultural form at Urban College can be seen as a discernment of the conditions of existence of its members within the social whole. Rather than entering the institution with these elements of culture fully developed, *students create a collective culture within the institution*. This culture, while not accidental, is also not imposed. Paradoxically, the very culture students create helps to ensure that the vast majority of them will remain in the ghetto.

Student cultural form at Urban College represents an impulse toward an understanding of the American ideology of equality of opportunity and the way in which this ideology has been translated into concrete practice in relation to blacks. In response to demands for equal educational opportunity in the 1960s, there was widespread expansion at the tertiary level. This expansion resulted in increased differentiation within higher education itself, and minorities are, as Olivas points out, confined largely to the less prestigious two-year sector. Students "see through" to the fact that they are offered an inferior education, and that even within this sector, the college will not work for them as a *group*. Success demands that they break from the collectivity and operate within dominant cultural categories. They must, as Bourdieu and Passeron suggest, absorb the cultural capital of the dominant classes if they are to "make it." This is particularly difficult in light of the fact that members of the black urban underclass possess the wrong educational decoders to begin with.

Lived culture must also be seen as a largely unconcious understanding of the role that education at this level plays *even if* students succeed. Given both segmented market processes and racism in American society, the community college degree in and of itself would do very little for most black students. Student cultural form, then, represents an understanding of the fact that education at this level not only doesn't work for the group, but also means less for individual blacks than whites.

Student culture thus sees through the ideology of the community college; it exposes the unequal position of blacks both as a collectivity and as individuals negotiating in a racist society. Student cultural form represents an unmasking of both the merit system as it relates to blacks and the fact that broader issues of distributive justice are ignored – issues which have constituted the core of the black struggle for hundreds of years. These insights are linked fundamentally to the position of blacks in the United States economy and the relationship between schooling and American economic structures.

The question must be asked, however, if the culture represents an understanding of the role of the urban community college in reproducing and legitimizing social inequalities despite an ideology which stresses mobility, why then, is the cultural level not more overtly political? There is potential on the cultural level for a thoroughly critical analysis of the mechanisms of educational selection and the role that the American ideology of equal educational opportunity plays in this process. Since the collectivity is reaffirmed at the cultural level, there is a basis for serious collective political action. This is even more true given the fact that there are moments of true conscious understanding of these processes. Why doesn't this happen? Why are insights at the cultural level only partial, falling short of transformative political activity? Chapter 7 explores these issues.

7
Analysis of culture—II

What happens to a dream deferred?
Does it dry up
like a raisin in the sun?
Or fester like a sore –
And then run?

Does it stink like rotten meat?
Or crust and sugar over –
like a syrupy sweet?

Maybe it just sags like a heavy load.

Or does it explode?

Langston Hughes, "Lenox Avenue Mural"

I have argued in chapter 6 that insights on the cultural level tend toward an exposure of the ideology of the community college and the role of education generally *vis-à-vis* blacks in the United States. What distorts such tendencies, rendering them partial? How are such tendencies broken up and ultimately applied to different ends – ends which serve fundamentally to reproduce, rather than challenge, existing structures?

An important point here is that the culture forged at the community college is a *group* culture. As individuals, students enter the institution with the intention of escaping the underclass. Individual students *want* to be "middle class" and see Urban College as a mediator between two worlds – that of the streets and the cultural mainstream. Once students are in the college, however, the group logic takes hold and these very same students create a collective culture that ensures that the vast majority of them will return to the streets. It is only those students who remain outside the collectivity that "succeed" in the institution.

It is critically important here that the collective is reinforced within the institution itself. While it is certainly the case that the black community has a strong collective tradition to begin with (stemming from historic oppression and response to such oppression on the part of blacks), the collective is strengthened by virtue of a shared community college experience. Given that student culture embodies the potential for transformative political activity, the question must be asked, why isn't this potential realized? Why does the cultural level remain relatively disorganized from within and politically weak?

Limitations

The notion "limitation" is useful here.[1] As in the case of working class whites, insights embedded within student culture at Urban College are prevented from going further by contradictions within lived cultural form itself. While black student culture expresses certain insights into the conditions of existence of its members, these insights are only partial. In the case of Urban College students, this incompleteness is linked to a collective faith in education itself. Despite a cultural form that suggests deep skepticism about what the community college will do for them as a group, Urban College students retain a profound faith in schooling and in the power and immediacy of knowledge. The contradictions embedded within student cultural form are thus particularly stark: elements of culture themselves represent *simultaneous insight and limitation*. As I suggested earlier, student culture makes a discernment of the difference between individual and group logics and their ideological confusion in education. At the same time, the collective faith in education – itself an element of culture – inhibits these impulses and renders them partial. *The culture itself serves to block the very insights it makes.*

It is important to point out here that the collective faith in education is itself an oppositional tendency in the black community. During slavery, it was against the law to teach slaves to read and write. Restrictions increased over time and numerous local laws supplanted already existing state laws. In some localities it was against the law simply to sell writing materials to slaves. Despite these prohibitions, literate slaves appeared everywhere, even on large plantations where the threat of severe punishment for such activities loomed large.[2]

The desire for literacy continued after the war and, as Genovese suggests,

> the freedmen's efforts to educate themselves and their children provides one of the most moving chapters in American social history and historians are finally giving it the attention it deserves. Northern white support played an important role, but the extent to which blacks with few resources and little experience scraped to pay for schools and teachers stands out like a miracle. (. . .) The desire for education everywhere exploded. For the freedmen, as for the slaves before them, it represented the Keys of the Kingdom.[3]

The attitude of Urban College students toward knowledge must be situated within this context. For blacks, an affirmation of learning has constituted a form of resistance to dominant ideology regarding their own position and posed a threat to the hegemony of the dominant classes (although not without its contradictory effects). It is this very affirmation that gave rise to the heightened struggle over schooling in the 1950s and 1960s. The continued struggle for education on a par with whites is an attempt to resist a current relegation of blacks to the position of unskilled labor and the increasing wagelessness associated with this position.[4] Thus, the desire for education is an attempt to gain ground within the existing system. While it constitutes an oppositional impulse, it represents at one and the same time partial accommodation to the existing regime.[5]

Just as the white working class affirmation of manual labor is partially determined by the broader white working class culture, black student affirmation of schooling and the power and immediacy of knowledge is partially determined by impulses within broader black cultural forms. Among black students, as among the white working class, these impulses are bound back finally, in complex ways, into the larger social structure. In the case of urban blacks, these very oppositional tendencies act to limit insights on the cultural level regarding the value of education for the group.

Elements of culture thus represent simultaneous accommodation and resistance. While elements of student cultural form see through the ideology regarding equal opportunity, other elements of this same form act to block these insights, rendering them truly partial. It is the partiality of insights which, in the final analysis, characterizes the culture students produce. Paradoxically, oppositional tendencies as described here can themselves be contradictory, thereby impeding the development of a fundamentally political culture.

The impact of ideology

The partiality of insights leads students to blame themselves. Despite a raised consciousness among blacks of their own structured subordination, students do, in the final analysis, take substantial responsibility for their *own* "failure." This breaks up and distorts a tendency toward true conscious understanding of the cultural processes outlined in this book. *A tendency to "blame the system" which is linked to a structural legacy of subordination thus exists side-by-side currently with a tendency to blame oneself.*[6] For example, students hold their neighborhood, lifestyle and problems with children responsible for what is, in fact, structurally induced. James, Jerome and George articulate this below:

> *James:* Now the attendance policy, I think, has a tendency to penalize students who really want to come to class but due to *their* lifestyle or *their* problems, or the neighborhood where they live, or problems associated with children in the household [my emphasis] that they [classes] sometimes are missed.

* * *

> *Jerome:* So, a lot of blacks are eliminated [from schools and good positions] through a whole lot of social mis-errors, not only blacks I would imagine all people – white too (. . .) but it is more pronounced, you can see it better in the black community than you can see [it] in the white where the average age of the teenage girl at 13, you know, five out of six, you know, got a baby already. You know, *it's a lack of training, and definitely, it's no question, clear across the board that it is a lack of home training* [my emphasis]. Then you get into a deeper

> psychological sort of thing; people accept the attitude that they just got a position in life, their position is never having any importance into it. They are willing to accept that. (. . .) They just give up.[7]

George's points below are particularly insightful. In two different discussions he stresses the fact that students, for a variety of reasons, blame themselves for "failure." The cultural level remains disorganized from within, and, as George's comments suggest, insights on the informal cultural level cannot compete with a well-articulated dominant ideology.

> *George:* This is why the school is failing in so many of its objectives. They [college personnel] don't understand those people. They just don't have the slightest fucking idea.
>
> And yet what's so tragic about it is that they [students] can't even articulate what it is that people don't understand. One of the reasons why they can't articulate it is because it's bending them out of shape. Too often black students become self-inverted racists because the kind of abstract thought that's shot in the curriculums [sic] are ethnocentric and racist.
>
> *LW:* (. . .) Why do students come one semester, maybe six weeks later drop out, then come back the following semester, then maybe drop out again?
>
> *George:* In my judgment (. . .) there is a search for the light. There is a search for some light but when they come there [Urban College] and they look around the rooms and the foyers and learning centers they do not find very much light, you know. So they retreat and when they retreat they're bombarded from every angle of their perceptions, of their objective observations, they're confronted with the idea that education *somehow* is the answer – *somehow* is the key. They got posters – Urban College is the key – and there will be the keys. One key says "brighter future," another says something else. Somehow or another they feel that maybe *they* missed the boat. Maybe it's not the school, maybe it's them. They become more negative in their self-opinion but conflicted by the contradiction that they become positive in their search for the light again. "Well, I didn't see it *that* time, it must have been me" – blame themself – but "God damn it, I'm going to find it," and they come back again.

George's comments are powerful. Despite the fact that students criticize faculty for not working hard enough, not caring enough, and so forth (see chapter 2), in the final analysis, students tend to hold *themselves* largely responsible for failure. Thus, while the student culture makes a collective discernment of the value of this type of education and schooling in general for the group, the collective is broken into its component parts by virtue of impulses which suggest that education *is* the key. As I argued earlier, these impulses are themselves oppositional within the black community. They are reinforced currently by a powerful dominant ideology which suggests that "education *is* the answer"; "anyone can make it if they only try hard enough"; and "if you fail, it is your fault." Since most *formal* barriers to equality have been struck down in response to the struggles of the 1950s and 1960s, this ideology has been distributed all the more widely through the black community. George comes closest when he states, "When they [students] retreat, they're bombarded from every angle of their perceptions, of their objective observations, they're confronted with the idea that education *somehow* is the answer – *somehow* is the key. (. . .) Somehow or another they feel that maybe *they* missed the boat. Maybe it's not the school, maybe it's them." Thus dominant ideology plays a key role here, but it does not determine student cultural form in any simple sense.

In comparison with the informal cultural level, dominant ideology is articulated and well-organized. It is, in short, formal, and literally permeates the entire society. As numerous analysts point out, it is distributed through newspapers, television, film, books, schools and welfare agencies.[8] As noted above, this ideology has been distributed all the more widely since formal barriers to equality have been dismantled since the 1960s.

Willis's points on ideology and culture are important here. He suggests that

> The fundamental weakness in cultural forms is the *mediated* nature of personal experience and validation as they overlay and are influenced by cultural penetrations. Though the latter are the ultimate basis of relevance and vitality in a culture they are never expressed explicitly. They are not direct resources for struggle, they only have a similarity *in the state of our analysis* with direct political statement: they do not replace policies or

> the level of conscious analysis. The very concreteness, denseness, buried radicalism, and relevance of informal cultural processes, and the very substance of their claim on individuals is their greatest weakness in the larger social context. The nature of informality as a mode of opposition in this society is that it reserves itself as the exception to the rule. It is blind to all of the other exceptions which together could overthrow the rule. It is unaware of its own "rules". The analysis of the world which actually directs its distinctively cultural responses remains silent. It is into this silence that ideology confidently strides. Whether right or wrong, whether penetrated or not it is *the* rule, it is *the* voice. It becomes the internal interlocutor for the weakness of cultural forms. Powerful ideologies, no matter what their content, always have the gift of formality, publicness and explicit statement. They can work within the scope of consensus and consent because nothing in oppositional *cultural* processes can displace their level of action and effectiveness.[9]

When Urban College students, as a group, differentiate themselves from the institution through absenteeism, tardiness and drug use, the insights (which are, at times, conscious) represented by such actions are prevented from going further. Dominant ideology plays two roles in this process. To begin with, the notion that education is *the* answer is encoded within student cultural form itself. While this may be historically oppositional, it nevertheless furthers current ideology regarding the value of education. Dominant ideology and cultural resistance truly do produce and reproduce one another. Ideology also works directly here. As George suggests, when students differentiate themselves from the institution, they are literally "bombarded" with suggestions that education is the key to success and that anyone can "make it." Unlike the relatively disorganized cultural level, ideology is organized and far from silent. Cultural form does not provide an alternative set of categories or vision. While the collective culture produced in the institution sees through ideology, ideology "confidently strides" into the space between the disorganized cultural level and political action. Despite the fact that the culture reflects insight into the conditions of existence of the group, dominant ideology serves to break up and distort these impulses. Dominant ideology is also encoded within student cultural form itself. It is this *combination* of blocks and ideological effects that limits cultural insights and prevents the development of a collective consciousness geared toward transformative political activity.[10]

"A heavy load"

Student culture is also limited by a well-founded sense of despair. In spite of optimistic expectations stemming from the struggles of the 1950s and 1960s, the median income of black families in 1978 remained at 57 per cent of that of white families. The median income is, in fact, at approximately the same relative level as that in the early 1950s and remarkably close to estimates of black–white income ratios in 1900.[11]

In the city in which Urban College is located, a feeling of despair is particularly well-founded. Industry is moving out of the northeast, in general, and the economic position of blacks is objectively worse than before. Men and women with thirty years at the steel plant are being laid off. Factories are closing everywhere, and jobs are increasingly scarce. There are, in fact, few opportunities for employment in the city in which Urban College is located. It is estimated that close to 50 per cent of black youth are currently unemployed and the welfare rolls continue to rise. Clifton and Leonard comment on this below:

> *Clifton:* I have some friends who got married. One, he just got laid off from work and she's working and they are getting into fights and they have bought new things and they are stuck, you know. He had a really nice job and they are going to be in trouble. They have a new car. . . . See, even now you can't count on a job, and if you buy all of this stuff, they might give you a line of credit, and you buy all of that stuff, it's got to be paid; if you don't pay, it's going to fold. And that's what they did; they didn't put anything away, credit cards and this and that – really messed them up.
>
> Another good friend of mine, like he's not working and she's not working, they are both laid off, you know, it's rough. They don't know, any day their car might get snatched; they got kids and rent, and it's going to fold, and you see, I know all that. (. . .) When you know all that you take that into consideration.

> These are difficult times, like you won't have something like the 60s again. These are difficult times. Hey, the 1970s you had to tighten the belt, and the 80s you're going to have to tighten it more. The 90s I don't know, it might be possible, I don't know.
>
> * * *
>
> *Leonard:* As far as the ______ area they [students] still don't see a future. Many people I went to grammar school, high school and college with, relationships that have been going on the last fifteen to twenty years of my life, most of those that I know of that have a two-year degree and the majority four-year degrees aren't even in the city any more. They left because there are no opportunities here, and there still are no opportunities here.

The sense that things are getting worse for blacks is a constant theme. As George argues:

> "I really believe that soon you'll have a small black middle class and the rest of the blacks will once again be slaves. Give them a guaranteed annual income and you have a class of slaves – people who have no say in their lives – just can be herded around like animals. We're moving toward that now. Most of these [students] have no basic skills. They can't read or write, can't do math, they don't know Malcolm X, John Coltrane, Bobby Seale, Huey Newton. They just don't know."

George's comments connote not only a sense of despair about the basic condition of black Americans, but the fact that felt subordination is no longer linked to a broader movement.[12] He suggests that students don't know Huey Newton, Bobby Seale, or Malcolm X.[13] Clifton also refers to the promise of the 1960s when he says; "These are difficult times, like you won't have something like the 60s again." Thus, a sense of despair runs through student culture like a fine thread. While students genuinely wish to escape ghetto poverty and feel on one level that education is a "way out," they also sense that the situation is hopeless – that they will never get out. The culture that is produced within the college reflects this desperation. Not only did conditions not improve for the majority of blacks in spite of the apparent gains of the 1950s and 1960s (and, indeed, they are objectively worse in the city in which Urban College is located), but there is, at present, no broader movement to impart hope for a better future, thus harnessing the cultural level.[14]

As students differentiate themselves from the institution, they link up with a well-developed sense of structured subordination. At present, however, this sense is characterized by hopelessness rather than political action. They are also met with a well-organized dominant ideology which suggests that education is the answer. Neither the disorganized cultural level nor the existence of a broader movement can compete currently with a powerful ideology. Neither provides an alternative vision.

Cultural and economic forms

In differentiating themselves from the institution, students are, in a sense, differentiating themselves from the cultural mainstream. In so doing, they fall back on their *own* culture which is linked dialectically to dominant culture and developed in opposition to this culture. Genovese's comments are still relevant here. Blacks, he argues, "learned to take the blow and parry it as best they could." Shut out by white racism from part of the dominant culture's value system, they simultaneously resisted that system by necessity and by "historically developed sensibility."[15] Blacks forged their *own* values (which are linked dialectically to dominant values) as a force for community cohesion. When Urban College students differentiate themselves from the institution, they return to a community which embodies oppositional cultural practices. As I suggested in chapters 3 and 5, opposition is encoded in such cultural elements as language and time.

The partiality of insights in student cultural form coupled with the fact that students fall back on their own culture, serves largely to reproduce the urban underclass.[16] When black students take up creative positions within the institution, they ensure their own future as part of the underclass as well as helping to provide the structural bases for their own "superexploitation." Given that black culture is a subordinate culture in the United States, students, by falling back on their own culture, are recreating, in part, the conditions of their own subordination. Genovese's comments on language are enlightening here.

The cultural relativists among the linguists have contributed a

> great deal toward an understanding of black English. They have properly insisted that it deserves to be treated with respect and that it could be expanded to do the work of any national language. But, as Gramsci has pointed out, dialects always must suffer in relation to developed national languages in their reduced ability to absorb the universalistic elements in world culture. This reduced ability arises from the realities of political life without regard for the intrinsic merits of the dialects themselves.[17]

While Genovese's comments relate specifically to language, black culture in general constitutes subordinate cultural activity in the United States. This is not to assess the value or virtue of such activity, but rather to see it starkly in terms of the realities of political and economic power. By reproducing an oppositional culture, students reinforce their own structured subordination *vis-à-vis* a dominant white culture.

It is here that the relation between cultural activity and the economy is important. As I argued in chapter 6, working class fractions are most beneficial to the capitalist class. Industry has capitalized on racism in American society to break strikes, and the continuing divisions by race have prevented the formation of a broadly based working class movement. Within this context, subordinate cultural activity serves to justify divisions between black and white workers. Differences in culture can be capitalized upon, thus providing a basis for division along racial lines in a society where, at least currently, such divisions are illegal.[18] While divisions by race would no doubt occur anyway to some extent (given a history of racism in the United States), the fact that blacks elaborate cultural forms that are different from those of whites in significant ways provides a justification for such division. Again, Genovese's comments are relevant here: "[Blacks] have developed their own values as a force for cohesion and survival, but in so doing, they widened the cultural gap and exposed themselves to even harder blows from a white nation that could neither understand their behavior nor respect its moral foundations."[19]

In short, the existence of a distinct black culture helps to provide a structural basis for continued "superexploitation." It also provides an evident underclass which can be partially exploited by the white working class itself in that it lessens their own exploitation.[20]

The paradox here is that it is the existence of this very culture that impeded the production of "racial subjects" over the years, enabling blacks to live with a minimum of decency and eventually challenge the entire racial order. To repeat Omi and Winant's point, "(t)he tremendous cultural resources nurtured among such communities, the enormous labors required under such conditions to survive and still further to develop elements of an alternative society can best be understood as combining with the continuous violent resistance (riots, etc.) (. . .) to constitute a racial *war of maneuver*."[21] In spite of its richness and strength, the existence of a distinct black culture contributes to the fractionalized nature of the working class – a fractionalization which ultimately benefits the capitalist class. While this fractionalization cannot be attributed simply to differences in culture (racism is, after all, fundamentally based on color), such differences are nevertheless related (albeit dialetically) to the current position of blacks in the economy. Class fractionalization is furthered by virtue of the fact that class/cultural tensions exist within the black community as well. It is significant that such tensions are also reproduced within the Urban College setting.

Once again, however, it cannot be assumed that all forms of racism are unequivocally positive for the capitalist class. As Wright has argued, capitalist expansion is related to labor power becoming a pure commodity, unfettered by ascriptive barriers.[22] While capitalism continues to benefit from an exploitation of such divisions, this is not to say that such divisions will *always* be uniformly positive in their effects for the capitalist class. When blacks produce oppositional cultural forms, they currently aid a divide and conquer strategy that has been and continues to be used by twentieth-century capitalists. At the same time, such distinctions are simultaneously reproductive and non-reproductive. It is possible that, at a future point, capitalist expansion will necessitate the erosion of such distinctions, and such erosion will be resisted at the cultural level. At the moment, however, urban blacks collude in their own oppression.

Student culture at Urban College is not determined in any simple fashion by prevailing economic arrangements. While it is, in the final analysis, rooted in such arrangements, cultural forms are not merely an "epiphenomenal expression of basic structural factors."[23] Cultural production always carries with it the *possibility* of producing alternative outcomes. In a sense, it really lives them out.[24]

That cultural form is not totally "determined" by economic form is optimistic in one sense and pessimistic in another. Unlike structuralist theories of reproduction, there is space for change. At Urban College, for example, student culture represents an understanding of what schooling will, in fact, do for the group, despite the extension to blacks of an ideology of equality of opportunity in response to the struggles of the 1950s and 1960s. There is, therefore, a *capacity* for serious political action. The situation is not entirely optimistic, however. Paradoxically, it is the students' own culture (as produced in the institution) which contributes to the maintenance of capitalism and their own continued superexploitation within this system. This does not, however, occur without a struggle. Can these tensions be worked on and with to encourage a more just and humane society? The last chapter explores this possibility.

8
Possibilities for action

I have argued in this book that black student culture at an urban community college acts primarily to ensure that the vast majority of students will return to the ghetto streets. In addition, the culture that students themselves produce encourages their own continued "superexploitation" as blacks in American society. This is in spite of the fact that students attend the college with the intention of escaping the urban underclass, and that the college itself embodies the principles of equality of opportunity and upward social mobility. Significantly, it is the culture that students *produce* within the college that makes a significant contribution to low "success" rates in traditional academic terms and the reproduction of a social structure that is strikingly unequal by class and race.

The shape and form of student culture cannot be seen as a simple response to factors within or outside the institution. While a high proportion of students are attempting to escape the ghetto streets and embody elements of street culture, students do not simply "act on" street cultural values within the community college setting. If this were the case, student "failure" could be attributed to the importation of cultural practices that, while "functional" on the streets, are non-functional in a mainstream setting. My analysis suggests that this is too simple. Students are acutely aware of the dichotomy between street and mainstream practices and they attend the college with full intention of learning to operate within the cultural mainstream. Students know that they must learn a new language, act on a different sense of time, plan for the future, and so forth. They are not unaware of mainstream cultural practices. Like all people who engage in subordinate cultural activity, Urban College students are cognizant of dominant culture, since their own culture developed historically in opposition to such culture. While such culture may be rejected, either consciously or unconsciously, it is, for the most part, not unknown.[1]

Student culture is not simply a response to institutional agents or practices either. There are those who might argue, for example, that faculty are directly responsible for the creation of student culture by their demeanor in the classroom. In the context of the urban community college, it is particularly easy to suggest that a largely white faculty creates the conditions for black student failure. While there may be some of this, once again, this cannot serve as a general explanation for the particular form that student culture takes. Faculty culture is itself dynamic and emerges in relation to a dynamic student culture (see chapter 4), Elements of faculty practice themselves develop in relation to students. It is, therefore, too simple to argue that faculty are totally responsible for student outcomes. While faculty certainly exert substantial impact on the shape and form of student culture, they do not and cannot "determine" such culture. To so argue would deny that students are also active shapers of their own lived reality.

Burton Clark in a well-known essay argues that community colleges serve a "cooling out" function in that they encourage students to pursue terminal rather than transfer curricula.[2] Clark argues that this is accomplished through remedial course requirements, the assignation of poor grades, and mandatory counseling interviews which assist students in choosing "appropriate" courses given their record. In this way, students *decide* to switch out of transfer curricula and accept their failure to attend a four-year institution as an *individual* failure.[3] At the same time, they retain a benign image of the sorting process.

Clark's formulation views student outcomes as a direct result of institutional agents, policies and practices. Through the day-to-day workings of the institution, students are sorted as to whether they will pursue their education or not. Students, in turn, learn to accept their status, thereby "choosing" an appropriate future and at the same time retaining a sense that the process is "fair." This can be seen as the converse of the student culture formulation described above. Rather than hold students responsible for their own failure by virtue of the culture which they bring with them into the institution, Clark holds the institution responsible for student outcomes. Neither position takes into account the way in which student culture and institutional agents and practices create aspects of the other. In the final analysis, neither captures the complexity of life within institutions.

Until now, only Howard London has conducted a serious study of the culture of a community college.[4] His study of a white working class institution in the United States provides valuable information regarding student culture and the relationship between this culture and institutional agents and practices. London suggests that students, due to their own class background, actively reject and at times transform meanings embedded within the institution. Working class students oppose what they perceive to be middle class meanings through incivility in the classroom, chronic absence, low level of effort and cheating. London carefully documents oppositional cultural practices as they are produced within the institution itself. These practices do not emerge simply by virtue of student class background; they emerge at least partially in relation to the institution. Incivility, for example, is directed at two kinds of teachers – those who teach liberal arts courses and those who teach vocational courses but are clearly identifiable as middle-class persons. The culture is particularly intense in courses that emphasize "theory" rather than practice. Significantly, it is these very cultural forms (which students create in relation to factors both within and outside the institution) that act partially to create institutional outcomes.[5] Students are not simply "cooled out" by virtue of the fact that they internalize institutionally imposed definitions, but themselves actively create and re-create forms of consciousness that in the long run help to sustain an unequal social structure.[6]

In a more radical vein, there are those who argue that student culture is determined in a simple fashion by prevailing economic arrangements. Institutions, and by extension cultures within them, are merely epiphenomenal; they are totally determined by economic structures and the existing distribution of power and wealth. Under this formulation, schools are seen solely as institutions of reproduction, as "institutions where the overt and covert knowledge that is taught inexorably molds students into passive beings who are able and eager to fit into an unequal social structure."[7]

In contrast, I have argued that black student cultural form is not totally determined by factors within or outside the institution. Culture is not "molded" totally by faculty or institutional practices, nor is it wholly "determined" by basic structural factors. While both internal and external factors exert a powerful effect on the shape and form of student culture, neither determine it in any simple sense. Lived culture really does exhibit a degree of autonomy – while not free floating (see chapters 6 and 7), it is also not thoroughly determined. In so arguing, I take a strong position against structuralists such as Bowles and Gintis.[8] Like London, I find that student culture cannot be reduced to a mirror image reflection of either institutional policies and practices or larger economic arrangements.[9]

That cultural form is only partially determined by factors within and outside the institution is both optimistic and pessimistic. If student culture were a mere response to institutional policies and practices, for example, how much more simple it would be to change than what is indicated by the complex pattern of cultural production uncovered here. It is also significant that the culture students themselves produce provides a basis for their own continued superexploitation. More optimistically, since the cultural level is at least semi-autonomous, there is always the possibility that culture will not be reproductive in the same sense. While, at present, the culture does not form a basis for transformative political activity, this may not always be the case. There are disjunctions and tensions in this process – tensions which at least open up the possibility of transformative action. If, as I have argued here, culture is relatively autonomous, there are spaces that make possible a number of practical interventions. Henry Giroux puts this well when he states: "while it would be naive and misleading to claim that schools alone can create the conditions for social change, it would be equally naive to argue that working in schools does not matter." He continues, "Needless to say, the power that schools have as both enabling and constraining institutions is often dependent on their articulation with other economic and political forces in the dominant society. But the relationship is a complex one, and to struggle in schools in order to transform the everyday practices and consciousness of teachers and students becomes meaningful only as part of a strategy to change the wider society."[10]

My analysis does not suggest simple solutions for practitioners. It is naive, as Giroux points out, to argue that schools alone can create the conditions for social change. It is equally naive to think that institutional agents and practices can totally remedy issues and problems that have structural roots. In this context, meaningful practice must be seen as a dilemma rather than something that can be engaged in if only we have enlightened administrators and faculty members. By way of addressing this dilemma, I offer a number of practical suggestions for those who live and work within urban community colleges. In so suggesting, I am assuming that college administrators and faculty sincerely wish to engage in meaningful action – that they, like students, genuinely desire higher success rates in traditional academic terms and that they do not sanction the strikingly unequal social structure presently in existence and the way in which the urban community college operates currently to sustain this social structure. The culture students produce within the institution is, in the final analysis, self-destructive. Not only is the urban underclass largely reproduced by virtue of the culture, but the potential for transformative political activity is minimized (see chapter 7). The suggestions below are aimed at helping students and institutional agents break this cycle.

Staffing patterns

It is critically important for urban community colleges to have a substantial number of minority faculty, particularly in the academic areas. Seventy per cent of the faculty at Urban College are white. Even more important is the fact that minorities are concentrated in low-status fields: Secretarial Science, Music, Physical Education and Child Care. Academic areas such as Science, English, Mathematics and Business Administration are staffed overwhelmingly by whites; Science and Mathematics are 100 per cent white. When black males obtain positions in the academic areas, they are hired one at a time in select fields. Black females have fared proportionally better, but, with the exception of the Social Sciences, they are concentrated in traditional "female" areas.

While perhaps unintended, such patterns serve to communicate to students that college knowledge, particularly of the most prestigious sort, is possessed most "naturally" by white men. The pattern of hiring for minority males also serves to highlight their "apartness" from the collective, thus exacerbating and reproducing tensions *within* the black community. Such tensions make it that much more difficult for individual students to attempt social mobility.

This study suggests that when students (as a group) differentiate themselves from the institution, they emphasize *certain* aspects of a highly contradictory culture. They drop in and out of school, arrive late to class and engage in extensive drug use despite the fact that they value education highly. The affirmation of schooling is also, in itself, contradictory: legitimate knowledge is valued and not valued (it is white, not black) at one and the same time.[11] The point here is that a higher proportion of black faculty in non-ghettoized positions would provide students with less reason to see the institution as "not ours" when differentiation occurs. It would also lessen the tendency for tensions internal to the black community to be reproduced in this site – tensions which only make it more difficult for underclass students to attempt "success."

It must be understood here that this is not primarily an argument for "role models," but rather a stark statement that we must break down the new severe tendency for institutional culture to appear white when students begin to differentiate themselves from the college. Present staffing patterns only serve to encourage this process. This is especially important given a history of race/class antagonism in the United States. Being white is not positive. Unless we seriously try to alter staffing patterns, there is little chance that cultures will not polarize in the manner described here.

Time and its use

One of the most powerful messages distributed through the college concerns the appropriate use of time. While all schools distribute dominant forms of time in that courses are divided into arbitrary time units and bells signal the beginning and end of class, post-secondary institutions rarely enforce official time. Urban College differs in that it attempts to regulate student use of time directly through a well-articulated attendance policy. More than any other single factor, the inappropriate use of time signals failure at Urban College.

While the institution's response to student use of time is understandable (see chapters 3 and 4), it nevertheless encourages the development of certain cultural practices. As the college emphasizes and rigidifies its position on the need to operate within dominant forms of time, students, as a collectivity, live their *own* time (which is embedded within the broader race/class logic) in opposition to dominant time, thus strengthening a fundamentally oppositional culture within the institution. While I am not suggesting that Urban College cease distributing dominant meanings (indeed, it must distribute certain dominant meanings), practices that serve no purpose other than to encourage oppositional cultural forms should be eliminated. The emphasis on time has not, thus far, prevented drop outs nor has it resulted in a higher success rate. Indeed, students correctly perceive that it does not operate primarily in their interest.

In so arguing, I am not insensitive to the fact that the state centers conflict in this area through grants and demands for attendance data associated with such grants (see chapter 3). The state does not, however, demand an attendance policy. The policy represents an attempt on the part of institutional personnel to mediate demands from the state and elements of student culture. It has not, however, been positive in its effects. Any policy which serves largely to encourage differentiation rather than integration should be eliminated.

Standard English

The case of standard English is different. Students must, if they are to challenge the class structure and their own position as underclass within it (whether individually or collectively), be fluent in what we call standard English. The college's position on this is rigid and I concur with this rigidity. This is not to argue that standard English is more intrinsically worthwhile than non-standard English, but to acknowledge the stark reality of language in American society.

The importance of standard English goes beyond its use value in the dominant society. While the use value attached to dominant and subordinate discourses in the United States is certainly different, skills such as reading and writing (which, after all, are coded largely in the dominant discourse) can be used for purposes of critical analysis and action. As Giroux argues, "subordinate groups must be given the opportunity to develop analytic and practical skills that they can use to understand and transform the relations that underlie the dominant culture, rather than simply being incorporated into its logic."[12] If students are to engage in a critical analysis of society and their own position within it, they must possess skills that will enable them to analyze dominant discourse about their position as well as those that will allow them to re-capture their own history. Subordinate language practices, in and of themselves, will not enable this form of analysis or reconstruction.[13] Again, however, this is not to suggest that the dominant culture is in any way superior to the culture out of which subordinate discourses are forged. It is simply to acknowledge that the cultural practices of subordinate groups are forged within relations of *both* domination and resistance, and bear the marks of both. Dominated groups must become familiar with the discourse of dominant groups if they are to challenge the class structure effectively.

The difference between standard English and dominant time should be obvious here. Students can and do profit from direct and systematic instruction in reading and writing. While students at times resent the imposition of standard English ("nobody talks like that"), they understand full well its importance and the necessity for such instruction. A comparable argument cannot be made for time. No adult in this society needs direct and systematic instruction in the appropriate use of time. Students know that they must adhere to dominant industrial clock time if they wish to maintain a job (assuming the availability of such jobs), and dominant time, unlike critical literacy, does not provide a basis for political action. I am not, therefore, advocating that urban community colleges cease the distribution of dominant meanings. In the case of standard English, it is critically important that they continue such distribution. I am suggesting that where the teaching of dominant meanings serves no other apparent purpose except to encourage the creation of oppositional culture, such curricular elements should be eliminated. Each institution must engage in a serious analysis of both the hidden and formal curriculum to determine which elements fall where.[14]

Faculty

Faculty do not possess the power to create and/or change student cultural form directly. Such form is rooted in larger social structural realities and cannot be changed easily by "enlightened" faculty or administrators. Faculty nevertheless contribute to the shape and form of student culture in some rather fundamental ways. It is therefore important for faculty to begin a process of self-analysis in order to unpack the way in which their own culture is linked dialectically to that of students. Well-meaning faculty contribute to the process of cultural production unbeknown to them simply because they are participants in a day-to-day drama. Faculty play an important role in the production of student consciousness – a consciousness which, at present, sustains an unequal class structure and the position of poor blacks within it. While students collude in their own oppression, faculty encourage this collusion. Again, this does not reflect an all-encompassing process of domination. The production of a culture that largely reproduces and legitimates social inequalities and antagonisms is a very human process; one which is mediated by people at the level of their own lived culture. Thus community colleges (like all educational institutions) must be seen as something other than "all encompassing footholds of domination."[15] Faculty and students at least embody the *possibility* of acting otherwise.

Faculty can take steps to develop a radical pedagogy, a pedagogy which, in Giroux's terms, embodies an analysis of "how the relations of domination in schools originate, how they are sustained and how students, in particular, relate to them."[16] A starting point here is for faculty to become more aware of their own role in the production of student culture. Faculty are eminently capable of developing these critical insights if so engaged. They can, as a group, raise to the level of their own consciousness some of the processes outlined in this book as well as go beyond these processes. They can read, discuss and reflect upon past experiences for insights. Committed faculty can begin a study group to look carefully at the process of cultural production and their own role in it. Discussion can then move to the level of developing a critical pedagogy. The question here must be, how can we, as faculty, alter our practice in accord with our insights?

Faculty are not, for the most part, aware of the dynamic nature of their own culture and the way in which their culture is linked dialectically to student culture. A first step is for faculty to become engaged in a critical analysis of their own situation *vis-à-vis* students, the state and so forth. While faculty often know *what* they are responding to (particularly in relation to the administration), they are usually less aware of how their own response to situations shapes aspects of consciousness and practice, which in turn impacts on student consciousness. Greater self-understanding constitutes a necessary but not sufficient condition for action within a larger political struggle. A serious analysis of this sort can form the basis of political action directed against the role that institutions like Urban College presently play in the maintenance of social and economic structures in spite of an ideology which suggests the opposite. Self-analysis can form the basis of "pockets of resistance that provide pedagogical models for new forms of learning and social relations – forms which can be used in other spheres more directly involved in the struggles for a new morality and view of social justice."[17]

Students

The same applies to students. Like faculty, students can profitably engage in an analysis of their own condition.[18] Once again, this must be seen as a process of developing a critical appreciation of their own situation. Students must become aware not only of what the institution does *to* them, but the way in which they collude in their own oppression, despite moments of exceptional and at times conscious, insight (this is terribly important; it is all too easy to blame the institution). Once again I am suggesting that self-understanding is a necessary condition for action. No one can successfully "teach" students (or faculty) about their own position. Students and faculty alike must engage in a process of self-reflection. Such self-reflection will go much further than externally imposed teaching ever could. While a book such as *Between Two Worlds* may provide a beginning for such reflection, it is only a beginning.

When students and faculty engage in this process they are engaging in a struggle aimed at understanding and changing their own conditions. It is my suggestion that this process begin separately; that students and faculty do not work together initially. Once this process is well underway, ideas should be shared in a non-hierarchical manner. Given unequal power, it is important that students engage in self-reflection before any sharing is attempted.

When interaction between students and faculty occurs, however, this may signal the beginning of collective struggle of some import. Conceivably it will help to break down the faculty/student polarization described in chapters 3 and 4. Student/faculty interests may be defined as closer, and faculty and students working together may ultimately represent a political action group of some consequence.[19] It is absolutely critical at this juncture for minorities to be well represented in non-ghettoized faculty positions. If this is not the case, the process of struggle across faculty/student lines will all too easily break down into its component parts. Both faculty and students will have to deal honestly and openly at some point with their own racism if this is to be effective.

The fact that an element of student culture is respect for knowledge is important here. Black students at Urban College already hold to the ideal that knowledge is positive and that it has emancipatory potential. Students firmly believe that knowledge can be used for collective action and the eventual betterment of their own condition as blacks (see chapters 6 and 7). It is, therefore, highly conceivable that students, as a group, will see the power of critical thinking as a tool of social transformation along the lines outlined here. This is in sharp contrast with the white working class. Willis's lads, for example, rejected the primacy of mental labor and its ethos of individual appropriation. In so doing, they closed off any possibility of pursuing an emancipatory relationship between knowledge and dissent.[20] The same can be said about students in London's study. The case of Urban College students is markedly different. Blacks in the United States already have strong feelings about the power of thinking as a tool for social transformation (both individual and collective) which can be capitalized upon for emancipatory ends. Students can, as a group, work to understand and articulate the conditions of their own existence. This is a fundamentally intellectual task. If this element of culture can be worked with, other, more self-destructive elements may fall away. Faculty may then become more aware of this element of student culture than they are presently. Ultimately, the disorganized cultural level may become more organized and manifestly political. All this can be accomplished by working *with* elements of culture that already exist. Students themselves, at the level of their own culture, do not close off the possibility of pursuing an emancipatory relationship between knowledge and dissent. It is for this reason that my suggested line of action has a relatively high probability of success.

The above recommendations should not be seen as simple solutions to complex problems. If my research has uncovered anything, it is the complexity of the relationship between the urban community college and the larger class structure. At present the college serves to maintain a class structure that is unequal by class and race. Despite intentions to the contrary, it also serves largely as an arena whereby the black urban underclass is reproduced. This is, nevertheless, a highly human process and, as such, offers the possibility of alternative futures to which we must turn our attention. We cannot change the past. Our goal must be to understand the past and use this understanding as a basis for collective action aimed at transforming the present and the future.

Appendix A

Methods

Participant observation, the technique employed here, is characterized by a period of intense social interaction between the researcher and the subjects in the subjects' milieu. Use of this technique enabled me to explore both the direct experiences of education and the way in which these experiences are worked over and through the praxis of cultural discourse. During the academic year 1979–80 I attended classes, conducted in-depth interviews with both faculty and students, and in general immersed myself in Urban College for three days a week for one full academic year. A record was kept of the day-to-day experiences and comments of students and teachers in classrooms, corridors, stairwells, offices, cafeteria and local coffee shop and bar.

Gaining access to Urban College was a time-consuming task. Initially I requested permission of the Vice-President, who was receptive to the idea, and he set up a meeting with faculty coordinators (department chairpersons). I met with the Vice-President in March 1979 and held a meeting with the coordinators in early May. In late May I sent a letter to all faculty members expressing a desire to conduct a study at Urban College commencing in the Fall, and solicited their help.

In late August (one week before classes were scheduled to begin), I met with each faculty member, re-stated the purpose of my study, and requested permission to observe their classes. Obtaining access to the field took over three months. Detailed field notes were kept during this period.

Data from urban settings have long been abused in the United States and faculty, in particular, were concerned about this possibility. If certain findings were to appear in the newspaper, for example, this might adversely affect county funding. For this reason I spent a great deal of time assuring faculty that I was not interested in Urban College *per se*, but rather life in *an* urban institution. All faculty members but two finally agreed to allow me into their classrooms. In some cases there existed an aura of suspicion as to my "real" intentions well into the first semester.

I was extremely sensitive to faculty/staff concerns. Urban College had just recently won a long hard struggle for a new campus and "bad publicity" could affect future funding. Since the press had been unfriendly to Urban College in the past, suspicions surrounding my initial presence were understandable. I nevertheless embarked upon my study in Fall 1979 with full knowledge that, in time, my intentions would be more fully understood and regarded as honorable.[1]

In the field

The participant observer enters the field with the hope that he or she can establish relationships with subjects characterized by trust and a free and open exchange of information. The researcher conducts himself or herself in such a way as to become "unobtrusive, part of the scene, people whom the participants take for granted and whom they consider to be non-threatening."[2]

Given deeply rooted race antagonisms in the United States, the fact that I was white in a largely black institution made it somewhat difficult initially to be unobtrusive. Like all students, however, I spent entire days on campus, taking classes and examinations. I, like other students, suffered through the crowded elevator, limited number of telephones, cafeteria food and generally poor physical facilities. Students began to see me everywhere and increasingly interacted with me. Unlike most white students, I was not part of a white clique, and, over time, I was trusted. Once students became aware of my intentions as a researcher they were more than happy to "tell their story." I took classes for four months before conducting any in-depth interviews. By the time I actually began interviewing, many students knew and trusted me. Had I not been trusted, I could never have elicited the type of information reported here.

During the first four months of field work, I took copious notes in all classes attended. I also recorded field notes after each and every observation period, as well as after more casual contacts with students and faculty. Any time I interacted with a student, faculty or staff member, either within or outside of the institution, I recorded field notes. Although precise data recollection may seem almost impossible in the abstract, in reality it is not difficult. It simply necessitates extreme concentration on the researcher's part and recording of interaction data as soon as possible after each observation and/or discussion.

Beginning in December, I started to interview students systematically. These in-depth interviews continued until June. A number of student interviews were conducted at the local bar where the proprietor hooked up my tape recorder and allowed me to spend literally hours taping. Other student interviews were conducted in the coffee shop across the street, and still others on campus. In all cases, the tape recorder was fully visible on the table and taping was done with the consent of the interviewee. I worked with a set of open-ended probe questions in order to encourage students to "tell their story" (see Appendix B). I shared these questions with students ahead of time and requested their permission to tape. No student (or later, faculty member) refused taping. Students were shown the "stop" button on the recorder and encouraged to push it if they wished to say anything "off the record." On occasion students exercised this option. Interviews ranged from forty-five minutes to well over three hours. I began interviewing faculty in February. Faculty interviews were conducted on the same basis (see Appendix B). Interviews with alumni were conducted in July and August 1980.

Data analysis

In qualitative methodology, data analysis refers to a process which attempts to identify themes suggested by the data. The virtue of this form of analysis is that themes not occurring to the researcher ahead of time can be "teased out" of the data during the analysis stage.

While data analysis is an ongoing process in participant observation research (the researcher explores themes throughout the course of field work), it is during the post-fieldwork stage that the researcher engages in the systematic construction of themes and the analysis and interpretation of data. The first step is to transcribe all taped material. This is a very time-consuming task and takes literally months to complete. While it is helpful to employ someone to transcribe tapes, this is nearly impossible without substantial grant support. It cost me three hundred dollars to have eight tapes transcribed by a secretary. While these happened to be extremely lengthy interviews, tape transcription is, in general, a very expensive task, both in terms of the researcher's time and of money. I transcribed most of my own tapes. Any researcher who does not have substantial support should plan on doing the same.

After transcribing tapes and assembling field notes, I was left with literally thousands of pages of material. Bogdan and Taylor's suggestions proved extremely helpful at this point.[3] As per their suggestions I coded important conversation topics and found that certain topics tended to occur and recur in conversations. This is a relatively objective way of categorizing qualitative data.

Once I read through the field notes and gained a sense of the important topics, I assigned a code to each of these topics. I then duplicated all notes and coded the duplicate copy by placing the appropriate code next to the relevant passages in the margins. I cut the duplicate by paragraphs, placing coded passages into manilla folders according to topic. When passages suggested more than one category, additional copies of such passages were made and placed in appropriate folders. The original copy of field notes was left uncut. Each passage was identified as to the page number of the field notes from which it was taken. In this way I could always go back to the original copy in order to contextualize a statement. After the coding was completed (again, the time involved here should not be underestimated), data were read, sorted and examined for patterns.

This process of data analysis enabled me to systematically identify salient cultural categories for both students and faculty. The virtue of this form of analysis is that such categories were suggested by the data themselves. This enabled me to identify truly core cultural elements in the Urban College setting, as well as to identify factors both within and outside the institution that contribute to the rise of located cultural form.

As part of this study I also administered several survey questionnaires to present students, former students (dropouts), and alumni. This was done largely as a favor to the college and the college incorporated these data into their Middle States Accreditation report. Questionnaires administered to students in English classes provided the demographic data reported in chapter 1. A copy of this instrument may be found in Appendix C.

Appendix B

Open-ended interview questions — students, faculty, alumni students

(1) How long have you been a student at Urban College?
(2) What curriculum are you in?
(3) What made you choose Urban College rather than another college?
(4) Whenever we attend a school or work anywhere, there are always things that we would like to see changed. If you could change anything at Urban College, what kinds of things would you like to see changed?
(5) Are you presently employed? What kind of work do you do?
(6) (If yes to 5) Is it difficult to go to school and work at the same time? Why?
(7) Do you plan to keep the same job after you graduate from Urban?
(8) Ultimately, what kind of job would you like to obtain?
(9) Do you think that you will be able to obtain this job? Why or why not?
(10) Do you think that your studies here will prepare you to get this job? Why or why not?
(11) If it were possible to change your studies here to ensure that you will obtain this job, what kind of changes would you suggest?

Faculty[a]

(1) When did you first begin to think of teaching in a community college? How did you come to teach at Urban College?

[a] Some of these questions are taken from Howard London, *The Culture of a Community College* (New York: Praeger, 1978).

(2) Were there any crucial points of decision when you could have chosen another path?
(3) Would you like to move on to another position in the future? To what? Why? Is there anything that inhibits your moving on?
(4) Did you have any difficulties orienting yourself to the community college?
(5) Do you see any differences between older and younger students? Male and female? Do you find yourself responding to them differently? If so, how?
(6) How do you define success in teaching at a community college?
(7) Is there anything that prevents you from being as successful as you would like to be in this position?
(8) Is there anything that you especially like about teaching in a community college?
(9) Is there anything that you especially dislike or would like to change about teaching in a community college? How do you approach these problems?
(10) Do you see any essential differences between the community college and four-year colleges?

Alumni

(1) When did you attend Urban College and how long were you a student there?
(2) What curriculum were you in?
(3) Did you continue your studies after leaving Urban College? If so, where?
(4) If yes to question three, do you feel that Urban adequately prepared you for further studies? If yes, how? If no, why not?
(5) If no to question 3, what are you doing presently?
(6) Do you see any relationship between your study at Urban and your present position? (whether employed or unemployed). If so, in what way? If not, why not?
(7) Did you seek employment after completing your studies at Urban? If so, how long did it take you to obtain a job? If not, why did you feel that you needed further training?
(8) If yes to question 7, do you feel that it took you an undue

amount of time to get a job? To what do you attribute this? Could you detail your experience in seeking employment?

(9) If you are working now, do you feel satisfied with the job that you have? If yes, why? If not, why not?

(10) If you do not feel satisfied, what kind of job would you like to obtain? What, in your opinion, prevents you from reaching this goal?

(11) Retrospectively, what did you like about Urban College?

(12) If it would be possible to change Urban College, what kinds of changes would you suggest?

(13) If you could do it all over, would you still go to Urban College? Why or why not?

(14) If yes, would you encourage your children to go to Urban College? Why or why not?

Appendix C

Student opinion survey[a]

Please circle the number of your response. If there is a blank space after a question, fill in the blank. Select only one response per item.

Part One: Background information[a]

(1) What is your age?

1 18 or under
2 19
3 20
4 21
5 22
6 23 to 25
7 26 to 29
8 30 to 39
9 40 to 61
10 62 or over

(2) How many semesters have you attended Urban College (excluding summers)?

1 One semester
2 Two semesters
3 Three semesters
4 Four semesters
5 Longer

If longer, how many semesters? ______________________

(3) Indicate your class level.

1 Freshman
2 Senior

(4) Are you mainly a full- or part-time student?

1 Full-time
2 Part-time

(5) Do you plan to continue your education after leaving Urban College?

1 Yes
2 No

(6) If you do not plan to continue your education, what job would you like to get after you finish your studies at Urban College?

____

If you do not know, write "do not know." ______________

(7) What is your sex?

1 Male
2 Female

(8) Of the following racial or ethnic groups, which do you identify with?

1 Afro-American (black)
2 Caucasian-American (white)
3 Asian-American (Oriental)
4 Puerto Rican or Cuban
5 Mexican-American (Chicano/Chicana)
6 Other ______________________________

(9) Are you the head of a household?

1 Yes
2 No

(10) Do you have children that you are directly responsible for?

1 Yes
2 No

If so, how many? ____________________

(11) Do you have a job outside of school (include work study or student assistant)?

1 Yes
2 No

(12) If you have a job, how many hours per week do you work (include work study or student assistant)?

1 1 to 10
2 11 to 20
3 21 to 30
4 31 to 40
5 Over 40

(13) If you presently work, what kind of work do you do?

Type of work ____________________
Place of work ____________________

(14) What type of work does your father do, or did he do?

____

If you do not know, write "do not know." ____________

(15) What type of work does your mother do, or did she do?

____

If you do not know, write "do not know." ____________

(16) How much education did your father have?

1 He had some elementary school.
2 He completed elementary school.
3 He had some junior high school or middle school.
4 He completed junior high or middle school.
5 He had some senior high school.
6 He completed senior high school.
7 He had some college.
8 He completed college.
9 He completed some other form of education (such as technical school or secretarial school).
10 I do not know.

(17) How much education did your mother have?

1 She had some elementary school.
2 She completed elementary school.
3 She had some junior high school or middle school.
4 She completed junior high or middle school.
5 She had some senior high school.
6 She completed senior high school.
7 She had some college.
8 She completed college.
9 She completed some other form of education (such as technical school or secretarial school).
10 I do not know.

(18) What curriculum (major course of study) are you enrolled in?

____

(19) If you do not plan to continue at a four-year college, what job do you *realistically think you will be able to get* after you finish your studies at Urban College?

____

[a] Adapted from Student Opinion Survey, American College Testing Program, 1975.

Part Two: College environment

Indicate your *overall level of satisfaction* with the following:

Academic

(20) Testing/grading system

1 Very satisfied
2 Satisfied
3 Neutral
4 Dissatisfied
5 Very dissatisfied

(21) The way the teachers teach in your major field

1 Very satisfied
2 Satisfied
3 Neutral
4 Dissatisfied
5 Very dissatisfied

(22) Preparation you are receiving for your future occupation

1 Very satisfied
2 Satisfied
3 Neutral
4 Dissatisfied
5 Very dissatisfied

(23) Sensitivity of male faculty toward students

1 Very satisfied
2 Satisfied
3 Neutral
4 Dissatisfied
5 Very dissatisfied

(24) Sensitivity of female faculty toward students

1 Very satisfied
2 Satisfied
3 Neutral
4 Dissatisfied
5 Very dissatisfied

(25) Material included in your courses

1 Very satisfied
2 Satisfied
3 Neutral
4 Dissatisfied
5 Very dissatisfied

Facilities

(26) Study areas

1 Very satisfied

2 Satisfied
3 Neutral
4 Dissatisfied
5 Very dissatisfied

(27) Campus bookstore

1 Very satisfied
2 Satisfied
3 Neutral
4 Dissatisfied
5 Very dissatisfied

(28) General condition of buildings and grounds

1 Very satisfied
2 Satisfied
3 Neutral
4 Dissatisfied
5 Very dissatisfied

(29) Classrooms

1 Very satisfied
2 Satisfied
3 Neutral
4 Dissatisfied
5 Very dissatisfied

(30) Library

1 Very satisfied
2 Satisfied
3 Neutral
4 Dissatisfied
5 Very dissatisfied

(31) Cafeteria

1 Very satisfied
2 Satisfied
3 Neutral
4 Dissatisfied
5 Very dissatisfied

(32) Gymnasium

1 Very satisfied
2 Satisfied
3 Neutral
4 Dissatisfied
5 Very dissatisfied

(33) Student center

1 Very satisfied
2 Satisfied
3 Neutral
4 Dissatisfied
5 Very dissatisfied

(34) Science lab

1 Very satisfied
2 Satisfied
3 Neutral
4 Dissatisfied
5 Very dissatisfied

General

(35) Sensitivity of male non-teaching staff toward students (for example, security, librarian, financial aid personnel, etc.)

1 Very satisfied
2 Satisfied
3 Neutral
4 Dissatisfied
5 Very dissatisfied

(36) Sensitivity of female non-teaching staff toward students (for example, security, librarian, financial aid personnel, etc.)

1 Very satisfied
2 Satisfied
3 Neutral
4 Dissatisfied
5 Very dissatisfied

(37) Racial harmony at this college

1 Very satisfied
2 Satisfied
3 Neutral
4 Dissatisfied
5 Very dissatisfied

(38) Student government

1 Very satisfied
2 Satisfied
3 Neutral
4 Dissatisfied
5 Very dissatisfied

Part Three: College services and programs

(39) Academic advising

1 Very satisfied
2 Satisfied
3 Neutral
4 Dissatisfied
5 Very dissatisfied

(40) Personal counseling services

1 Very satisfied
2 Satisfied
3 Neutral
4 Dissatisfied
5 Very dissatisfied

(41) Math lab

1 Very satisfied
2 Satisfied
3 Neutral
4 Dissatisfied
5 Very dissatisfied

(42) English lab

1 Very satisfied

2 Satisfied
3 Neutral
4 Dissatisfied
5 Very dissatisfied

(43) Financial aid services

1 Very satisfied
2 Satisfied
3 Neutral
4 Dissatisfied
5 Very dissatisfied

Part Four: General statement

In the space below please feel free to express

(1) Other feelings about Urban College; and (2) suggestions for improvement

(1) Other feelings ______________________________

____

____

____

____

(2) Suggestions for improvement ______________________________

____

____

____

____

____

____

____

Thank you for your cooperation. We hope that our findings benefit both you and future generations of students.

Notes

1 Introduction

1 See, for example, Harvard Sitkoff, *The Struggle for Black Equality 1954–1980* (New York: Hill & Wang, 1981). H. Rap Brown's statement is on page 217. Extensive statements by Martin Luther King, Malcolm X and other important figures of this period may be found in chapters 6 and 7 of Sitkoff's book.

2 This is not the true name of the college. All names of students and college personnel are also fictitious.

3 Michael Reich, *Racial Inequality* (Princeton: Princeton University Press, 1981), p. 18.

4 Reich, *Racial Inequality*, p. 19.

5 Reich provides impressive statistical evidence to this effect. See Reich, pp. 17–75. Quoted material can also be found on p. 18 and p. 74.

6 Sitkoff, *The Struggle for Black Equality*, pp. 236–6.

7 See Reich, *Racial Inequality*, p. 25 and chapter 7; and Stanley Masters, *Black-White Income Differentials* (New York: Academic Press, 1975), chapter 2, as cited in Reich, p. 25.

8 Reich, *Racial Inequality*, p. 27. See also Ann Schnard, "Residential Segregation by Race in U.S. Metropolitan Areas: An Analysis Across Cities and over Time" (Washington, DC: Urban Institute, 1977); Annemette Sorenson, Karl Taeuber and Leslie Hollingsworth, "Indexes of Racial Segregation for 109 Cities in the United States, 1940 to 1970," *Sociological Focus* (April, 1975), cited in Reich, p. 27.

9 Reich, *Racial Inequality*, p. 66.

10 See, for example, "Fact Sheet on Institutional Racism" (New York: Foundation for Change Inc. and Council for Interracial Books for Children, August 1975).

11 Douglas Glasgow, *The Black Underclass* (New York: Vintage Books, 1971), pp. 8–9. In the United States today, blacks constitute a relatively high proportion of the permanently trapped urban poor. See also Elliott Liebow, *Tally's Corner* (Boston: Little Brown, 1967); and Melvin Williams, *On the Street Where I Lived* (New York: Holt, Rinehart & Winston, 1981).

12 See Richard Edwards, *Contested Terrain* (New York: Basic Books, 1979).
13 Bettylou Valentine, *Hustling and Other Hard Work* (New York: Free Press, 1978).
14 Valentine, *Hustling and Other Hard Work*, p. 118.
15 Jagna Wojcicka Sharff, *Life on Doolittle Street: How Poor People Purchase Immortality*, Final Report, Hispanic Study Project, Department of Anthropology, Columbia University, 1980.
16 Sharff, *Life on Doolittle Street*, p. 23.
17 See A. Bequai, *Organized Crime: The Fifth Estate* (Lexington, Mass.: 1979).
18 Samuel Bowles and Herbert Gintis, *Schooling in Capitalist America* (New York: Basic Books, 1976).
19 Omi and Winant suggest that

> Hegemony is the thoroughgoing organization of society on behalf of a class which has gained the adherence of subordinate as well as dominant sectors and groups. Often, summarized as a rule by means of a combination of coercion and consent, hegemony is better understood as the creation of a collective popular will by what Gramsci calls intellectual and moral leadership. The exercise of hegemony extends beyond the mere dissemination of "ruling class" ideas and values. It includes the capacity to define, through a vast array of channels (including the basic structures of economic, political, and cultural life) the terms and meanings by which people understand themselves and their world.

See Michael Omi and Howard Winant, "By the Rivers of Babylon: Race in the United States," *Socialist Review*, vol. 71, vol. 13, 5 (September/October 1983): 43.

20 See, for example, Michael Apple, *Education and Power* (Boston: Routledge & Kegan Paul, 1982); Michael Apple and Lois Weis, eds, *Ideology and Practice in Schooling* (Philadelphia: Temple University Press, 1983), chapter 1; Henry Giroux, *Theory and Resistance in Education* (South Hadley, Mass.: Bergin & Garvey, 1983); Richard Johnson, "Histories of Culture/Theories of Ideology: Notes on an Impasse," in Michele Barrett *et al.*, eds, *Ideology and Cultural Production* (New York: St Martin's Press, 1979), pp. 49–77; Geoff Whitty and Madeline Arnot, "From Reproduction to Transformation: Recent Radical Perspectives on the Curriculum from the USA," *British Journal of Sociology of Education* 3, 1 (March 1982); Martin Carnoy, "Education, Economy and the State," in Michael Apple, ed., *Cultural and Economic Reproduction in Education* (Boston: Routledge & Kegan Paul, 1982), pp. 79–126; and Roger Dale, "Education and the Capitalist State," in Apple, ed., *Cultural and Economic Reproduction*, pp. 127–61.
21 Martin Carnoy, "Education, Economy and the State," p. 114. Martin Carnoy and Henry Levin elaborate their model of education further in *The Dialectics of Education and Work* (Stanford: Stanford University Press, 1983).

22 While mediation takes place in large part though the state supported education system, Carnoy reminds us that capitalists also attempt to deal with contradictions in the base directly. As he states,

> (C)ontrary to the stress put by Althusser on the ideological reproduction of labor power and the relations of production through the state apparatuses, we cannot forget that capitalist relations in production are reproduced *in the base itself* by three principal means: (a) a reserve army of unemployed, created in various ways, which produces fear among workers of leaving their jobs, and thus slows down or prevents organizing into unions, increasing productivity and keeps downward pressure on wages; (b) Taylorism, speed-up, and segmentation of labor markets, which attempt to increase productivity and control workers' use of time, and divide workers against each other; and (c) the favorable accumulation of capital and the resultant increase of average wages.

Carnoy, "Education, Economy and the State," p. 114.

23 Apple, *Education and Power*; and Dale, "Education and the Capitalist State."

24 Dale, "Education and the Capitalist State," pp. 146–7.

25 Apple, *Education and Power*, p. 15.

26 Apple, *Education and Power*, pp. 52–8.

27 Omi and Winant, "By the Rivers of Babylon," p. 58.

28 Ibid., p. 56.

29 Paul Willis, *Learning to Labour* (Westmead, England: Saxon House, 1977). For an essay review of Willis, see Michael Apple, "What Correspondence Theories of the Hidden Curriculum Miss," *The Review of Education* 5 (1979): 101–12.

30 Willis, *Learning to Labour*, p. 19, as cited by Apple, "What Correspondence Theories of the Hidden Curriculum Miss."

31 Harry Braverman, *Labor and Monopoly Capital* (New York: Monthly Review Press, 1974).

32 Angela McRobbie, "Working Class Girls and the Culture of Femininity," in Women's Studies Group, ed., *Women Take Issue* (London: Hutchinson, 1978), pp. 96–108.

33 Ibid., p. 104, as cited in Apple, *Education and Power*, p. 44.

34 Robert Everhart is a recent example here. See Robert Everhart, *Reading, Writing and Resistance* (Boston: Routledge & Kegan Paul, 1983).

35 While there have been some excellent studies of raced persons in schools, there has been no detailed analysis of race as a factor in the production of culture using the framework outlined here.

36 Willis, *Learning to Labour*, p. 3.

37 It must be kept in mind that I am studying adults, not adolescents. For this reason, I did not attach myself to one particular group such as the "lads." While adults in tertiary level institutions certainly maintain informal groups, there is not the same emphasis on the maintenance of the group as there is among secondary school

students, for example. Part of the reason for this is that adults are not compelled by law to attend school, nor to be on campus eight hours a day. There is, therefore, less need to "hang" with one's friends in order to make the institution tolerable. Thus, while the cultural processes explored here are, as I argue throughout, *group* processes, the group logic is not mediated in the same way as studies by Willis, McRobbie and Everhart suggest.

38 The growth of community colleges is also linked to demands for education among working class whites.

39 Those who emphasize this aspect of the community college include R.R. Fields, *The Community College Movement* (New York: McGraw-Hill, 1962); E.J. Gleazer, *This is the Community College* (Boston: Houghton Mifflin, 1968); and Carnegie Commission for Higher Education, *The Open Door Colleges* (New York: McGraw-Hill, 1970).

40 See Jerome Karabel, "Community Colleges and Social Stratification," *Harvard Educational Review* 42, 4 (November 1972): 521–62; Ellen Trimberger, "Open Admissions: A New Form of Tracking?", *The Insurgent Sociologist* 4, 1 (Fall, 1973): 29–42; and Burton Clark, "The 'Cooling-Out' Function in Higher Education," *The American Journal of Sociology* 65 (May 1960): 569–76.

41 The new Urban College has a day care center. See footnote 42.

42 Since the time of this research, Urban College has been relocated in the downtown area. The struggle to obtain a permanent site for Urban College went on for ten years. During this period, no fewer than twenty-three potential sites were seriously proposed and publicly reviewed. From 1970 to 1978 approximately 158 articles appeared in a local newspaper about the college. Most of these address the issue of a new site for the campus.

43 Urban College, *Self-Study Report* (submitted to Middle States for accreditation), 1981, p. h.

44 See Clark, "The 'Cooling Out' Function in Higher Education." Clark himself has recently suggested that the transfer/terminal distinction and the meaning of the transfer track have been blurred somewhat since the time of his original writing. See Burton Clark, "The 'Cooling Out' Function Revisited," in George Vaughan, ed., *New Directions for Community Colleges: Questioning the Community College Role* (San Francisco: Jossey-Bass, 1980): 15–31.

45 Urban College, *Self-Study*, p. 6.

46 Urban College, *Self-Study*, pp. 6–7.

47 Urban College, *Catalog*, 1981–2, p. 17.

48 The zip codes of students enrolled in Urban College during the 1979–80 academic year indicate that 90.3 per cent live in the city. Of these, 72.1 per cent live in the city center, while 18.2 per cent live on the periphery. The remaining 9.7 per cent live in the suburbs and surrounding towns. Urban College, *Self-Study*, p. 2.

49 These data were obtained through questionnaires administered to all students in Day division English classes in March, 1980.

Questionnaires were administered by a carefully trained group of Urban College students in order to maximize accuracy in responses. Since forms were administered to students in English classes, results are skewed slightly toward newer students.

50 London finds a distinct difference in student culture between "younger" and "older" white working class students in City Community College. See Howard London, *The Culture of a Community College* (New York: Praeger Publishers, 1978). This distinction does not hold for students at Urban College. Anthony's comments on the black community are interesting here.

[on status within the community]

Anthony: It all depends on what age group you are talking about. Old age group means a job, punching a clock, or going to work every day. Young blacks, it is just the opposite.

LW: What do you mean by young?

Anthony: I would say the age groups – high school age to about 35, or 15 to 40.

51 This represents an estimate obtained by means of the questionnaire described in footnote 49.

52 Tuition Assistance Program (TAP) is a state grant for all residents who are full-time students. Net taxable income must be less than $20,000. Amounts range up to $740 per year. The entire tuition of most Urban College students is paid under this grant. Basic Educational Opportunity Grant (BEOG) is a Federal grant for all students who are US citizens and whose income ranges from low to moderate level. The amount of the award is based upon congressional appropriation, but should range from $176 to $1138 per academic year. Most students at Urban College who receive this grant receive checks of approximately $500 per semester. Educational Opportunity Program (EOP) is designed to educate students throughout the state whose academic and economic backgrounds did not prepare them for college. EOP provides both academic and financial support. Students are eligible for more than one type of financial aid. Urban College, *Self-Study*, p. 6; and mimeo sheet distributed to all students entitled *Academic Financial Aids*. The percentage breakdown provided in the text is on page 6 of the *Self-Study* report.

53 These figures are based on results of the survey undertaken in Spring 1980. See footnote 49.

54 Data on mother's occupation suggest that mothers hold slightly more "prestigious" occupations than fathers. This must be interpreted with caution, however, since relatively "prestigious" jobs for women such as teacher's aid or nurse's aid pay very little.

55 Joyce Ladner, *Tomorrow's Tomorrow* (New York: Anchor Books, 1972), p. 135.

56 Carol Stack, *All Our Kin* (New York: Anchor Books, 1972), p. 135.

57 Stack, *All Our Kin*, p. 108.

58 These essays were written for a Business Organization class. Jennifer

is a white student. Approximately 37 per cent of white women at the college have children. As noted earlier, it can be estimated that 70 per cent of black female students have children.

59 Stack, *All Our Kin*, p. 28.

60 It must be remembered that Odessa is only 25. When I noted that she is still "quite young," her response was "I don't feel young."

2 Elements of culture

1 Paul Willis, *Learning to Labour: How Working Class Kids Get Working Class Jobs* (Westmead, England: Saxon House, 1977); and Howard London, *The Culture of a Community College* (New York: Praeger Publishers, 1978). Such comparisons must be made cautiously, however, especially in the case of Willis's "lads." The United States has had a less overt set of class antagonisms than Britain, and working class cultures will differ somewhat simply on that basis. In addition, the lads attend school by law whereas community college students attend by choice. Despite these caveats, the comparisons promote fruitful discussion about cultural form and its relationship to the economy.

2 Fathers of students typically hold such jobs as construction worker, longshoreman, telephone worker, fork-lift driver and industrial machinist. See Richard Edwards, *Contested Terrain* (New York: Basic Books, 1979) for a discussion of the Traditional Proletariat.

3 Periods of wagelessness are probably far more common now than they were at the time of Willis's study.

4 Willis, *Learning to Labour*, p. 19.

5 The pattern for females is different. London also suggests that "older" students do not exhibit these behavioral manifestations of lived cultural form.

6 London, *Culture*, especially chapter 3.

7 It is significant that Urban College students, in the final analysis, also hold *themselves* responsible for failure. I will discuss this at a later point.

8 See Willis, *Learning to Labour*, pp. 62–77 for a discussion of the teaching paradigm.

9 In point of fact the vast majority of the teachers are white. I will pursue this point further in chapter 3.

10 See Jean Anyon, "Social Class and School Knowledge," *Curriculum Inquiry* 11, 1 (1981): 3–41; and Jean Anyon, "Social Class and the Hidden Curriculum of Work," *Journal of Education* 162, 1 (Winter 1980): 67–92.

11 Willis, *Learning to Labour*, p. 26.

12 London suggests that absence from class is a "means of dissociating [oneself] from slavish adherence to official expectations." As such, it was defined positively. See London, *Culture*, p. 68.

13 This is an important element of the "hidden curriculum" and will be subject to more extended analysis in chapter 3.

14 If students attend regularly during the first three weeks, their name appears on the final class list and they receive grant checks whether they attend regularly after that point or not. Students are not necessarily aware of this, however. The discussion between two faculty members below is instructive here.

> *1 February 1980**
> [informal discussion in the hall]
>
> Phil [a Mathematics instructor] had given a report to the faculty at yesterday's meeting. He argued that attendance did not "drop off" significantly after checks were issued. Indeed there had been large-scale drop-out *before* checks came out.
>
> Sam [a Business Administration instructor] wanted to point something out to Phil. He suggested that if students attended class consistently the first three weeks of school, they get their check anyway.
>
> Phil asked if the students knew this.
>
> *Sam:* "The sharpies do." He told Phil to check with the financial aids office to see whether this was the case. He said it took him a long time to find this out, but indeed it's true. He said Phil "might be right and might be wrong." It's something for him to think about.

15 The attendance policy allows two hours of absence for each hour of credit. This means that six absences are allowed for a three-credit course. Faculty reserve the right to count "lateness" as absence. This is the second semester 1979–80 policy; the first semester policy was somewhat different. See chapter 3.

16 Not all students receive BEOG and TAP monies. Some have EOP grants (Educational Opportunity Program) and others receive Veterans' benefits or social security payments. The main source of financial aid to students, however, is BEOG and TAP.

17 While there has been some attempt on the part of the administration to stop this practice, the attempt is not without its contradictory effects. Since faculty and ultimately administrative jobs depend upon student headcount in the state system, it may not be in the college's best interest to deny admission to students even if they engage in this practice.

18 In the 1979 graduation ceremony, only one black student received an Associate's degree in Radiologic Technology. Since many students go through the formal graduation when they have not in fact met all requirements, this is not generally a good source of graduation rates by race.

19 Diane is a white female, approximately 50 years old. I will explore white response to elements of black lived culture at the end of the chapter. It is also the case that older women, both black and white, are largely exempt from the group logic examined here.

20 It can be assumed, because of grant requirements, that these students have always taken a full load. At the time of this writing, Jerome had left Urban College (without completing the Associate's) and was taking courses at another local institution.

21 Urban College Task Force, *Student Enrollment, Retention and Placement*, 1976–81 Data Bank. These are estimates based on number of admits per given year and number of graduates two and three years later.

22 As noted earlier, individual faculty are free to develop their own policy with respect to lateness.

23 These are interesting comments in light of my earlier discussion of the relationship between the economy and the state. See chapter 1.

24 See Paul Corrigan, *Schooling the Smash Street Kids* (London: Macmillan, 1979).

25 "Horse" is heroin.

26 Faculty occasionally comment on this. Phil [a Mathematics instructor], for example, told me that a number of the students in his classes come stoned. One of the students even asked him how he kept from laughing at some of the "off the wall" questions. He said that indeed some of the questions "come from left field. They just seemed to come from nowhere; they were not related to any of the topics they were discussing in class."

27 My two research assistants and myself were approached on numerous occasions throughout the year by students and asked to "share a joint" with them.

28 Marijuana is more common in large part because it is relatively inexpensive.

29 The importance of an apartment and its relationship to selling drugs is expressed by Anthony, a Business Administration student, below.

> It's getting harder to find a job. You don't want to stay home with your mom and pop once you are 19 and 20 years old, so you go out to the streets to get a job to take care of yourself. How do you get your money? It's beautiful, you know, the parents are there whenever you need them, but to call yourself an adult now, I want my own apartment, I want to go out, I want to party, I want to get me a car. And if you can't get a job to get any of these things, then how do you do it? How do you get these things? Sure, you can stay at home until you get 90 years old. But you reach a certain age, you want to be on your own. With the unemployment ratio being as great as it is, what do you turn to to get this money and get these things that you want to do? So if I can get enough money together to get my first quarter pound, or my first pound, I can go from there.

It is important to point out, however, that blacks, for the most part, do not control drug traffic in the United States. Drug sales in the ghetto are dependent upon the availability of drugs in the larger marketplace, which is not, in the final analysis, under black control. Bequai has argued persuasively that the structure of the illegal (or irregular) economy closely parallels that of the legal one, with high monopolistic earnings at the top, and low-paid, unstable, risky jobs at the bottom. As in the legal economy, blacks occupy positions in the illegal sector largely at the bottom. See A. Bequai, *Organized Crime: The Fifth Estate* (Lexington, Mass.: Lexington Books, 1979).

30 The essay is reproduced here exactly as written.

31 It is significant that students "share a joint" or otherwise engage in drug use collectively. It must be pointed out that the logic examined here is a group logic; it does not lie in any individual act. I will discuss this further in chapters 6 and 7.

32 See footnote 21.

33 A list was compiled of all Urban College graduates by curriculum from 1975–8 (Associate degree only). Student race was estimated on the basis of residence zip codes. Four zip codes are associated with black neighborhoods during 1975–8. While there are certainly some blacks who reside in white neighborhoods and vice versa, I am confident that the breakdown in Table 2.3 is reasonably accurate. The one neighborhood that is now "transitional" was almost totally white until 1978. Data presented in Table 2.3 may understate slightly the proportion of black graduates since blacks who live in white neighborhoods are likely to be of a higher status than those who live in ghetto neighborhoods and therefore more likely to graduate. Such individuals would not, of course, appear as "black" in these calculations.

34 General Studies implies no particular committment to specific academic or vocational goals. Fewer credits transfer to four year institutions and it is commonly thought of as a "second class" curriculum. General Studies allows ten free electives whereas Liberal Arts, for example, allows six.

35 A new curriculum, Paralegal Assistant, also draws a high proportion of white students.

36 These data were obtained through questionnaires administered to all students in Day division English classes (see Appendix C). Questionnaires were administered by a carefully trained group of Urban College students in order to maximize accuracy in responses. Since forms were administered to students in English classes, results are skewed slightly toward newer students. Results are likely to be skewed slightly toward black students as well, since a relatively greater proportion of blacks take the required English course more than once.

37 Although I cannot substantiate this claim, it was alleged that, since Urban College was shifting location within the year (out of the ghetto), a greater proportion of whites attended the school during the academic year 1979–80 than during previous years.

38 An Urban College party, for example, held on 7 September 1979 at a local bar, drew approximately fifty black students and only a few white students. Frank, a Business Administration instructor, commented to me that only black students showed and that this

always happens "whenever a party is on *this* side of street; if it were downtown, only white students would show." *While there is no overt hostility between black and white students in classes, "at the end of classes, they don't see each other at all."*

39 The majority of white students at the college are working class. It cannot be assumed, however, that white student cultural form in this predominantly black institution parallels that depicted by London. White lived culture in Urban College will be linked dialectically with urban black culture (as produced within the institution) as well as broader white working class cultural forms. Whites in the college take education more seriously, for example, than students in studies by London, Willis or Corrigan. I suspect this represents an attempt on the part of whites to distance themselves from what they judge to be the "non-serious" nature of black students with respect to education. Some whites, however, are less enthusiastic about schooling than others. Jay, for example, is reminiscent of London's students.

LW: You feel you can learn here [Urban College] if you really want to?

Jay: Oh, definitely. Like if you have a good head. I feel that I have a good head, but like I say, my girlfriend and neighborhood it conflicts all the time. Striving for the best and then falling back and being a player. No responsibility, that's what it boils down to. (. . .) It's fun, living your life with no responsibility and then dying. But I like to be in the latest design clothes and the nicest car. I know you have to hit the books to get somewhere, but the way the world's going today, you don't know which way to go. Don't know what to do, where to go, what to learn, where to learn it. I think about going into the Air Force (. . .) every time I discuss it [the future]. When I think of my folks they're shot.#

Most whites interviewed, however, talked less about personal dilemmas and more about how they differed from blacks.

40 Some black students, like Anthony and Belinda, blame the institution for not using better judgment with respect to admissions (see chapter 3). While Anthony and Belinda resent the attendance policy and feel that this effort to control their time is due in large part to poor admissions criteria, there is no comparable sense among black students that an individual's education suffers because of others' absence.

41 While I cannot provide exact figures, most white students receive some form of financial aid as well. The relative amount of such aid may be less, however.

42 Dick is very specific in his reference to "southern blacks.' He states the following:

Dick: The RT [Radiologic Technology] was sort of a clique. (. . .) As far as the other students, considering that the majority of them were black – we really didn't associate with them. (. . .) Culturally they were behind us. There was a big cultural gap.

LW: What do you mean by cultural gap?

Dick: Well, I worked in California. The blacks there are highly civilized. When I came back here I found that the blacks were uncivilized. It was really kind of a surprise to me because I had been away from it for a number of years. The blacks out there I could relate to as a person. When I came back here it was sort of a cultural shock. (. . .) I've been back here for five years; I'm becoming sort of a bigot myself. The southern blacks came up here and brought up a lot of their culture. I find it very degrading. They're slow in action, slow in moves, and always lagging behind. The American thing is sort of to move up and improve yourself. Basically from what I see from the southern blacks, they don't care.#

43 I will explore the relationship between student culture and the pace of learning more fully in chapter 4.

44 There was some hostility on the part of black women toward white women who dated black men. Paula, a Business Administration student, dated George for a period of time. She told me that a number of black women who knew George would not speak to her in the hall, even when she said "hello" to them first. Interracial dating was not common, however, and blacks and whites basically kept to themselves.

3 "Thirty years old and I'm allowed to be late!"

1 Paul Willis, for example, pays no attention to the internal workings of the school as they might affect the lived culture of the lads. While he suggests, following Bourdieu and Passeron, that "it is the exclusive 'cultural capital' – knowledge and skill in the symbolic manipulation of language and figures – of the dominant groups in society which ensures the success of their offspring [in schools] and thus the reproduction of class position and privilege," he does not investigate these processes directly. See Paul Willis, *Learning to Labour: How Working Class Kids Get Working Class Jobs* (Westmead, England: Saxon House Press, 1977), p. 128. See also Pierre Bourdieu and Jean-Claude Passeron, *Reproduction in Education, Society and Culture* (London: Sage Publications, 1977).

2 I use the term "hidden curriculum" to refer to the day-to-day interactions and regularities of classrooms and schools that tacitly teach important norms and values. This is distinct from the form and content of school knowledge – the overt curriculum – that is found in texts and other materials distributed by teachers. This parallels Michael Apple's use of the term. See Michael Apple, *Ideology and Curriculum* (Boston: Routledge & Kegan Paul, 1979); and Michael Apple, *Education and Power* (Boston: Routledge & Kegan Paul, 1982).

3 Bowles and Gintis, for example, present a largely mechanistic view of

the hidden curriculum. See Samuel Bowles and Herbert Gintis, *Schooling in Capitalist America* (New York: Basic Books, 1976).

4 In highlighting the active role of students in shaping aspects of institutional life, I do not mean to imply that students and institutional agents possess equal power. Clearly this is not the case. Students do, however, as a group exert considerable power over the shape and form of institutional life. The way in which this acts to shape their own culture and ultimately maintain an unequal social structure and deeply rooted antagonisms, despite moments of exceptional insight, is very important.

5 Michael Olivas, *The Dilemma of Access: Minorities in Two Year Colleges* (Washington, DC: Howard University Press, 1979), p. 64.

6 The social science unit has its own unique history in the college. A top administrator explains predominately minority hiring in the Social Science unit as follows:

> What that really probably means is that (. . .) there are some very very strong [black instructors in that unit]. _______ is a strong woman, _______ is a very strong human being and they look around and they feel that there is a great deal of racism at Urban College and they feel that the only way to impact that is to bring on as many blacks as they have the right to bring on [and] that's what they do. In fact, I think that there is a lot of racism at Urban College in terms of making hiring decisions in certain units (. . .) and I think that in certain instances people feel quite good about that, that they don't have to respond to any kind of larger system in making those kind of determinations. That's a point of some discomfort [for me] but it is also a difficult front to move on.

7 It has been argued, of course, that sociology is relatively receptive to women because of its focus on the family.

8 While female faculty occasionally teach literature, the English department hires on two lines: one reading and one writing. Female faculty occupy the reading lines.

9 Olivas, *The Dilemma of Access*, p. 62.

10 It must be emphasized here that this is not a conscious process. It must be seen in relation to broader race, class and gender logics.

11 As noted in chapter 1, over 90 per cent of full-time students receive some form of grant money. The vast majority receive Basic Educational Opportunity Grants (BEOG) and Tuition Assistance Plan (TAP) monies.

12 This, of course, represents a misunderstandng of the way in which faculty are paid.

13 During the previous academic year, in an article in the student newspaper, the Vice-President referred to those students who drop out after receiving their grant checks as "phantoms." He came under some criticism for this statement by the student body.

14 It is highly questionable, of course, whether it is "humane" to ask students to produce an obituary.

15 There were eight issues of the newspaper in 1979–80. Of these, five carried major pieces on the subject.
16 We observed over fifteen classes during the first week of school.
17 *Urban College Student Newspaper*, vol. 5, no. 3, December 1979, p. 1.
18 *Urban College Student Newspaper*, vol. 5, no. 3, December 1979.
19 The Child Care Unit, for example, has made the policy more rigid.
20 As pointed out in chapter 2, footnote 14, students do not necessarily know that they receive BEOG grant checks if they attend a specified number of classes during the first three weeks, despite their attendance during the remainder of the semester. As of second semester, however, students did know that names would be dropped from the class roster if they did not meet the three-week requirement.
21 John Horton, "Time and Cool People," in Lee Rainwater, ed., *Black Experience Soul* (New Brunswick, New Jersey: Transaction Books, 1979), p. 31.
22 *Urban College Student Newspaper*, vol. 5, no. 3, December 1979, p. 1.
23 While this may have constituted a quorum, this was not a well-attended meeting. Had the vote been to abolish the attendance policy, it is not clear to me that the decision would have stood.
24 The administration of certain grants, such as Veterans' benefits, demands a careful accounting of student attendance. Faculty turn these data over to the Financial Aids Office each semester.
25 The fact that class attendance is treated here as a commodity to be bought and sold is, of course, an interesting point.
26 Since the college is designated a Full Opportunity Program, all applicants who have high school or General Equivalency Diplomas are admitted. It is, therefore, not possible to exercise greater care in the selection of students as Anthony and Belinda suggest. Students are admitted on a "first come, first served" basis.
27 Clyde is not correct, however. The first semester policy stipulates six absenses for a three-credit course. The vast majority of courses at Urban College are three credits. This represents just one of many misunderstandings about the policy despite the fact that it is constantly discussed and clarified.
28 While most students resent the policy, a small minority do not. The case of Loretta, a black female of about 48, is an example here.

Loretta: With regard to financial aid, I think the students should be made aware that the grant money is not automatic. The attendance policy has to be enforced; you have to attend classes. (. . .) There's always going to be a few people that are intent upon ripping off the system, and if it's explained in the beginning and you have a hard fast rule I think it'd sort of lessen this, because the people wouldn't bother. (. . .) The new attendance policy [second semester] you can have twelve absences. Well, that's fine for some classes, but if you were in a class like chemistry or accounting and you missed twelve classes, to me you'd blow the whole thing. You have to be there, I think.

LW: So you don't think the attendance policy is tough enough?

Loretta: No, I don't. I think twelve absences is far too many. They should still leave it up to the discretion of the instructor depending upon what course he's teaching. I feel that the instructor should be the boss in his class at all times. (. . .) There are some courses you can't *miss* twelve classes – not and get anything out of them – like accounting.

The important point here is not that Loretta thinks the policy should be more rigorous, but that she, in contrast to the majority of students, is willing to grant the institution the right to have such a policy to begin with.

29 Anthony once again reveals that respect for knowledge is embedded within the culture. It is an enigma to him that he could tell who was going to drop out of school whereas institutional personnel seemed not to notice. As he states, "I'm quite sure that someone in administration would see the same things that I saw. (. . .) Because they have been exposed to this kind of thing much more so than I have, so what I am saying is that *they should have the knowledge* [my emphasis] that is greater than I have as far as school and people go." Anthony's position is that knowledge ought to be useful in solving problems. Jerome also takes this position below.

I think they should have them a psychologist over there, maybe a pool of them at Urban College, and have it a part that every student go through some type of professional, you know, evaluation. Because there is many people with problems up there. (. . .) Some of the problems are more minute psychological than any other thing. They [students] just need that assurance, that little extra push to make them perform, you know, and this is what is lacking.

The point here is that both Anthony and Jerome pinpoint problems at the college and argue that such problems can be alleviated by those with knowledge (administrators, psychologists). This once again implies a respect for knowledge that is not apparent in the white working class.

30 It can be argued that the college survives at the present time because such institutions represent one outcome of racial contest in the state. Thus the state supports these institutions out of its *own* legitimation needs rather than institutional outcomes *per se*. While I believe that this is in fact the case, this may or may not be so in the future. The attempt to control student time can be seen as an attempt to enhance outcomes before the state no longer needs to legitimate itself in this way. Although institutional personnel may not articulate it in precisely this manner, they are partially conscious of exactly this dynamic.

31 The issue of attendance is also tied to faculty culture which will be discussed at length in chapter 4.

32 Numerous scholars have argued this point. See, for example, E.P. Thompson, "Time, Work Discipline and Industrial Capitalists," in *Past and Present* 38, December 1967; and Eugene Genovese, *Roll*

Jordan Roll: The World the Slaves Made (New York: Vintage Books, 1976). See also Paul Willis's discussion of time and abstract labor in *Learning to Labour*, pp. 33–7.

33 Tamara K. Hareven, "Family Time and Historical Time," *Daedalus* 106, 2 (Spring 1977), p. 59.

34 Horton, "Time and Cool People," p. 31.

35 Eugene Genovese has argued that oppositional time embedded within the black American subculture developed out of the plantation experience. "It combined," he suggests, "the ostensibly natural sense of time found among traditional agriculturalists with an attitude of disguised disobedience – of apparent shiftlessness – which makes a slave class at once sullen, 'stupid', and uncooperative and yet enormously resourceful at doing what it wants to do." See Genovese, *Roll Jordan Roll*, p. 293. Variations in time, argues Genovese, develop in opposition to dominant forms of time which exist primarily to benefit certain classes.

36 Horton, "Time and Cool People," p. 40.

37 Ibid., p. 42.

38 There is a material basis for this as well. As Horton notes, there are not enough cars or money for individual dates, so everyone converges in one place. The fact that there are few cars means that a crowd can be sustained for an indefinite period of time.

39 See Horton, "Time and Cool People," p. 44.

40 Ibid.

41 At another point, George suggested that "blacks got no money but they live pretty well – they buy nice suits and clothes and cars at a reasonable price – village economy. It has nothing to do with the economy of the larger society – it has a life and sense all its own."

4 The role of faculty

1 Howard London, *The Culture of a Community College* (New York: Praeger Publishers, 1978).

2 Scholars working within the critical tradition have not paid enough attention to this point. While many persons working in the area of education and cultural and economic reproduction are sensitive to the creation of cultural form among students, there has not been equal sensitivity to the fact that faculty also produce their own culture in particular sites. Faculty behavior and attitudes are at least partially created in response to located student cultural forms. This is not to deny the importance of dominant ideology as distributed through media, teacher education programs and so forth, but to argue for the relational quality of the production of faculty culture in particular sites of struggle.

3 Information was obtained through formal interviews as well as informal interactions with faculty. All formal interviews were taped with the permission of the respondents. See Appendices A and B.

4 Dennis also suggests that "being a cop, I'm used to dealing with minorities. So I felt comfortable."

5 As the discussion below suggests, Bill, an English instructor, also had previous contact with ghettoized minorities and therefore felt "comfortable" when he first came to Urban College. This does not, however, lessen the tendency to view students as "other" than himself. In fact, he may have been predisposed toward this to a greater extent than faculty with no previous contact.

LW: (. . .) When you first came to the school did you have any difficulty orienting yourself?

Bill: No, none. I had taught four years at ________ . It was a girls' vocational high school. It was probably I'd say the lower socioeconomic level of girl. (. . .) The students had similar problems to the kind the students here have, economically, culturally and socially, so I had no qualms about the type of student that I was coming to serve and I had no difficulty at all.

6 An objective test here refers to one with a forced choice format.

7 This is not an inconsequential point. There has been far too little attention paid to the way in which curricular form emerges in educational institutions. It is not *simply* a form of control applied to specific groups. Although Linda McNeil does not focus on student race or class, I am in agreement with her basic argument regarding the shaping of curriculum. See Linda M. McNeil, "Defensive Teaching and Classroom Control," in Michael Apple and Lois Weis, eds, *Ideology and Practice in Schooling* (Philadelphia: Temple University Press, 1983); Linda McNeil, "Negotiating Classroom Knowledge: Beyond Achievement and Socialization," in *Journal of Curriculum Studies* 13, 4 (1981): 313–28.

8 For a discussion of the contradictory pressures on educational institutions (and by extension school personnel), see Michael Apple, *Education and Power* (Boston: Routledge & Kegan Paul, 1982), especially pp. 120–34; and Michael Apple and Lois Weis, "Ideology and Practice in Education: A Political and Conceptual Introduction," in Apple and Weis, *Ideology and Practice in Schooling*, pp. 1–33. See also Roger Dale, "Education and the Capitalist State: Contributions and Contradictions," in Michael Apple, ed., *Cultural and Economic Reproduction in Education: Essays in Class, Ideology and the State* (Boston: Routledge & Kegan Paul, 1982), pp. 127–61.

9 Faculty at Urban College, like faculty at the university level, are basically in control of their own curriculum. Clearly such "choice" is dependent upon what is available in the marketplace. See Apple, *Education and Power*, chapters 2 and 5.

10 Alex is Acting Academic Dean; see chapter 3.

11 Jim did, however, on another occasion, mention students as a reason for enjoying his job. Over lunch (February 1980), he stated that he "likes teaching at Urban College" and finds the "students at [the two suburban campuses] rather boring." He taught some at both, and finds the "middle class too complacent." He suggests that students at

Urban College "are very interesting and a novelist would be able to write a great deal about the urban existence in a campus of this sort." He can't do it, but he recognizes it "as a fertile area." Basically, however, faculty did not mention students as constituting a reason for enjoying their work. If they did, it generally paralleled Jim's sentiments that the students are "interesting."

12 By contract, faculty teach five courses per week. In addition, many faculty teach one or two courses off-load for additional money.

13 This parallels the position of white students on campus, as I discussed in chapter 2.

14 London has categorized faculty in the community college as having conservative, liberal or radical perspectives. While this may be true, subsequent practice in the classroom may not follow from such perspectives. See London, *The Culture of a Community College*, chapter 5.

15 I do not mean to imply that Eboe has not experienced racism as a black man residing in the United States. Rather I am suggesting that his culture is not that of a black American.

16 It also must be noted that middle class black Americans know full well what white society expects of them. Generally speaking, for a black man or woman to "make it," they must exhibit qualities far in excess of what would be demanded of a white male or female in the same position.

17 This is obviously because the relationship has been historically antagonistic.

18 See Eugene Genovese, *Roll Jordan Roll: The World the Slaves Made* (New York: Vintage Books, 1972) for an excellent discussion of simultaneous accommodation and resistance in the production of culture. I will discuss this further in chapter 7.

19 While this individual is truly marginal in that he fits neither within ghetto culture nor middle class black culture, he is, by his own admission, more closely aligned to what he calls the "village economy." It is significant that George did not pursue his Bachelor's degree, although he would be a full-time faculty member if he had. Although he completed his Associate's degree, George exhibits some of the same contradictions as students at Urban College. One difference, however, is that he is acutely aware of this. As he states,

> Blacks have become accustomed to the posture we're in. And the thing that fucks me up about it (. . .) is that I'm realizing that I'm part and parcel of the whole experience. (. . .) I know that I've got to go back and get me some more schooling my damn self. All those things that I'm talking about now I'm very much part of, and that's why I'm very sensitive to them.

20 On another occasion, George suggested the contradictory nature of these impulses. "On the one hand they [students] want education so they can 'make it'; on the other hand, they smoke dope and gamble in the Student Center. These are the inside pressures and the pressures of the peer group."

21 While I am suggesting that polarization along class/cultural lines emerges at least partially within the college itself, it is, of course, possible for faculty to enter the college as blatant racists. While I met only one such faculty member during my year at Urban College, his comments below are telling.

> One of the first problems I ran into was back in 1972 when I was doing job interviews for a _______ class as part of a unit and I ask students "married?" They'd say "no." "Children?" They'd say "yes." That kind of threw me because I was used to the puritanic concept, that is, you're married, you have children, if you're not married, you have none. It seemed very common that many of the students here would have a number of children from a number of different fathers. They had no problem raising them. There didn't seem to be any kind of social stigma to the fact that you have a lot of fathers for your children.
>
> I was also concerned originally with the black-white relationships between male and female. White girl with a black boyfriend or black girl with a white boyfriend. Here it's accepted, but it was quite a shock to me at first in terms of my own puritanical viewpoint.
>
> (. . .) I almost think there is a congenital problem with respect to math in the black race. They just can't do math. You see [a female student], she's doing very poorly in Accounting II.
>
> Another black male we had here – our graduate – I got him an entry level position in management at [a local department store]. Do you know he failed the basic math test for clerks? Incredible! It's a real problem.

22 This is the same argument I made with respect to white students in chapter 2.

23 This is not to deny the very real politics surrounding Urban College that may necessitate "a good fight." It is significant, however, that faculty enjoy action outside the classroom to a greater extent than they do action within the classroom.

24 While this is not my primary focus here, such statements reveal quite clearly that gender tensions are reproduced as well.

5 The individual versus the collective

1 This point is discussed at length in chapter 1.

2 See Carol Stack, *All Our Kin* (New York: Harper & Row, 1974).

3 Ibid., p. 28.

4 The norm of cooperation has been depicted by Valentine and others. Male street networks have been shown to be cooperative as well. See Bettylou Valentine, *Hustling and Other Hard Work* (New York: Free Press, 1978); Melvin Williams, *On the Street Where I Lived* (New York: Holt, Rinehart & Winston, 1981); and Jagna Wojcicka Sharff, *Life on Doolittle Street: How Poor People Purchase Immortality*,

Final Report, Hispanic Study Project, Department of Anthropology, Columbia University, 1981.

5 There are, in fact, some women who always bring their children to class.

6 It must be pointed out, however, that it is not only black females who bring their children to class. Some white females also engage in this practice, although to a far lesser extent. In part this is linked to the fact that a much higher proportion of black female students have children. The case of Paula, a white female in Business Administration, is illustrative here.

> Paula had her 4-year-old daughter with her. She said she can't afford day care any more – "it's just too expensive." She said "working women really get screwed since there is no free day care. Many women are divorced and they have kids. They use their own sick days and vacation days to take care of their sick kids. They use most of their money to keep the kids in day care?
> *Paula:* Whatever happened to the proposals in the early 1970s for federally supported day care?
> *LW:* Well, they didn't do anything because people started talking about the sanctity of the home.
> *Paula:* That's a lot of bullshit. There is no sanctity of the home any more. Many women are divorced. We *have* to go to work just to support ourselves. In order to get a decent job we have to go back to school and how can we go back to school unless we have someone to take care of our kids? Things are really bad now.*

In general however, white females did not bring their children, if they had them, to class.

7 Again, however, it must be stressed that this polarization is not vicious or even overt on campus. It is casual in the sense that black and white students simply do not mix. While there may be individual exceptions to this, the groups do not associate with one another. This can lead to a very "harmonious" racial situation. In fact, results from a Student Opinion Survey (See Appendix C) conducted during March 1980 reveal that students are very satisfied with racial harmony on campus. Students were asked whether or not they are very satisfied, satisfied, neutral, dissatisfied or very dissatisfied with each of twenty-four areas of Urban College. "Racial harmony" elicited the most positive response. Urban College, *Self-Study Report* (submitted to Middle States for accreditation), 1981, Display III 5 A.

8 These names were mentioned because Anthony was aware that I knew Randy and Jerome.

9 There is, in fact, extensive advertising. It is interesting that Jerome perceives that students attend Urban College because of a "word of mouth situation" rather than in response to the quite costly advertising campaign.

10 This cannot be generalized to the white working class as a whole. See chapter 2.

11 An effort was made to contact all students who graduated during the years 1975–8. Data reported here are drawn from in-depth interviews with those that were contacted and agreed to the interview. Twenty students were interviewed during the summer 1980.

12 I do not mean to imply here that if only students would adopt the attitudes outlined, they would succeed in school. Rather I am suggesting that there is a *relationship* between a set of personal/behavioral characteristics and "success" at Urban College.

13 School knowledge, in general, embodies dominant cultural categories. This argument has been advanced by Michael F. D. Young, "An Approach to the Study of Curricula as Socially Organized Knowledge," in Michael Young, ed., *Knowledge and Control* (London: Collier-Macmillan, 1971); Pierre Bourdieu and Jean-Claude Passeron, *Reproduction in Education, Society and Culture* (London: Sage Publications, 1977); Basil Bernstein, *Class, Codes and Control, Volume 3: Toward a Theory of Educational Transmissions* (London: Routledge & Kegan Paul, 1977); and Michael Apple, *Ideology and Curriculum* (Boston: Routledge & Kegan Paul, 1979).

14 While there is opposition to the attendance policy, for example, there is no expressed opposition to dominant forms of time *per se*. Opposition to standard English occasionally takes the form: "Nobody talks like that."

15 In fact, however, a number of students do wear designer jeans. Many such consumer items are available through what George refers to as the "village economy."

16 Fashion History is, in fact, the history of white upper class fashion. George had the following comment on the course:

> You know what it helps do – it helps the pimp. It helps the pimp – that's what it does. (. . .) While they're [students] going to school they're building a mentality that is in pursuit of a disneyland, of a fantasyland, of a Mahagony [referring to Diana Ross's film about a black model]. (. . .) To get a chance to be models. So what happens is that the school will take them to a couple of modeling shows, they'll put on a modeling show at school, they live that out you know. It's bullshit. (. . .) If they could ensure them going to the New York Institute of Fashion Technology [sic] and give them all six- or seven-month apprenticeships with certain jobs if that's what they want to do, you know, get paid for it, it's all about the money.

17 Paul Willis, *Learning to Labour: How Working Class Kids Get Working Class Jobs* (Westmead, England: Saxon House Press, 1977), p. 1.

18 See Nell Keddie, "Classroom Knowledge," in *Knowledge and Control*, Michael Young, ed. (London: Collier-Macmillan, 1971), pp. 133–60.

19 Keddie, "Classroom Knowledge," pp. 154–5.

20 Anyon argues persuasively that the knowledge distributed through

schools is closely tied to the social class of students. See Jean Anyon, "Social Class and School Knowledge," *Curriculum Inquiry* 11, 1 (1981): 3–42. See also Edgar Litt, "Civics Education, Community Norms, and Political Indoctrination," *American Sociological Review* 29 (February 1963): 69–75.

21 For example, 35 per cent of first-time students in Spring 1980 had below a tenth-grade reading level and only 21 per cent of new admits had a reading level above twelfth grade. Urban College, *Self-Study*, Display II 5A.

22 Sharp and Green argue similarly when they speak of the ideal "good" pupil being that individual whose teacher-pupil intersubjectivity is high. Rist also discusses the nature of classroom stratification in terms of the shared culture of teachers and students. See Rachel Sharp and Anthony Green, *Education and Social Control* (London: Routledge & Kegan Paul, 1975); and Ray Rist, "Student Social Class and Teacher Expectations: The Self-Fulfilling Prophecy in Ghetto Education," *Harvard Educational Review* 40, 3 (1970): 411–51.

23 Thirty-six per cent of female graduates during the years 1975–8 were in these fields. The figure includes both black and white females.

6 Analysis of culture — I

1 Faculty perspectives and practice and aspects of the hidden curriculum cannot be considered a *mere* response to student culture either. See chapters 3 and 4.

2 Willis raises this question on p. 119 of *Learning to Labour*, I employ his basic framework in chapters 6 and 7. See Paul Willis, *Learning to Labour* (Westmead, England: Saxon House Press, 1977).

3 Bisseret and others have pointed to the way in which sexist terms and metaphors dominate our linguistic usage. So as not to further this practice I employ Willis's term "penetration" only when I quote directly from Willis's work. See Noelle Bisseret, *Class, Language and Ideology* (London: Routledge & Kegan Paul, 1979) as cited in Michael Apple, *Education and Power* (Boston: Routledge & Kegan Paul, 1982).

4 Willis, *Learning to Labour*, p. 119.

5 Ibid.

6 Ibid.

7 See Harry Braverman, *Labor and Monopoly Capital* (New York: Monthly Review Press, 1974); and Michael Burawoy, "Toward a Marxist Theory of the Labor Process: Braverman and Beyond," *Politics and Society* 8, no. 3–4 (1978): 247–312. This is not, of course, without its contradictory effects. See Richard Edwards, *Contested Terrain* (New York: Basic Books, 1979).

8 Willis argues that while capitalism can sacrifice individualism, it cannot sacrifice division. The lads recreate at the level of their own

culture a distinction that is fundamentally useful to the capitalist class. The extent to which such "divisions" are functional to capitalism will be discussed at a later point.

9 Willis, *Learning to Labour*, p. 119. As Willis argues,

> It is the specific combination of cultural "insight" and partiality which give the mediated strength of personal validation and identity to individual behavior which leads in the end to entrapment. There really is at some level a rational and potentially developmental basis for outcomes which appear to be completely irrational and regressive. It is, I would argue, only this contradictory double articulation that allows a class society to exist in liberal and democratic forms: for an unfree condition to be entered freely. (pp. 119–20)

The case of American blacks is somewhat different, of course, since what Ogbu calls the caste-like status of minorities has legally prevented blacks from assuming certain positions until the 1960s. See John Ogbu, "Equalization of Educational Opportunity and Racial/ Ethnic Inequality," in Philip Altbach, Robert Arnove and Gail Kelly, *Comparative Education* (New York: Macmillan, 1982) pp. 269–89.

10 This is a very important point. Lived culture cannot be seen as free-floating.

11 This must be seen as a debate with the structuralists such as Althusser and Poulantzas. The debate over the relationship between base and superstructure is very intense currently and both Willis's work and my own highlight the relative autonomy of the cultural level. For a discussion of the culturalist/structuralist controversy see Michael Apple, ed., *Cultural and Economic Reproduction in Education: Essays on Class, Ideology and the State* (London: Routledge & Kegan Paul, 1982), chapter 1; Richard H. Johnson, "Histories of Culture, Theories of Ideology," in Michele Barrett *et al.*, eds, *Ideology and Cultural Production* (New York: St Martin's Press, 1979), pp. 49–77; and Henry Giroux, "Hegemony, Resistance, and the Paradox of Educational Reform," *Interchange* 12, no. 2–3 (1981): 3–26. For a structuralist perspective see Louis Althusser, "Ideology and Ideological State Apparatuses," in *Lenin and Philosophy, and Other Essays* (London: New Left Books, 1971); Nicos Poulantzas, *Classes in Contemporary Capitalism* (London: New Left Books, 1975); and Samuel Bowles and Herbert Gintis, *Schooling in Capitalist America* (New York: Basic Books, 1976).

12 Willis, *Learning to Labour*, pp. 120–1.

13 Ibid., p. 121.

14 This is Willis's point. As he states, "(i)t is no accident that different groups in different schools, for instance, come up with similar insights, even though they are the products of separate efforts, and thus cohere to make distinctive class bonds" (p. 121).

15 The reason, in my opinion, why so many educational "reform" efforts have failed to alter interactions and outcomes within

educational institutions is because they have not taken into account carefully enough the cultural level. "Reforms" such as the "effective schools movement" are doomed to failure for precisely this reason. The record of failure historically speaks for itself.

16 Gender operates differently *within* class and race categories. It must also be stressed that students of different class, race and gender backgrounds will also be given different types of educational experiences. While Bowles and Gintis's "correspondence theory" is too mechanistic, their notion that educational messages will be distributed differentially according to student class, race and gender is not totally incorrect. What we must guard against is a tendency to ignore the way in which class, race and gender cultures *themselves* work at least partially to shape the type of education which groups receive.

17 Ogbu, "Equalization of Educational Opportunity," p. 270.

18 Michael Omi and Howard Winant, "By the Rivers of Babylon: Race in the United States," *Socialist Review*, vol. 71, 13, 5 (September/ October, 1983): 54.

19 Omi and Winant, "By the Rivers of Babylon," p. 55.

20 See George Rawick, *From Sundown to Sunup: The Making of the Black Community* (Westport, Conn.: Greenwood Press, 1972); Herbert C. Gutman, *The Black Family in Slavery and Freedom, 1750–1925* (New York: Vintage, 1976); as cited in Omi and Winant, p. 54.

21 Omi and Winant, "By the Rivers of Babylon," p. 56.

22 Eugene Genovese, *Roll, Jordan, Roll: The World the Slaves Made* (New York: Vintage Books, 1972). See especially chapters on the black work ethic and language. The extent to which blacks had a well-developed sense of being an oppressed group under slavery is the subject of intense debate among historians currently. I am not necessarily taking Genovese's position on this particular matter. See James Anderson, "Aunt Jemima in Dialectics: Genovese on Slave Culture," *Journal of Negro Slavery* 61, 1 (1976): 99–114. I am indebted to David Gerber for calling this debate to my attention.

23 I do not mean to imply that the struggle among working class whites was "easy." I am simply pointing out that, until recently, whites struggled in the public sphere to a greater extent than blacks.

24 Jerome Karabel, "Community Colleges and Social Stratification: Submerged Class Conflict in American Higher Education," in Jerome Karabel and A.H. Halsey, eds, *Power and Ideology in Education* (New York: Oxford University Press, 1977), p. 235.

25 See Karabel for documentation of this point, p. 233.

26 Ralph Turner argues that the American system of education keeps the "contest" open for as long as possible in contrast to "sponsored" systems of mobility. The American ideology of equal educational opportunity whereby the individual, if he or she only tries hard enough, can always "make it," has been instrumental in the success of the community college movement. See Ralph Turner, "Sponsored

and Contest Mobility and the School System," *American Sociological Review* 25 (1960): 855–67.

27 In fact, minorities are enrolled disproportionately in the two-year college sector. For an excellent analysis of the position nation-wide of minorities in higher education, see Michael Olivas, *The Dilemma of Access: Minorities of Two-Year College* (Washington, DC: Howard University Press, 1979).

28 Karabel, "Community Colleges and Social Stratification," pp. 233–4.

29 Ibid., p. 234.

30 See Michael Olneck, "The Effects of Education," in Christopher Jencks *et al.*, *Who Gets Ahead?* (New York: Basic Books, 1979), pp. 150–170. While Olneck does not assess the effects of an Associate's degree *per se*, we can assume that black students with only community college degrees are still at even more of a disadvantage relative to whites than blacks who complete the Bachelor's. See also Joseph Schwartz and Jill Williams, "The Effects of Race on Earnings," in Jencks *et al.*, *Who Gets Ahead?* pp. 191–212; and Erik Olin Wright, *Class Structure and Income Determination* (New York: Academic Press, 1979), chapter 8.

31 Willis, *Learning to Labour*, p. 128.

32 While it may not be easy emotionally for an individual to separate himself or herself from any community it is more difficult materially in some communities than others. I have discussed this point at greater length in chapter 5.

33 See Karabel, "Community Colleges and Social Stratification," and Fred L. Pincus, "False Promises of Community Colleges: Class Conflict and Vocational Education," *Harvard Educational Review* 50, 3 (1980): 332–60.

34 As Pincus argues, however, even if such curricula were available, the majority of students may not be able to obtain jobs. It is nevertheless noteworthy that there are few vocational programs at Urban College. The only truly applied programs are Child Care, Secretarial Science, Radiologic Technology, Paralegal Assistant and Criminal Justice. As I suggested in chapters 2 and 5, the Radiologic Technology program is largely closed to black students and jobs in Secretarial Science and Child Care pay little and offer few benefits. Paralegal Assistant and Criminal Justice are new programs and their outcomes are not yet clear. Interestingly enough, the curricula which lead to reasonably well-paying, stable jobs such as Data Processing, Nursing, Automotive Technology and Computer Technology are not available at Urban College. They are, however, available at the suburban campuses which serve a predominantly white clientele.

35 Pierre Bourdieu and Jean-Claude Passeron, *Reproduction in Education, Society and Culture* (London: Sage, 1977), as cited in Willis, *Learning to Labour*, p. 128.

36 See Michael F.D. Young, "An Approach to the Study of Curricula as Socially Organized Knowledge," in M.D. Young, ed., *Knowledge and Control* (London: Collier-Macmillan, 1971), p. 8, as cited in

Michael Apple, *Ideology and Curriculum* (Boston: Routledge & Kegan Paul, 1979), p. 31.

37 Jean Anyon's study of United States history textbooks makes concrete Young's notion that there is a dialectical relationship between access to power and the opportunity to legitimate dominant social categories. See Jean Anyon, "Ideology and United States History Textbooks," *Harvard Educational Review* 49, 3 (August 1979): 361–86. For other studies of school culture as a commodity and its relationship to economic arrangements see Joel Taxel, "The American Revolution in Children's Fiction: An Analysis of Literary Content, Form and Ideology," in Michael Apple and Lois Weis, eds, *Ideology and Practice in Schooling* (Philadelphia: Temple University Press, 1983), pp. 61–88; and Landon Beyer, "Aesthetic Curriculum and Cultural Reproduction," in Apple and Weis, *Ideology and Practice in Schooling*, pp. 89–113.

38 Nell Keddie argues this point exceptionally well. See Nell Keddie, "Classroom Knowledge," in Young, *Knowledge and Control*, pp. 133–160.

39 Willis, *Learning to Labour*, p. 128.

40 Ogbu, "Equalization of Educational Opportunity," p. 272.

41 Part of the reason this is the case, of course, is that legislation designed to promote equality is not enforced to the full extent.

42 See Edwards, *Contested Terrain*. Numerous studies suggest that secondary jobs exhibit a persistently small return to education, for example, and this is particularly true for black workers. See Robert Buchele, "Jobs and Workers: A Labor Market Segmentation Perspective on the Work Experience of Middle Aged Men," unpublished paper submitted to the Secretary of Labor's Conference on the National Longitudinal Survey of the Pre-Retirement Years, Boston, 1975; Martin Carnoy and Russell Rumberger, *Segmented Labor Markets: Some Empirical Findings* (Palo Alto: Center for Economic Studies, 1975); David Gordon, "Class Productivity and the Ghetto: A Study of the Labor Market Stratification," PhD dissertation, Harvard University, 1971; Paul Osterman, "An Empirical Study of Labor Market Segmentation," *Journal of Industrial and Labor Relations*, 1975, as cited in Edwards, *Contested Terrain*, p. 170.

43 See, for example, Michael Piore, "Notes for a Theory of Labor Market Stratification," in Richard Edwards, Michael Reich and David Gordon, *Labor Market Segmentation* (Lexington, Mass.: D.C. Heath, 1975).

44 There is no question but that women also constitute a distinct class fraction. See Edwards, *Contested Terrain*, pp. 194–9; and Wright, *Class Structure and Income Determination*, chapter 9.

45 This is, of course, true for women as well.

46 Michael Reich, *Racial Inequality* (Princeton, New Jersey: Princeton University Press, 1981), p. 197.

47 See Michael Reich's excellent review of literature related to this point

in *Racial Inequality*, chapter 6. See also Philip Foner, *Organized Labor and the Black Worker, 1619–1973* (New York: Praeger, 1974).

48 For an analysis of the class fraction struggle over welfare, see Frances Fox Piven and Richard A. Cloward, *Regulating the Poor: The Functions of Public Welfare* (New York: Vintage Books, 1971); and Richard A. Cloward and Frances Fox Piven, *Poor People's Movements: Why They Succeed, How They Fail* (New York: Vintage Books, 1979).

49 As Erik Olin Wright suggests, fundamental class interests "refer to interests defined across modes of production (i.e., interests in capitalism vs. socialism), whereas 'immediate' interests refer to interests defined within a given mode of production." He suggests that while white and black workers may have conflicting immediate interests, they still share fundamental class interests. This is true of class fractions in general, not simply blacks and whites. See Wright, *Class Structure and Income Determination*, chapter 2 and p. 205.

50 Edwards, *Contested Terrain*, p. 203.

51 See Reich, *Racial Inequality*, chapters 6 and 7 for an exemplary analysis of this issue.

52 The notion that all forms of racial discrimination are totally reproductive is similar, argues Wright, to analyses of the state which argue that every state policy in a capitalist society is orchestrated by the capitalist class to serve its own interests. "Such 'instrumentalist' views of the state and ideology," argues Wright, "minimize the intensely contradictory character of capitalist society." See Wright, *Class Structure and Income Determination*, p. 201.

53 Wright, *Class Structure and Income Determination*, p. 201. I am indebted to Wright for his points on the contradictory nature of class fractions as they relate to the capitalist accumulation process.

7 Analysis of culture — II

1 Paul Willis, *Learning to Labor* (Westmead, England: Saxon House Press, 1977), p. 119.

2 Eugene Genovese, *Roll, Jordan, Roll: The World the Slaves Made* (New York: Vintage Books, 1974), pp. 561–6.

3 Genovese, *Roll, Jordan, Roll*, p. 565.

4 For a discussion of education as it relates to the relegation of blacks to unskilled labor and the increasing economic marginality associated with this position in the United States and England, see John Ogbu, "Equalization of Educational Opportunity and Racial/Ethnic Inequality," in Philip Altbach, Robert Arnove and Gail Kelly, eds, *Comparative Education* (New York: Macmillan, 1982), pp. 269–89; and Mike Brake, *The Sociology of Culture and Youth Subcultures* (London: Routledge & Kegan Paul, 1980), chapter 4.

5 It must also be noted here that schooling provides a focal point for resistance among black youth. The black collective relation with

schooling is thus contradictory: schooling is both affirmed and rejected by strands within the broader class/race subculture.

6 I, therefore, do not totally agree with Ogbu's position that caste-like minorities will always hold the "system" responsible for individual failure.

7 It is interesting that within this context Jerome once again affirms college knowledge. He suggests that "they should have them a psychologist over there, maybe a pool of them at Urban College, and have it a part that every students go through some type of psychological, you know, evaluation."

8 For analyses of dominant ideology as encoded within commodified culture see Todd Gitlin, "Prime Time Ideology: The Hegemonic Process in Television Entertainment," *Social Problems* 26 (February 1979): 251–66; Michael Apple, "Curricular Form and the Logic of Technical Control," in Michael Apple and Lois Weis, eds, *Ideology and Practice in Schooling* (Philadelphia: Temple University Press, 1983), pp. 143–65; Landon Beyer, "Aesthetic Curriculum and Cultural Reproduction," in Apple and Weis, *Ideology and Practice in Schooling*, pp. 89–113; and Will Wright, *Sixguns and Society* (Berkeley: University of California Press, 1975).

9 Willis, *Learning to Labour*, p. 166.

10 It is important to point out here that the group logic does not embody an affirmation of underclass life and associated practices in the same way that cultural practices among working class males embody a voluntary giving of manual labor. Urban College students are attending school to escape the underclass and they "choose" to be there. The important point is that the group logic operates to ensure that, as a group, they can't escape. The vast majority of students end up as part of a permanently trapped population of poor people. I suspect that a comparable study of black secondary school students would uncover a subjective identification with the urban underclass that parallels the subjective giving of manual labor described by Willis. This is an excellent topic for future research.

11 See Michael Reich, *Racial Inequality* (Princeton: Princeton University Press, 1981), p. 19. See my chapter 6 for a more extensive discussion of the position of blacks in the American economy.

12 Kelly and Nihlen discuss the importance of a women's movement in making cultural resistances "count" among girls. See Gail Kelly and Ann Nihlen, "Schooling and the Reproduction of Patriarchy: Unequal Workloads, Unequal Rewards," in Michael Apple, ed., *Cultural and Economic Reproduction in Education: Essays in Class, Ideology and the State* (Boston: Routledge & Kegan Paul, 1982), pp. 162–180.

13 This is not to deny the very real struggle that continues in the state sector. It does not compare, however, to that of previous decades.

14 As Willis points out, however,

> In one sense the reason why these cultural penetrations [referring to the lads' culture] and associated practices fall short of

> transformative political activity is simply the lack of political organization. No mass party attempts to interpret and mobilize the cultural level. This is too facile, however. The lack of political organization itself can be seen as a result of the partiality of the penetrations – not vice versa. The cultural level is clearly partly disorganized from within. (p. 145)

The presence of a larger movement could provide students with a vision for the future which they do not currently have. Part of the reason why such a mass movement does not exist at present is precisely because the cultural level is internally disorganized as a result of the concessions made *vis-à-vis* equality of opportunity in response to the struggles of the 1960s.

15 Genovese, *Roll, Jordan, Roll*, p. 294.

16 There is, notes Willis, "precisely a partial relationship of these penetrations to that which they seem to be independent from and see into." Willis, *Learning to Labour*, p. 119.

17 Genovese, *Roll, Jordan, Roll*, p. 440.

18 There were a number of important court decisions, beginning about the 1940s, which recognized certain forms of segregation as being unreasonable. In the 1950s and 1960s the last vestiges of legal segregation were struck down. Highlights here are Brown v. Board of Education; the Civil Rights Act of 1964; and the Elementary and Secondary Education Act, 1965. There are currently nine United States anti-discrimination laws and a Presidential executive order enforced by different agencies and requiring different remedies if violations are proven. Two key laws which relate to race are Title VI of the Civil Rights Act of 1964 which prohibits discrimination on the basis of race, color, or national origin against students of any school receiving federal assistance, and Title VII of the Civil Rights Act which prohibits discrimination against *employees* on the basis of race, color, national origin, religion or gender by any employer in the United States who employs 15 or more people. This also includes employment agencies and labor unions. See Perry Zerkel, *A Digest of Supreme Court Decisions* (Bloomington, Indiana: Phi Delta Kappa, 1978); and Teacher Standards and Practices Commission, *Discrimination and the Oregon Educator*, 2nd ed (Salem, Oregon: Teacher Standards and Practices Commission, 1980).

19 Genovese, *Roll, Jordan, Roll*, p. 294.

20 This is Willis's point. See Willis, *Learning to Labour*, p. 152.

21 Michael Omi and Howard Winant, "By the Rivers of Babylon: Race in the United States," *Socialist Review*, vol. 71, no. 13, 5 (September/October 1983): 55.

22 Erik Olin Wright, *Class Structure and Income Determination* (New York: Academic Press, 1979), chapter 8.

23 Willis, *Learning to Labour*, p. 174.

24 Ibid., p. 172.

8 Possibilities for action

1 Consider, for example, American comedians such as Richard Pryor whose humor is based on these cultural differences.

2 See Burton Clark, "The 'Cooling Out' Function in Higher Education," *American Journal of Sociology* 65 (May 1960): 569–76.

3 Clark has recently suggested that the transfer/terminal distinction and the meaning of the transfer track has been blurred somewhat since the time of his original writing. See Burton Clark, "The 'Cooling Out' Function Revisited," in George Vaughan, ed., *New Directions for Community Colleges: Questioning the Community College Role* (San Francisco: Jossey-Bass, 1980), pp. 15–31.

4 Howard London, *The Culture of a Community College* (New York: Praeger Publishers, 1978).

5 One can raise questions, however, as to London's explanation that it is "status anxiety" which translates into powerful peer pressures defining those students who express high academic aspirations as deviant.

6 The community college in the United States plays a key role here in that it provides an arena whereby working class white males, through their own lived culture, reproduce necessary division in an increasingly proletarianized white-collar world.

7 Michael Apple, *Education and Power* (Boston: Routledge & Kegan Paul, 1982), p. 14.

8 Samuel Bowles and Herbert Gintis, *Schooling in Capitalist America* (New York: Basic Books, 1976).

9 It must be noted that London does not address these theoretical issues directly.

10 Henry Giroux, "Pedagogy, Pessimism, and the Politics of Conformity: A Reply to Linda McNeil," *Curriculum Inquiry* 11: 3 (1981): 218.

11 This underlines Henry Giroux's point that "(s)ubordinate cultures are situated and recreated within relations of domination and resistance, and they bear the marks of both." See Henry Giroux, *Theory and Resistance in Education* (South Hadley, Mass.: Bergin and Garvey Publishers, 1983), p. 229.

12 Giroux, *Theory and Resistance*, p. 230.

13 In his discussion of Gramsci, Genovese states that,

> dialects always must suffer in relation to developed national languages in their reduced ability to absorb the universalistic elements in world culture. This reduced ability arises from the realities of political life without regard for the intrinsic merits of the dialects themselves. Thus, Gramsci argues for the progressive role of the Italian language in Sicily, not because he thought the Sicilian dialect intrinsically inferior to Italian, which itself began as just one dialect in Florence, but because he was committed to the principle of Italian national unity.

See Antonio Gramsci, *Modern Prince* (New York: International Publishers, 1959), as cited in Eugene Genovese, *Roll, Jordan, Roll* (New York: Vintage Books, 1976), p. 440.

14 Bourdieu and Passeron have argued that it is the exclusive "cultural capital" of the dominant groups in society which ensures the success of their offspring and thus the reproduction of privilege. This is because educational advancement is controlled through testing of precisely those skills which "cultural capital" provides. An emphasis on standard English obviously works to the benefit of those groups who already possess this language. To argue that standard English should not be distributed through schools, however, is to ensure that subordinate cultural activity will forever remain subordinate and that groups who carry such cultures will have no access to dominant culture. Much as I agree with Bourdieu and Passeron's point here, I strongly support the continued distribution of certain dominant meanings. Pierre Bourdieu and Jean-Claude Passeron, *Reproduction in Education, Society and Culture* (London: Sage Publications, 1977).

15 See Giroux, "Pedagogy, Pessimism and the Politics of Conformity," p. 215.

16 Henry Giroux, "Theories of Reproduction and Resistance in the New Sociology of Education: A Critical Analysis," *Harvard Educational Review* 53, 3 (August 1983): 293.

17 Giroux, "Theories of Reproduction and Resistance," p. 293.

18 This has been done at City University of New York (CUNY). See the Newt Davidson Collective, *Crisis at CUNY* (New York: Newt Davidson Collective, 1974). I am indebted to Ellen DuBois for bringing this to my attention.

19 There is some precedent for this at Urban College in that students and faculty worked together on several occasions when the issue of a permanent site for Urban College was being debated.

20 This is Henry Giroux's point. See Giroux, "Theories of Reproduction and Resistance in the New Sociology of Education," p. 284.

Appendix A Methods

1 This did, in fact, happen. By the end of the study, many faculty members regarded me as an "insider."

2 Robert Bogdan and Steven J. Taylor, *Introduction to Qualitative Research Methods* (New York: John Wiley & Sons, 1975), p. 41.

3 Bogdan and Taylor, *Introduction to Qualitative Research Methods*, especially chapter 4. In practice, I followed their suggestions regarding data analysis almost totally.

Index